Of All the Nerve

Critical Performances

Series editors: Lynda Hart and Paul Heritage

Combining performative texts with critical theory and personal reflection, each volume in the series pairs a performance artist/playwright with a critical theorist in a dialogue aimed to elucidate both disciplines. These books are designed both as critical introductions to the artists and as scholarly introductions to the field at large.

Of All the Nerve
Deb Margolin: SOLO

Edited and with Commentaries by Lynda Hart

CASSELL
London and New York

Cassell
Wellington House, 125 Strand, London WC2R 0BB
370 Lexington Avenue, New York, NY 10017–6550

First published 1999

British Library Cataloguing-in-Publication Data
A catalogue record for this book is available from the British Library.

ISBN 0-304-70318-4 (hardback)
     0-304-70319-2 (paperback)

Library of Congress Cataloging-in-Publication Data
Margolin, Deb.
     Of all the nerve : Deb Margolin SOLO / edited and with
commentaries by Lynda Hart.
          p.   cm.
     Includes bibliographical references.
     ISBN 0-304-70318-4 (hard cover). — ISBN 0-304-70319-2 (pbk.)
     1. Performance art—United States. 2. Women—Drama. I. Hart,
     Lynda, 1953–   . II. Title.
     PS3563.A648037   1999
     812'.54—dc21   98–31201
                                                              CIP

Typeset by BookEns Ltd, Royston, Hertfordshire
Printed and bound in Great Britain by Biddles Ltd, Guildford & King's Lynn

Contents

Acknowledgments

I must acknowledge, in no particular order, those people without whose support I would not have been able to persist in this demented and exquisite profession: Harold and Elaine Margolin, Neal Kirschner, Rebecca Rose, Virginia Mayer, Madeleine Olnek, Cruz Irizarry, Peggy Shaw, Lois Weaver, Ellie Covan of Dixon Place, Mark Russell of Performance Space 122, Margot Lewitin and Ronnie Geist of the Women's Interart Theatre, Mickey Rolfe of The Rolfe Company, Inc., Louis Kirschner, Randy Rollison, S.F. Belman, Peggy Phelan, Christopher Collins, Rae C. Wright, Noel Simmons, Joni Wong, Camden Toy, Kevin Seal, Kristin Garrison, Jo Bonney, Gabrielle Hamilton, Lillian Slugocki, Aimee Schneider, Robin Schatell, Terry McCoy, Amy Sommer, Allie Michelle Sommer, Shelley Michelson, Aviva Weintraub, Joseph Roach, Laurie Stone, Salley May, Amy Meadow, Andy Davis, Dona Ann McAdams, Elin Diamond, Una Chaudhuri, Julie Malnig, Ann Daly, Leslie Satin, Mary Kay Dauria, Nicole Adelman, Mr. Turner, Lou Viola, Martha Wilson, Mary Salter, Hana Iverson, Amy Reich, Rachel Abbey, Ken Levinson, Reno, Dan Crozier, Janie Pipick, Jennifer Lee, Claudia Barnett, Rhonda Blair, Karen Kolhaas, Kent Alexander, Alisa Solomon, Amy Zorn, Carol Belsky, Janie Iadipaolo, Marlene Shwartz of Soho Rep, Lisa Jo Epstein, Beth Willinger, Mimi Town, Len Steinbach, the census-taker whom I forced to play Ophelia to my Hamlet one afternoon when he just came to ask how many adults lived in my apartment, Ed Benson, the women of WOW, the guys from Gusto House, Dale Goodson, Aaron Beall, Beverly Bronson and A Repeat Performance, Linda Gui, Diana Arecco, Jamie Leo, Joel Giguere, Lynda Hart for her commitment, persistence, vision and remarkable grace and, without in the least being able to describe the depths of how and why, my beautiful children Bennett and Molly Kirschner.

Deb Margolin

1

Introduction: A Love Letter

Lynda Hart

Beginnings are always arbitrary. The gap between the present tense of this 'speech' and the text you will read is a daunting chasm. I am not a 'critic' who generally writes 'about' artists' work. Deb Margolin's work speaks eloquently for itself, and yet I find myself in the position of 'introducing' it. The critic/artist couple is a relationship like all others – vexed with identifications, projections, displacements, dis-identifications, incorporations, and, one hopes, moments of bliss that make continuance possible. Collaborating on this collection with Margolin has contained far more of those blissful moments than one usually dares to hope for, and it is *because* of them that my introduction risks falling into rhapsody, which is a risk in academic discourse. Deb once told me, when I find myself disappearing into that space of utter silence where no language seems ever possible again, to send her an envelope of confetti, to tear bright party papers into tiny bits, fill the envelope with them and mail it. And she will know then where I have gone, and come find me. I keep an envelope with her name and address written on it, and a stamp, just in case. In a sense, this introduction is that envelope of party-colored papers.

It is so seductive to search for beginnings, to find the originary moment. Where was Margolin's desire to perform engendered? And what has kept it living in the midst of the colossal obstacles that bar the way to any woman's desire to lead an artistic life? Perhaps it was that moment she often speaks of when a man she met, a moving man by profession, who thought he was the Messiah, stopped his van on the Brooklyn Bridge in heavy traffic, bowed his head, and offered this prayer: 'Almighty God, may our efforts amuse you

1

enough.' Margolin has said that she uses comedy because it is the 'weapon of the powerless.' Certainly this man who moved pianos moved her, and perhaps his hilarious but nonetheless beautiful prayer was for her a founding moment in the way she brings comedy to bear on the most serious issues.

Or perhaps it was when she first saw *Electra Speaks*, by the Women's Experimental Theater Project, where she saw women 'working from some very primary, very unembellished, personal impulse,' and carried away with her two vivid, unforgettable images: one of a woman simply drawing an invisible line on the stage with her toe, and defiantly crossing over it; the other of a woman sitting in a chair, turning her head mechanically back and forth, chanting – 'get married, get married, get married, get married.' These were radical acts for a generation of women who had been indoctrinated into the belief that their personal experiences were not only vastly removed from the stuff of artistic expression, but not even credible *as personal experience*.

Perhaps it was the night she attended Spiderwoman Theater's performance, *An Evening of Disgusting Songs and Pukey Images*, and watched each woman in the troupe come forward and boldly pronounce her 'flaws.' Margolin describes it this way: 'And one by one, they took their place, and stridently announced what was wrong with them in the eyes of the conventional world, and it was hysterical, and it was radically political. And it made me think that I wanted to do that, and furthermore, that I could.' These are a few of the moments that have stayed with her throughout her career, and of course they are all beginnings, each arbitrary but no less foundational.

So let me begin, again, with the story of how she came to know what writing for the theater meant. And did it. Collapsible boundaries. Margolin describes the evening in which she discovered what it meant to write for the theater. And how to do it. It was an 'apocalyptic' moment in her life, 'a very cusp, an evening when my life changed completely and forever.' Margolin's friend, her best friend for many years, who had suddenly and inexplicably ceased communication with her, just as abruptly and magically returned to her, and told her that she had been away for a year engulfed in the world of theater. She had met two women, Lois Weaver and her partner, Peggy Shaw, who were working on a performance about three women who had spent their lives in Virginia, living in almost complete isolation, in a world of their own. They were relatives of Lois Weaver, who desired to perform their lives, together with Peggy

Shaw. The woman they had engaged to write a script disappeared, and they asked Margolin's friend if she would 'bring that little Jewish friend of yours who likes to write' to a workshop. Margolin went to the workshop and, finding it rather incomprehensibly silly, took the train back to Boston. There she received a phone call, asking her if she had managed to write anything. Margolin lied, assuring them that the script was well underway and that she was in control, knowing full well that she had neither written a single word nor even given it a thought. She then went to bed with a sound conscience. But there was a buzzing in the room, a mosquito. And a cat kneading her chest with its paws. These calls from the wild made her leave her bed, and with pad and pencil in hand she locked herself in her friend's bathroom, took up her tools on the dirty circular rug of many colors, and wrote through the night. Scenes, monologues, songs, dialogue – eight hours of nearly 'automatic' writing. And with nothing to say, nothing to tell, Margolin collapsed her boundaries, inspired perhaps by the cat and the mosquito, who had learned no respect for her personal space. She wrote a significant part of the body of what would become *Split Britches*, the signature piece for what then became The Split Britches Company, three women whose work has forever changed – and made – the history of feminist performance art.

That night on the bathroom floor, Deb Margolin had a fire in her pocket. She had had one there before. She would have one there again. The fire would enter into the *Split Britches* script, and into the three-woman troupe, which came to be known as a 'company with fire in its pockets.' And that fire would continue to burn hot and mysterious in the most unexpected moments of her solo performances. It is, perhaps, difficult to keep in mind that all of Margolin's work, however fantastical, is resonant with the corporeality of her daily life. As a college student, she was walking the streets in New York one day, feeling spiffy in her short red jacket with a zipper up the front, when she reached into her pocket and was burned. There was a fire in her pocket, perhaps from a carelessly tossed-in smoldering cigarette or match, perhaps from spontaneous combustion. But a fire, a real fire. And her zipper was stuck. So she began rolling around on the ground to put out the flame, probably without making too much of a spectacle of herself, given New Yorkers' general nonchalance about unusual behavior. She never forgot that incident. And many years later, it came to her as a monologue in the mouth of Della, one of the three characters in *Split Britches*, the sister whom no one could remember in detail, except in euphemistic allusions – 'She was tall.' *Who was she?* these three women wanted to know. Conjecturing that she was a woman who had desires that couldn't be named in her isolation, with only the company of her two relatives to explore her impulses with, Margolin gave Della a voice for her desires, collapsing her own boundaries, stealing a moment from the history of her own college girl to transform into the passion of a woman who had probably nothing to tell. Margolin gave Della language, hence manifesting her identity, in these words:

DELLA: Once I saw a whole farm burn down. And all the cows and chickens. And the fire went out and brought in other creatures from miles around . . . big black birds that flew upside down next to the fire. And the fire held them there with a string tied to their wings in order to scare all the animals to death. I seen a chicken fall over and the fire went up and ate up its whole body and burped out a big white smoke! I heard dogs barkin' but there wasn't no dogs. And I got fire eatin' inside of me. I can feel it but you can't see it. And that makes me a person with a secret. I can feel it in my eyes. I can feel it in my chest. And I can feel it other places. . . . And that fire can make ashes out of me if I ain't careful. Once I had a fire in my pocket. I put my hand in and pulled it out real quick, and I said, why'd I do that? And I looked in my pocket, and there was the fire, lookin' up at me just cute and sweet as a pretty girl. . . . But then it starts to hurt. So you got to beat it. You got to put it out . . . (p. 57)

That monologue, that night, that beginning, was eighteen years ago, and Margolin has never left the theater since. She cries 'theater' in a crowded fire, or anywhere else that she finds herself. She has said that the theater is the safest place in the world for her, that she suffers from *offstage* fright. But when she is on, she's on, and her nerves are all firing.

Of All the Nerve, the title of this collection of Deb Margolin's solo performances, throws down the gauntlet, takes the dare, pricks up your ears. The writing you will encounter here has a certain quality of that which is usually 'unspeakable.' In my notes scribbled in the margins of a steno pad I carried to a conference on performative writing, I find this entry: 'Performative writing is that which speaks when there is nothing left to tell.' This citation refers me to yet another, a conversation I had recently with Margolin, in which she told me that she called a poetry professor who had moved her deeply many years ago and left an indelible impression on her psyche. She spoke of the *nerve* it took to make that phone call, to reach out across the decades knowing that she might not be remembered among the thousands of students he had taught, but how she had taken that leap of faith in order to tell him that she did remember him, and that he had changed her life. He told her that he was no longer a poet. She responded that that would be like her saying she was no longer a Jew, and reminded him that he had once said these words: 'When you reach the inevitable, it doesn't make sense to keep talking.' And then they kept talking. And she spoke to me of what they had said to one another.

Love, passion, pleasure, fear, tenderness, longing, yearning – desire and the excruciating terror of its death – are encapsulated here. And this is what you can seek and expect to find in Deb Margolin's work, these small moments, these most innocent and ordinary exchanges, that are nonetheless the very warp and woof of what constitutes our lives, and makes our deaths meaningful. 'There's desire. There's death, there's desire. And what else is there to talk about?' Margolin asks.

Desire. No one knows what desire is. As feminist critics and theorists, we have written volumes trying to follow its smoke. We have argued endlessly about various identity positions and their relation to desire; we have tracked through the wilds of psycho-analytic theory searching for subjects that are not one nor anywhere to be found; we have held hand mirrors, stood in front of full-length ones, cupped compacts in the palms of our hands, and wandered about through myriad funnyhouses. We have found lost objects and lost found objects, mourned the losses of things we never had, forgotten or never known the differences between grief and joy, put all our cards on the table and hidden our hands. Identities, identifications, dis-identifications, displacements, divorces, deser-tions, deliriums. We have remained alone, together. No one knows what desire is. But Margolin says that she writes from that place, that place that no one can know. And I believe her.

I believe her the way that June believes May in the last script that Margolin wrote for the Split Britches Company, *Lesbians Who Kill.* Writing that excites the desire to *perform* – erotic writing, writing that makes me want to say out loud, for no good reason, *'and the word became flesh,'* is hard to come by. Margolin's writing has circulated through my erotic life in ways too tender, painful, and exhilarating to enunciate. These are some of her words that quicken my pulse:

Once we picked wild raspberries together by the railroad tracks. At night. Ridiculous. She said she knew where they grew, and I loved to make preserves. She said we couldn't go during the day, it was forbidden. Against the law! Of course we went at night . . . raspberries . . . little clusters of edible garnets . . . the darker, the sweeter . . . when they're at their prettiest, they're too young to eat . . . and the raspberry bramble is so protective of her bower . . . thorns . . . we brought metal pots . . . it was dark, and there was that odd, hot wind, and we crouched down where the trains passed, we were eye level with the train wheels, like being in the mouth of an animal. She forbade me to cry out when the thorns burned my skin, and in the dark I crushed more berries than I picked . . . it was torture, not knowing when the pain was going to come, and trying not to scream when it did, and the trains kept coming. By morning my fingers were blue with berries and blue with blood and my lips were blue with cold and the horizon was purple as if we'd crushed all those berries against the sky. All those raspberries hidden somewhere in the sunrise . . . she washed my hands for me . . . sucked the bruises . . . even that reads like a dream to me, but she says she never dreams. And I believe her.

When I hear these words, my 'critical' training unravels. Who would not want to steal these words, eat them? When she calls, I respond. It is hard to find the words. I would paint her if I could, in primary, pungent sounds. Would the paint run on such a delicate canvas? Will it run so fast I cannot catch it? Would it be futile to try to follow? Am I not afraid that the richly textured paper will suck up all the colors before I can mold them into shapes? Yes, yes, yes. Is this what Beckett meant when he said that when one cannot go on, one goes on? Yes. Therefore, I will continue.

The texture of the pages you hold now in your hands is merely a canvas. The performances are lost before they can be held. See her when you can. Get as close as possible. Like the boys in *Of Mice, Bugs and Women* who press her up against the metal gate and while away their summers painting her lips, wrestling for control of the slick tube of pink gloss as it peeps out from its shelter. Listen to her words and hear them softly breaking through, touching places that are old and dark and dank. Her eyes on my screens, penetrating. She wore my body on her dress. I watched her touching it. She said it was inappropriate, and it was, but we noticed that we were not pretending. Reality is a ruse to hide the Real of our desires, or so Lacan says. And I believe him. Not because these words hold any authority, *per se.* But because I like the way they roll around on my tongue, speaking in tongues. Like gospel singers whose voices build to an ecstatic frenzy, and make my body rock. The stones roll. But not as in Sisyphus's labors that had no pleasures. Unless he came to know that he was himself the stone that he was rolling.

In an interview, Margolin has said: 'I allow desire to lead me. The thing about daily life, the mystical, the revelatory aspect of daily life, is that I will allow myself to explore something if it compels me. I don't have to know why it compels me. I don't even have to be able to defend the compulsion. ... If I can be said to have a religion, it is that there is resonant beauty in daily life, and that anybody who wants to admire that beauty and make use of it, for any artistic purpose, can do so.' She speaks eloquently and lovingly of the beauty in her collaboration with Split Britches, her 'education, [her] school, [her] theater school.' But she paid a price for that education: 'I was asked to, and willingly gave up, a sexual identity, in favor of my ability to put language to a collective ideal. And in service of my learning theater and in service of my exploring other aspects of my identity where I was not mainstream and where I wasn't comfortable. And for me, that was the Jewish identity, it was the brainy one, it was the one who talked too much. So that was the dynamic.'

Catherine Clément has written that 'identity is a mere outer skin that constantly distorts one's relations with others. Yet there is no other way to have relations with others, since without identity there is no language ... no social life, only an autistic existence ... one needs this knight in shining armor.' If there is no language without identity, there is also no identity without language. And herein lies one of the deepest paradoxes of collaborative performance. Collapsible boundaries are both exquisitely beautiful and terrifyingly dangerous. Writing and performing that emerges from the most minute particulars of our personal lives is a love that has not achieved Luce Irigaray's poignant dream of a love that would be exchanged as 'neither gift nor debt.'

For that to happen, we might have to discover or invent a way to have relations with others without identities. Performance tries to take place in the present. But there is always a gap – either anticipatory or recollective. Identities, as I have argued elsewhere, are always belated. They are after-effects, and not easily linked to causes that precede them. Effects, perhaps *without* causes. In this sense, identities are reminiscences, and thus 'hysterical.' Or perhaps they come before; they are premature. Still shadows, but rather than shadows that follow the image of oneself refracted in the light, they precede it. And we follow them. In either case, they create the illusion of having already been – whether behind us or before us. We are always running to catch up with them, or waiting for them to arrive. In *O Wholly Night*, Margolin says that she leaves the book on identities open. To leave something open is an act that must be negotiated very carefully, performed to appear as if it were done carelessly – *as if* – the great words of the theater.

So what about these knights in shining armor? Surely as feminists we can search for ways to dispense with these armed riders who more often than not are none too skillful. One of the many ways that I experience the beauty of Margolin's work is in the feeling she creates of waiting *with*, rather than waiting *for*. A waiting without the anxiety of forward movement, without projection. A looking about, a keen attention. Noticing and appreciating what already is, rather than what is behind or before us. Like the infant in *O Wholly Night* that she takes from the arms of its desperate mother, Margolin's performances hold our attention, not because they keep us in suspense by making promises that no one can keep. But simply because she holds us. The present happens in rooms that she is in.

Chronology of a Career

In the mid-1980s, Margolin was working as a typesetter, like so many other women performers doing whatever she had to do to make a living so that she could have a life in the theater. Split Britches, the company that she had co-founded with Lois Weaver and Peggy Shaw, won a Villager Award for Excellence in 1982, and in 1986 an OBIE award , but such distinguished accolades did not translate into hard currency. Her solo career can perhaps be said to have begun when Ellie Covan, whom Margolin describes as a 'vastly amusing frontierswoman,' called her from Dixon Place, one of the longest-running and most pioneering venues in New York's downtown theater world. She wanted Margolin to do a solo performance. In her customary Beckett-like manner, Margolin said absolutely not, then booked the show. This was the beginning of *Of All the Nerve*, originally titled, *Of All, the Nerve*, but no one ever understood Margolin's comma. Such a seemingly simple gesture can, of course, change the entire meaning of a show. Nonetheless, Margolin dropped the comma, and *Of All the Nerve* became her signature. In its original form, it contained work that does not appear in the text printed here. On the cover photograph of Performance Space 122 program, Margolin appears glaring defiantly into the camera with a gavel grasped between her teeth. She is almost snarling, but there is also a weighty hilarity barely contained just behind her aggressive posture. In one monologue that is now lost from this script, Margolin portrayed Miss Tennessee, a beauty pageant contestant in the combined bathing suit and talent competition, who paraded her assets while performing Hamlet's 'To be or not to be' soliloquy. Of course all performance is 'lost' when it is performed, if not *before* it is performed, but some traces of these lost moments will be kept in Margolin's archives that Tulane University has recently acquisitioned.

Margolin then began working regularly at Dixon Place, as well as other downtown performance art spaces, such as WaWa Hut, Gusto House (now defunct), Lizard's Lounge, Café Bustelo, Theater Club Funambules (now Nada) and other venues that allowed her the space and freedom to develop her full-length shows. In 1988, most of what would become *Of All the Nerve* was presented at Soho Repertory Theatre in a first full-length solo performance.

Margolin, Shaw, and Weaver, still performing as Split Britches, were invited to be artists-in-residence at Hampshire College, where Margolin was subsequently invited to deliver the commencement address (see Bibliography). When she returned to New York, *Of All the Nerve* debuted for a full run at Performance Space 122 under the artistic directorship of Mark Russell. Madeleine Olnek served as dramaturge, production assistant, sound designer and comedic director, with Lois Weaver of Split Britches tending to transitions and acting work.

In 1990, *970-DEBB* opened for a full run at P.S.122 with Madeleine Olnek directing. Again it featured pieces that had been developed at Dixon Place. Margolin was working with two comic talents, Dale Goodson and Kevin Seal, with whom she was involved in a postmodern sketch-comedy group. *970-DEBB* had a run at the Women's Interart Theater on West 52nd Street, reopening there in July 1991. During this second run, Margolin was pregnant, and the extravagant dancing in the show, requiring much lifting and turning, became increasingly difficult for her and her dancing partners. Stormy Brandenberger, the choreographer, kept making adjustments to the dance as Margolin grew heavier and heavier, and Linda Gui, the costume designer, kept letting out her leotard. Following in the tradition of using whatever material and circumstances are at hand to make the show, Margolin's pregnancy during this piece, in which she plays an over-educated sassy call-girl, became not an obstacle but an integral part of the performance.

Late in 1991 came *Gestation*. Written and rehearsed during her seventh and eighth month of pregnancy, it premiered at Theater Club Funambules on Ludlow Street in a series then curated by artistic director Camden Toy. Madeleine Olneck served again as dramaturge and director, and the show, slotted for a midnight spot at this small theater, actually premiered at 1:30 a.m. Once again, the timing of the moment coincidentally, yet artfully, complemented the show's emphasis on Margolin's insomnia-induced early-morning deliriums.

In the two years between *Gestation* and *Of Mice, Bugs and Women*, Margolin collaborated on a play, *The Breaks*, with actress/writer/performer Rae C. Wright, which opened at P.S.122 in 1992 and continued its run at the Interart Theater in 1993. This play won honorable mention for the Jane Chambers Playwrighting Award in 1993. During this time she and the other two Split Britches, Lois Weaver and Peggy Shaw, were artists-in-residence at the University of Hawaii, where Margolin scripted a play for thirty students, *Valley of the Dolls's House*, loosely revisiting Henrik Ibsen's famous play, *A Doll's House*. While there, she also began writing and testing out the four monologues that would comprise *Of Mice, Bugs and Women*, which premiered at the Atlantic Theater under the auspices of Karen Kohlhaas for a weekend. Its full-length run occurred in October 1994 at P.S.122, with dramaturgy by Madeleine Olnek, Kent Alexander as director and Beverly Bronson as set designer.

Late in 1994 and early in 1995, she began developing *Carthieves! Joyrides!*, another piece that evolved from a promise she made to Ellie Covan at Dixon Place. *Carthieves* was also performed a few times at The Knitting Factory in New York, and she brought it to the American Theater in Higher Education's 1995 conference in San Francisco. Randy Rollison of Here Theater worked with her as both dramaturge and director, and the show opened in the fall of 1995 for an extensive run at Here.

In 1996, the Jewish Museum commissioned *O Wholly Night and Other Jewish Solecisms*, and it was first performed at the Jewish Museum on April 26, 1996. Later that year, it moved to Interart Theater and ran for several months under the directorship of Margot Lewitin, with a new set and lights provided by a grant from the Anita Brill Scheuer Foundation. Margolin also took this show to Tulane University in the fall of 1997, as Zale Writer-in-Residence.

Her most recent script, *Critical Mass*, opened at P.S. 122 on February 27, 1997. Developed over a period of four months, *Critical Mass* was directed by Jamie Leo, and once again Madeleine Olnek served as dramaturge. Margolin describes *Critical Mass* as a play 'in a sense designed by all the actors who inhabited it as well.' In this volume, it is the only performance in which she writes full parts played by actors other than herself.

Deb Margolin has carved out for herself a place in the theater that pays homage to her ancestors and her peers, while at the same time being richly original. Her work has been honored and recognized in multiple ways. She has received grants as a Franklin Furnace Artist (1986), been a New York Foundation for the Arts Performance Fellow (1990–91), served on the Board of Governors of the New York Foundation for the Arts (1992–96), and has been featured as a performance artist in *Harper's Magazine* (1988). In addition to the scripts contained in this volume, she has written a number of other shows for herself as well as for other performers (see Bibliography). Margolin has performed on university campuses across the U.S.A., from small Southern state colleges to Ivy League universities. The Los Angeles, Boston, and Philadelphia Women's Festivals have all hosted her; and her work has been aired on television's *Comedy Central* and *HBO Downtown*. Her ever-expanding audience testifies in its diversity to the wide appeal of this work, which cuts across boundaries of race, class, gender, sexual identities, age, ethnicities, and various other categories, which often become imperatives among marginalized groups. It is a precarious act of balancing to accomplish such attractions, without erasing differences among her constituencies. Margolin's special blend of comedy and the sublimity of the everyday creates performances that are at once easily within one's grasp and yet somehow just enough beyond it to repeat the seduction.

Deb Margolin in *Of All the Nerve*. Photo: © Dona Ann McAdams.

2

Of All the Nerve

(The set for Of All the Nerve *features an old-fashioned telephone booth, way upstage center, with a ringable phone in it; the upstage-right corner of the set is the central hanging point of a huge white cloth which falls down onto the floor like a window dressing on either side of its affixed point. Underneath this huge, blanketing cloth are all the costumes and props the* PERFORMER *needs, withdrawn at different points in the performance from beneath it. A piano, somewhat downstage right, completes the set. The show begins with lights coming up and down several times on the* PERFORMER, *who is clad in a pink and gold peignoir and obtrusively chewing gum; each time the lights come back up, she has changed position, but the gum-chomping is like the North Star, fixing her persona in clear opposition to her luxurious costume or any other dignities. Finally, the third time the lights catch her, she says:)*

PERFORMER: Don't hate me because I'm beautiful . . . find some other reason!

*(*PERFORMER *spits her gum out in a vulgar fashion, and it lands wherever on stage it may. Lights go down again. When they come back up,* PERFORMER *has retired to the phone booth, where she sits lighting a cigarette in a most soigné manner. She then puts the cigarette in a glass ashtray, walks out of the booth and approaches the audience.)*

PERFORMER: It's just a nerve. When I speak to you, it's just a nerve of yours my whisper brushes. It bounces off the plush of your earlobe, falling in silence down the very channel of hearing. It brushes soft hairs, turns to chemical power, changes speed; brushes from the spine to the neck to the brain to the mind. Then it travels down the front of your body: through the chest, grazing a thigh, lingering by the ankle. My voice in your ear. *(phone rings)* It's just a nerve. *(phone rings)* Of all this, it's just a nerve.

*(*PERFORMER *turns and wistfully regards ringing phone, without having the slightest intention or emotional ability to answer it. Three more rings and the phone stops. Then, with clear will, she raises the ashtray with burning*

13

*cigarette to the presentational shoulder level of someone in a television adver-
tisement, smiles, and approaches the audience once again.)*

PERFORMER: Ladies and gentlemen, it is now my privilege
and my pleasure to be able to introduce to you my mother.
(speaks to cigarette in ashtray) MA? *(turns to audience)* – ladies and
gentlemen. *(to cigarette)* Ma? You know, my mother frequently
comes to my shows, but it is rare that she gives me the honor of
being able to introduce her to you in such a personal way. *(to
cigarette)* Mom, ladies and gentlemen. You know, my mother is
so funny! Nobody makes me laugh like my mother. As a matter
of fact, one time we were watching *Fury* on television and Pete
got caught in a mine that collapsed . . . and then they broke for a
commercial from Nabisco. And Mom spent the entire commercial screaming, 'Hang on, Pete! Hang on, Pete!' *(turns to ashtray)* Isn't that something? *(to audience)* Isn't she something? *(to
ashtray)* Well, uh, Mom, I'm going to put you back on the piano
and I'm going to talk to the people for a little while, okay dear?
–You can't see on the piano, dear? – Well, I can't put you on the
floor, dear, it's against the fire regulations, hon. – Well, where
do you want to sit, Mom?! *(turns to audience and fake-laughs; turns
back to ashtray)* Okay, dear, I'll put you on the piano and I'll turn
you around – make sure you can get a good view, okay, dear?
Good. Thank you. – Oh, yes, Mom, of course I'll give you a
kiss, sure. I'd be glad to! *(PERFORMER takes a drag from the cigarette, starts coughing violently; she turns to audience.)*

I love her, but she kills me. *(She crosses to her right and gently,
painfully, places ashtray on the piano; adjusts its position several times,
and speaks to the burning cigarette within it.)* Can I get you something,
Mom? – okay sweetie.

(She crosses once again to center stage, smiles; then, to audience)

Ladies and gentlemen, I am so delighted that you asked me here
tonight to talk to you about the pressing modern problem of
loneliness. Now I myself am not lonely. My mother and I are very
close. So there's no loneliness there. And my two sisters aren't
lonely, either! They're both married so there's no problem there.
And my cousin Deedee isn't lonely, either. I saw her
Thanksgiving, and she's just fine. And her parents, my Aunt
Betty and Uncle Leon, live in Newington, Connecticut, and
they're not lonely, either. And my Aunt Myrna and my Uncle

Eli are both in Austin, Texas, and they're not lonely, either. And their three lovely kids Vicki, Ronnie and Steve are not lonely in any way. So you can see, it just doesn't run in our family.

Just the same, it's an interesting modern problem! I'm frequently asked when I give these small lectures how is it that I managed to avoid the scourge of modern loneliness, and when I think about it, I like to reflect on my formative years during the ages of five to seven. And during that time, I thought I had Kitty Carlisle hanging upside down from her high heels by a coat hanger in my bedroom closet! Now I suppose that is a common fantasy among young girls. But for me it was very special. I remember my mother would be doing the dinner dishes, and I would steal food from the dinner table and bring it to her there in the closet, screaming, 'Here, Kitty! Here, Kitty!' and that gave me a sense of responsibility, too. Oh, sometimes I used to worry that perhaps the blood was rushing to her head but, now that I think about it, I'm sure it was a very rewarding time in her life. I know it was for me!

Well, I'd like to talk now just a little bit about the history of modern loneliness. Loneliness was invented in 1964 by Joni Mitchell, and has been marketed with great success to people the world over. Now, I have had the privilege of being able to study some of the characteristics of lonely people and one of them is that lonely people have a heightened sense of things, don't they? Why colors, and odors, and sounds, and lights seem huge and larger than life to them, don't they? Why, even mundane things like *car horns* sound like . . . *mooses lost on the range* to them – or wherever it is that mooses hang out . . . excuse me just a moment. *(She takes several steps backward, withdraws into herself and sings.)* 'Home, home on the range! Where the deer and the antelope play! Where seldom is heard a discouraging word and the skies are not cloudy all day.' *(to audience)* Well! I wish they mentioned more animals in that song, don't you?

Yes, well! Another one of the characteristics of lonely people is that they always seem to see themselves as travelers, don't they? As solitary sojourners alone on a road by themselves, now, don't they? Oh, lonely people can be seen everywhere – at an airport or a train station or a bus depot with a knapsack or a suitcase, can't they? And even modern music seems to support this trend! We have songs like: *(sings)* 'I am on a lonely road and I am trav-lin', trav-lin', trav-lin' . . . Lookin' for something, what could it be?' *(speaks)* And we have songs like: *(sings)* 'I'm-a-leavin' on a jet plane, why, I – I don't know when I'll be back again.' *(speaks)* And we have songs like: *(sings while snapping fingers and stamping foot)* 'Trailers for sale or rent! Rooms to let for fifty cents!'

(A moment of silence while the ramification of this lyric sinks in. She becomes profoundly agitated.) Fifty cents! Rooms to let for *fifty cents*! I took a calculator recently and I figured out what fifty cents would get me in my apartment! Fifty cents would get me exactly *twenty-seven seconds* in my apartment! Now, I'll show you what that looks like! *(simulates walking up several flights of stairs, opening a door with a key, walking into a room while taking off her coat)* 'Oh! Another dirty roach!' *(steps on roach)* 'Oh, I didn't do those dishes, did I ?' *(phone rings)* 'Oh . . .' *(walks over to phone and picks it up)* 'Hello! Yes, Joanne. Yes, fine! How was your day? Good – good. Yes, Joanne, the most remarkable thing happened . . .'

(She looks up at audience and hangs up the phone with prosecutorial vengeance; extracts fifty cents in coins from the coin return of the pay phone, walks out of the phone booth, onto the stage, and hurls the coins onto the floor with all her strength, scattering them in all directions; they join the spit-out gum somewhere in the mystical recesses of the stage. Finally:)

That was fifty cents in my apartment!

Yes! Well! The data seem to strongly support that the level of loneliness has something directly to do with the public transportation in a place, doesn't it? I mean, we live in a lovely island! I mean . . . it's a small, slimy sort of a place, isn't it? And yet it takes *longer to get somewhere than to do what you went there to do!* And that's only one way! Then you have to trip back, don't you? I mean let's say you want to get from 14th Street and First Avenue to Canal Street, let's say. And you go down there . . . and it's a time warp down there! Light years go by! Leap years pass! By the time you get out, your sisters are married and having babies, and your mother's taking laxatives regularly! Then there's some girl you went to high school with and she says, *(in a husky, uninterested voice)* 'Oh, hi, Debbie. What have you been doing with yourself?' And you say, 'Well, I took the LL crosstown and changed for the Number 1 to Canal.' I mean, what are you supposed to say, really?

You have to do something when you're down there, don't you? What are you going to do, you're going to read the billboards, aren't you? What do you get when you read the billboards but roaches, hemorrhoids, and Carolina Long Grain Rice! Can't go far with that, now, can you? So what are you going to do? You're gonna read the paper. The man sitting next to you is reading your paper. It's time to turn the page – you wanna turn the page – you *can't* turn the page, can you? So you don't read your paper. You read his paper. It's time to turn the page – he wants to turn the page – he does turn the page, doesn't he?

Excuse me, just a moment.

(walks over to piano, picks up ashtray and lovingly looks at it, asking) Can I get you something, Mom? Oh, you wanna go out? Okay. *(snuffs out the cigarette)* Okay, sweetie. Yes. Yes, I'll tell them. *(puts ashtray back on top of piano; approaches audience once again)* My mother has asked me to make a small announcement, and that is that if, for some reason, you don't find this discussion particularly entertaining or informative, you're welcome to come back next week and see my dramatic presentation in which I play Siamese twins with a kosher butcher.

Well! New York has two beautiful, beautiful terminals, doesn't it? Grand Central Station and Penn Station! Oh, Grand Central Station, with all its echoes and stars, and from everywhere comes the sound of intimate conversation! And when you follow that conversation to its source, you discover you were right. What could be more intimate than eighty homeless people talking to themselves! And Penn Station, with all its energy of a shopping mall, like near where I grew up in Paramus! And the man who announces the station stops is fantastic! Oh, I love lists! Laundry lists, waiting lists, hit lists, shopping lists . . . but the way he announces the station stops! 'This is the 9:40 Stamford local, making all local stops to Stamford and stopping at Mt. Vernon, Pelham, New Rochelle, Larchmont, Mamaroneck, Harrison, Rye, Port Chester, Cos Cob, Greenwich, Old Greenwich . . . New Greenwich . . . Middle Aged Greenwich . . . *(something transformative happens; PERFORMER seems to have glimpsed the flickering strobe lights of a sudden, virulent rage)* Young Upwardly Mobile Professional Greenwich! High-Roller-In-Las-Vegas-With-Maybe-Just-A-Little-Bit-Too-Much-Money Greenwich! Not treating women too well at home or in the workplace Greenwich! Don't let Jews into the country club Greenwich! *Fuckin' blowing up the*

Greenpeace ship and then they arrest a couple of men when what about the God-damned Prime Minister Greenwich!
And Stamford. All aboard, please.

(A silence. PERFORMER *struggles to recover her composure; she seems shocked to have lost it so quickly and so thoroughly. The scar of that loss haunts her ensuing remarks.)*

Well. I love to be alone, don't you? And one of the greatest celebrations of solitude is going to the movies, isn't it? Oh, I love to go to the movies and when I go, I like to bring along with me my *suitcase*. Oh, it's great to bring your suitcase! If there's room, you put it on the seat next to you, and if there's not, you put it on the floor and put your feet up on it! Which of your friends would let you do that? Oh, I went to the movies recently. It was a budget picture, I remember, starring George Segal, Susan Ansbach and Kris Kristofferson, in which Miss Ansbach had jilted Mr. Segal for Mr. Kristofferson. Now he doesn't do it for me, and besides, his name is redundant and I *hate waste*! I mean, why doesn't he just call himself KRIS TOFFERSON instead of KRIS KRISTOFFERSON? I mean why should I stand around saying KRIS all day? Do I look like a person with nothing better to do?

Well! And they were having trouble in the projection booth, I remember. And the dialogue would be going along and then all of a sudden *(imitating speech in slow motion) shoughm boughm boughm.* And then, once again they would get it fixed and then all of a sudden *shoughm boughm boughm.* Well, just the same I followed the plot! In which Miss Ansbach had jilted Mr. Segal for Mr. Tofferson! And then in walks Mr. Segal and he rapes her under the grand piano! Oh she enjoyed it! All women do, you know. And they're lying there breathing with their 'hah-huh-hah' *(moves hands up and down suggesting heaving of a woman's chest)* And the camera man is right down there with them! Well, if you were a camera man, where would *you* be? And with the 'hah-huh-hah'! And then in walks Mr. Tofferson! And he's towering above them, you know, and his nose casts a shadow on his pants, you know. And with the 'hah-huh-hah'! And he says, 'I'm going to tell you something I've waited my entire life to tell somebody.'

And she says, 'What is it?'

And then the *shoughm boughm boughm*!

(Picks up coat from floor. Clutches it to her chest.)

Well! Does anybody know what it is that he said?

(After a long pause, PERFORMER *retires to phone booth to change costume, stepping all the way into booth and shutting the door. As she strips off her peignoir, the theme music from* Masterpiece Theater, *as rendered from a touch-tone telephone keypad, is heard. The performer then emerges from phone booth in black leotard and tights; hair pulled back. The following monologue is the halting, correctable speech of an irritated NERVE CELL in the brain of an arrogant, marijuana-addicted man. NERVE CELL's movements are axonlike and jerky; her arms frequently roll upwards in waves, or laterally, with flat palm facing the audience, indicating the processing of neural information, particularly when encoding memory or conducting a lexical search.)*

NERVE CELL: Excuse me. I do not give these tors – tors – tars – TOURS! I do not give these TOURS! on a regular basis, so you'll excuse my oddball NO! INCORRECT stomach pain / first loss / mother touch / return / SOCIAL AWKWARDNESS! *(moves hand and arm in an upsweeping motion)* Excuse my *social awkwardness!* As must by now be perfectly obvious, I am a deep-process ganglion nerve cell in some guy's brain.

I was told you would be showing in ... INCORRECT PREPOSITION / rise from beneath the surface of reality to go from possibility to fact / UP! I was told you would be showing UP, and that I was to acquaint you with my life and work. But I was not told that I would have to do it while this guy was awake. His name is Essent, an old British name. But his parents were sentimental and so they named him Evan, which made his name Evan Essent. Have you heard this word? It means vanishing, fleeting, tending to become imperceptible. My attitude is APHORISM ON – so what else is new? – APHORISM OFF.

My job is to pass and process. First I process, then I pass. It is like a government. And the stimuli make their way through the tangled legislature of the senses and end up on my desk. I am like your governor Koch-omo INCORRECT! mayor first Governor second / sounds like *ecce homo* / *ecce homo* / che homo / che homo / Koch says I'm no homo / CUOMO! Governor CUOMO! And the stimuli are like the death penalty or some other issue. *(Sounds of music – something like an advertisement for*

Agree shampoo – emerge from a TV offstage.) Oh, shit! He has turned on the TV. Something has come in . . .

(Throughout cell's effort to process commercial, during which a silky voice sings: 'Use your mind! To improve your body! New Agree! Agree Shampoo!' the cell is processing frantically, with arms rolling upward in waves, and feet moving side to side.)

Agree. Agree. Agree. Agree . . . in the sense of feel concurrent . . . no . . . align . . . no . . . harmonize . . . MAYBE . . . rest sense here . . . to be accommodated . . . no . . . to live in concord or without contention . . . no . . . to be appropriate . . . no . . . to be grammatically correct . . . no . . . to arrive at a settlement . . . no . . . to be of one mind . . . no . . . return to holding sense: HARMONIZE . . . on second thought no . . . denotational possibility . . . STRONG . . . couched in soupy music . . . YES . . . product name . . . YES . . . of what? Some tacky HAIR SPRAY . . . sexy women . . . fans blowing . . . does Jan use it? . . . process left . . . return tongue reflex to genital area . . . retain: yes, no . . . waiting . . . YES! Words left . . . music right . . . *(singing)* hm hm hm! Hm hm hm hm hm hm! *(speaking)* Go, guanine, up fourth, right, short term . . . words: USE YOUR MIND TO IMPROVE YOUR BODY! down left, long term, cancel, two parts adenosine, punstart, annoying adage, come-back-in-the-middle-of-nowhere-on-Third-Street, acetylcholine 1 pump 2 long term random, stop: proper name! Meaning-wrap-around: pleasant and harmonious.

Excuse me. I am like an air-traffic controller for associated words and images. I decide what lands where and at what altitude. For example. If it is short term you will use it tomorrow night at a cocktail party to impress some chock . . . chock . . . CHICK! To impress some CHICK! And if it is short term, you will be eighty years old and remember some useless Yiddish word as you sit in an old-age home clutching your purse and a sweater. Oh, things get annoying. I get annoyed up here. But my one instrument of revenge is that I have the power to recall unwanted data, particularly songs, and torment him. For example, he had a childhood friend who used to sing a song that went like this! It went like this! *(singing)* 'Movies movies, M-O-V-I-E-S. Movies movies, M-O-V-I-E-S. Myst'ry, murder, comedy! Love suspense and history! Movies movies, M-O-V-I-E-S.' *(song stops)* Now that is annoying, isn't it? So when he sniffed glue in the sixties and I was almost killed, this song was all he could think about for three months. He had to quit his job and get treatment for tinnitus!

So I am located right about . . . here . . . drop down grey velvet cord corpus callosum under left smooth heart-hope . . . HERE! *(hand sweeps over head slowly and stops just over region between back of neck and shoulders)* Here. It is a plush middle management position from which I receive and pass. And the stimuli come in down here. *(points hand down to feet)* Down here. It is the in basket down here . . . the *(begins searching for proper noun)* Lysol denote / having not / needing foot / move walk change to high heels at work / desk curve / line cool / Opium perfume / MasterCard International / shoe denotational left find: REEBOK! The REEBOK! The REEBOK section down here! This is the in box down here. And the stimuli come pass in through here and they take the form of chemical electricity. Now you probably think of electricity as something you get when you plug in your openercan . . . openercan . . . INCORRECT / can / cannot / possibility . . . no . . . return / openercan / reverse. / canopener / juncture open . . . CAN OPENER! When you plug in your CAN OPENER! But electricity is all silk baby MOOD CHANGE!

(Cell begins frantic processing.)

Want want lip tooth snow lost bear lost body /
people in snow, tension of animal / light blue light dying blue on snow /
retina screaming for its food: blue light! Blue light! / Kiss me, he says,
kiss me / kiss me there in the bear-fear and blue light!

(Processing finishes.) Sorry, a memory to send. You call them memos in your office, we just add R-Y in here.

So the chemistry of this information enters the Fastfood left short REEBOK area and passes through here *(indicating stomach area)*: the long lean part of the cell, and that is like – ANALOGY ON: when a child lifts a kitty under its arms and its whole body just sags right down it makes me think about a kitty . . . ANALOGY OFF.

(A loud, droning sound; CELL bends awkwardly over to one side. Long pause)

Oh, shit. He is smoking a doppie. A doopie. A doobie! He is smoking a DOOBIE! *(chuckle)* I will do the best I can to continue *(chuckles)* but I promise nothing. And then the stimuli pass on *(chuckle)* the stimuli pass up through here *(chuckle)* and then I give! And then I give! And I give through the teeth – INCORRECT! And I give through the nose – incorrect. *(chuckle)* And I give and I give and I give and I give and give. And I give at the office. *(chuckle)* And I give at the office. And I give and give and give at the office . . . *(begins processing)* women who love too much by some man, hate him! Man throws money out window and then jumps himself, beggars stepping over death to get the bills, stepping over death to get to bills, stepping over death to get to bills, Buffalo Bill's defunct who used to ride a watersmooth silver stallion just like that one two three four Jesus he was a handsome man and what I want to know is how do you like you like your blue-eyed boy mr. death e.e.cummings! *(chuckles more)* And then something happens to click me off . . . click me off . . . click me off . . . PISS ME OFF! Please, mother, I'd rather do it myself . . . headache . . . Bufferin! *(Sound of Agree commercial is heard again from offstage; CELL, unhinged from cannabis, begins to sing:)* Happy birthday to you, happy birthday to you, happy birthday dear . . . blank note denotational . . . Happy Birthday To You!

(CELL falls to ground on its back and lies there; finally, out of corpse of CELL image, PERFORMER rises. She walks slowly to a cascade of white cloth on stage floor, lifts it and extracts JAZZ MUSICIAN's sweater, puts it on slowly and walks to piano, stage right. There she sits down, and begins his story.)

JAZZ MUSICIAN: I'm outta work. I'm a jazz musician. Sounds like bull, right? Listen. *(Plays quick blues riff on piano.)* I'm outta work. Fired me. They said I couldn't keep a beat. I got a great sense of rhythm, they say I can't keep a beat. It's really hard. It's hard to keep a beat pure! Even the heart has variations. Arrhythmia they call it. I get that. Arrhythmia. But I got chops, licks. I'm a restaurant, right? Hey, steaks chops licks! Every business got its own language, right? I got fired. The guitarist said I couldn't keep a beat. It's okay. It's okay.

There's nothing like jazz, it's okay. It's okay, it's like swimming in the ocean, like drowning, like getting saved and wishing you had died. It's time to die, they fish you out too

22

quickly. The thing I like about jazz is the absence of judgment. Like Bach, you take Bach, take Beethoven, Bach and Beethoven are the Supreme Court of tone ... the absolute law, the beauty of the law. See with jazz, jazz is the opposite, see, jazz is like civil disobedience. It's oceans during a storm, it's all broken, it's laws like vows waiting to be broken.

So that bastard said I couldn't keep a beat ... the beat is important, sure ... it goes like the days go, it goes *(tapping rhythm on his thigh with his hands)* Mon-day ... Tues-day ... Wednes-day ... Thurs-day ... Fri-day ... Satur-day ... Sunday and ... Mon-day Tues-day ... It's like one after the other, right, it's like a spine going down somebody's back, it's *(tapping)* vertebra-disk vertebra-disk vertebra-disk. But you know, time is funny. I worry – I worry when I start to time something that I'm going to start to time it between the beats instead of right on the mark. The beat ... between beats ... a lot happens. There must have been a moment when time started ... a gunshot or something ... absolute time, he says that doesn't exist, Einstein says that, and I'm sure that's true, but there must have been something, right, some tiny harbor that time got sent out from like a dinghy boat. Or like Noah sending out a dove to look for dry land.

You know sometimes I think that being born is like being given a chance to solo. No, that sounds really stupid, right, but think about it. Think about it. You get this time. You start with a melody and you do something with it! You take it outside, take it far, then you bring it back to the melody to die. Shit! I heard Wayne Shorter last week take the solo of a lifetime, O my God ... they had this woman piano-player ... Patrice Rushen ... fools Rushen where angels ... yeah ... she was an angel ... she had long dark hair and long dark fingers ... lady fingers ... the audience looked real funny from the side, I was sitting on the side, you know, I had to turn my head to see the show, if I just looked straight ahead I saw all these people ... as though they had come to see me but just got momentarily distracted ... they looked like pouring rain ... they looked like grass wet and stuck together with rain, it was oddball ... this piano-player, she wrote a song that was like ... O, beautiful ... it was like when you put a stethoscope to the chest of a child and listen to the slow ... listen to the health ... listen to the waiting ... a hand cupped for a bird to sit in ... I can't explain ... a perfect space to take a solo in, a dance floor, a cage for the jazzbird . . . yeah . . . beautiful structure, okay, so they spell the structure, she's leading them, they repeat it, they repeat it again, its back arches, it waits to be entered, it craves the solo, here comes Wayne Shorter! Okay, Jesus. He comes into that solo like an inheritance, he touches every corner of the time . . . he bounces off it, hugs it, rides it like a funny car, he's in love, he comes home with flowers, he holds her head in his hand, one note one note one note for years, one note through the changing seasons of other chords . . . Okay, have you noticed this? When you hold one note while chords change, it's like being yourself, your same self, while the seasons change: Winter, Spring, Summer, Fall, and it's you . . . you . . . you . . . you.

He stands up, he does it, he lays down, he undoes it, O God. They said I can't keep a beat . . . I can't. No one can! The beat . . . if it doesn't want to sit with you, it ain't gonna, you know? It's going to leave you. It's going to leave you. It's going to get up and leave you like someone who found a younger lover. Good luck when the beat leaves you. In the hospital you hear boooooop! From that heart machine. Wonder what key that's in. Could write a tune.

So I can't keep the beat, can't keep it, I admit it. I throw it away, because, you know why? Because it's too steady . . . it makes me feel like something unavoidable is coming toward me and I can't get out of the way . . . I don't even want to . . . it's funny . . . you know, you reach that point where nothing can stop it . . . fail safe . . . there's no going back . . . I get so excited . . . I can't even believe it's going on . . . *(plays the classic children's song, but with a minor and dissonant quality to it)*

> *Frère Jacques, Frère Jacques*
> *Dormez-vous? Dormez-vous?*
> *Sonnez les matines, sonnez les matines,*
> *Ding dang dong, ding dang dong.*

. . . and when you know a tune, when you love a tune so much you never want it to end . . . you hold every note . . . hold it . . . and you know every note that passes brings you closer to the end, but you wouldn't have it any other way . . . you're aching for what hurts you the most . . . it's too incredible . . . you need to be a movie star to deal with shit like that . . . I throw it away . . . I'm scared. I get scared . . . *(laughs)* . . . like meeting the perfect person ... you know when I was a kid I spent a lot of time scared, and when I learned to write, by mistake I spelled 'scared' SACRED.

(JAZZ MUSICIAN freezes for a moment; when PERFORMER stands, he is gone. She walks over to cascaded white drape, lifts a small corner of it and extracts WAITRESS's uniform from under it: a dress, small apron, hair-net. The following lines are spoken by PERFORMER in a personal, offhand manner as she changes into WAITRESS's uniform.)

PERFORMER: You know, I have always felt that the stage was the safest place in the world. Really. People ask me, do I get stage fright. Nope! Uh-uh! I get *off-stage* fright. I mean, I'm fine out here. The minute I leave, everything goes to pieces. I mean, really, the stage is very safe, when you think about it: no sheriffs can serve you papers, no lover's going to give you the axe or anything. Nobody's going to call you on the phone. You're hiding behind a wall ... a kind of wall that's made only out of a little lace and belief, and yet it's so powerful nobody can touch you. You can kill yourself, but nobody else can touch you. Well, Frank Rich comes to mind as a kind of exception, but even he can't do it right then, he's got to wait till press time. I always think of it as part of the journey home. Performance is a part of my trip home. I stand and think: there's no way home but straight through the show. That's the way home is. Kind of like an underground tunnel, when I think of it; a smelly underground tunnel, stinking of piss but littered with beauty. I have always felt very safe and protected when I get out on ...

(Phone rings. WAITRESS, now in full uniform, walks over to pay phone. Before answering phone, waitress pulls out order pad and pencil from her apron pocket; we now see her, lucid and irritable, at the end of her shift waiting tables and fielding telephone take-out orders at the Chelsea Coffee Shop.)

WAITRESS: *(answering phone)* Yeah, alright hello Chelsea Coffee. Yeah. Yeah, alright. Alright, your address, hon? *(writes in pad)* Right, your phone number? Right, hon, and your order? Yeah, that's a ... that's a tuna on white. Yeah, any lettuce with that? No? Mayonnaise, tomato? No? Any vegetable or fiber whatsoever with this order? *No?* Alright, hon, that does it! That's fuckin' disgusting, hon! I'm not gonna serve that! No, I'm not! No, hon, you call me back when you get an idea, alright?

(WAITRESS hangs up phone testily, exits phone booth and grabs a broom from behind it. She begins sweeping up, and suddenly catches sight of someone, invisible to the audience, who's just walked in to the restaurant. She addresses him while sweeping.)

WAITRESS: *(smiling with her eyes)* Yeah, hi, how ya doin'?

(Phone rings; she lifts one finger in an entreaty for visitor to wait; puts down broom, gets pad and pencil out, returns to booth and answers it.)

WAITRESS: Yeah alright hello Chelsea Coffee! Yeah. Yeah, alright hon, the special today, pastrami on rye, it's a buck eighty, alright? Yeah, alright, hon. Right, your address? One. Yeah, one what, hon? Oh, yeah, yeah. One nineteen west twenty-third . . . yeah, alright, look, hon, is this the Vaughn Gallery? Yeah, alright hon . . . alright, well you're disgusting people and we're not servin' you the special, alright? Alright. Keep in touch!

(She slams the phone down; resumes sweeping and flirting with mysterious stranger.)

WAITRESS: Well, yeah, I'd be glad to finish telling you this story, you know? Just sit still, don't be a stranger, alright? I'm here till closing.

(Phone rings; again, she excuses herself with a gesture to visitor, readies pad and pencil and answers it.)

WAITRESS: Alright hello Chelsea Coffee. Yeah. Yeah! *(pleasantly)* You're 80 Eighth Avenue, right? Yeah! How ya doin? Yeah! Alright, hon, your phone number again? Alright hon, and your order? Yeah, that's a grilled . . . a grilled cheese with bacon . . . yeah, alright, look hon didn't you have that *yesterday?* Yeah, alright hon! Hon! Look through the menu and pick something else, alright? Hon, don't eat the same thing every day, that's humiliating, alright? Alright hon. You give me a call, alright? I'll see ya.

(She hangs up; resumes sweeping and flirting.)

WAITRESS: Alright we were at the party, right? He shows up at the party, right, he tells my husband Joe he wants to take me to a play, alright? He tells my husband Joe he's gonna take me to a play, and Joe says, 'Fine, fine!' Now nobody says 'Fine, fine' except on the Andy of Mayberry show, is that true or not?

(Phone rings; she rushes to phone booth to do battle.)

WAITRESS: Alright hello Chelsea Coffee! Yeah. Alright hon your address? Yeah, no. Yeah, no, hon, we only deliver within a ten-block radius, alright? No hon, not a radio, a radius, hon. Hon, that's ten blocks in either direction, alright? No, hon, a *radius*. Hon, it has nothing to do with nuclear power, hon, it has to do with circles! Hon if you draw a circle . . . hon, draw a circle . . . hon, you got a piece of paper? Hon, *get yourself a piece of paper*. Good! Now hon, *draw a circle*. Good! Alright hon, now *put a dot in the center of the circle*. Good! Alright, now hon, *draw a line that connects the dot to the outside part of the circle*. No hon it doesn't matter which edge. Any edge, hon – hon *anywhere*! That's the beauty of this, *you just draw the line*! Good. Exactly. Yes, like the spoke of a wheel. Alright, hon, now put a little ten next to that, alright? Alright hon, there it is! A ten-block radius, alright? Alright look hon, I know the city isn't round, it's just a concept. Not a concert, hon, a *concept*, an idea. *(furiously)* Look hon! This is a restaurant, it's not some kind of a fuckin' math seminar, alright? You give me a call, alright?

(She bangs the phone down and shakes off customer's stupidity; replaces pad and pencil in her pocket and returns to her sweeping and storytelling like the postmodern Cinderella that she is.)

WAITRESS: *(to visitor)* Alright, so he takes me to Beckett, alright? He's wearing a *tuxedo* and he takes me to *Beckett*. He smells like strawberries, and he takes me to Beckett. And I couldn't hardly see, he's leanin' right over me the whole time like a street lamp over a tenement building, alright? And it was that really weird Beckett play where nothing happens. *(listens)* Oh, nothin' happens in any of them? Oh. Well, it was that one that had those two men, Vladimir and Estrogen. And then they brought some guy in on a *leash* and he's talking about sports for a half an hour, for no reason, can you imagine that? A half-an-hour lecture about sports for no reason. I'm thinkin' what the hell is this, then all of a sudden I *get it*! That's what it means! Because things happen for no reason . . . that's the point of this thing . . . that things happen for no reason! All these people paid fifty bucks for seats, for no reason, alright?

(Phone rings; she is becoming increasingly irritated by these interruptions. She stops sweeping and answers.)

WAITRESS: Yeah alright hello Chelsea Coffee! *(pause)* Yes we serve more things than coffee! Hon, we call it Chelsea Coffee, because it's short for Chelsea Coffee House – or shop, alright? Chelsea Coffee Shop. Right, hon! Now coffee in this case is a *synecdoche*: using the part for the whole, alright? Right, like 'tread the boards' or 'chase the skirts', alright? Oh, no, hon. Metonymy's somethin' different. No, hon, *metonymy* is when you use one thing to represent something else to which it has like a logical relationship, alright? Like *the bottle* for a strong alcoholic beverage, alright, hon? Alright, now would you like to order? Yes, hon, we serve coffee, I just told you that! Hon, just because we serve more things than coffee does not mean we don't serve coffee! Now hon, you're throwin' out the baby with the bath water! No, hon, that is not a synecdoche, it's an *aphorism*! Now would you like to order? Alright, and *what is that order? (in an unregenerate rage)* You want tea?!! *Then what the fuck are we talkin' about coffee for!*

(She hangs up the way some people have a car accident, exits phone booth and animatedly resumes her sweeping and her story.)

WAITRESS: So, I never been to a theater like this before! It's all ritzy and big, and I've never seen anything like it. There's nothin' in it! Like you can tell that rich people go there cause there's nothin' in the whole place, it's empty! Even the bathroom is weird. It says 'WOMEN: VACANT.' Like women are some kind of transient motel or somethin'.

(Phone rings; she is beyond irritation, and determined that this will be the last call. She answers phone without removing pad or pencil.)

WAITRESS: Alright hello Chelsea Coffee. *(pause)* Chelsea Coffee. *(pause)* Hon, you need it a third time? Chelsea Coffee! Oh, delivery. No, hon. No. Wrong. It is wrong. Hon, wrong number. Check it out, look it up, hon. Wrong. Alright?

(She hangs up phone and comes out of booth with her broom; looks quizzically at her visitor, who seems to have a question about her approach to this last telephone customer.)

WAITRESS: Yeah well he wanted to order food and I did not want to take his order. So in that sense he had the wrong number, y'understand me? It was a wrong number not of *form* but of *substance*, y'understand me? Anyway! So he is starin' at me the whole time – starin' and starin' and starin'. So I says 'Why you starin' at me?' and he says 'Oh, no. I'm not starin' at you.' And he says 'My eyes are botherin' me . . .' and then he says 'Are my eyes crossing?' and I says 'No. *I think they're waiting for the light.*'

(At this moment, the physical reality of the coffee shop falls away, but the WAITRESS herself remains. Into this demi-reality, fully alive, she steps forward and addresses the audience warmly.)

WAITRESS: Yes, I love language. Of course I love language. How else are you going to scream for help? I mean, you got some terrible emergency; maybe you were born with it. And your back stiffens and your heart rate triples and you raise your arms and you open your mouth and – something! You have to say something! You have to say something!

(WAITRESS inhales sharply and urgently as if to speak; phone starts ringing. She removes her hair-net and apron slowly; with these gestures, the WAITRESS is gone from the stage. PERFORMER walks over to the phone, picks it up.)

PERFORMER: Hello? Well . . . I don't know. Would you like me to check? Surely. Hold on just a moment please.

(She exits booth and approaches audience, using her hand to shade her eyes from glaring stage light.)

PERFORMER: Excuse me . . . is there anybody by the name of Bonnie Josephs in the house? Because if there is . . . could you please leave immediately. Your motor vehicle has exploded, and it is currently in flames with pieces leaping from it, and the aforementioned flames are threatening to consume the only viable bodega on Second Avenue, so could you please attend to that promptly? Thank you.

(She returns to telephone; says a few more words to caller and hangs up; returns center stage and stands there briefly, just smiling.)

PERFORMER: *(warmly)* It is uncharacteristic of me to just come forward in the middle of a performance and start talking. I mean I don't tend to believe in that. I've always felt that if you want to do something, just go ahead and do it. If you want to do a show, do a show. If you're going to read a poem, clear your throat and read a poem. If you want to do a dance, warm up and do a dance; why all the chit-chat yick-yack? I don't really see the point of that. Well, it's very hard to get a theater space, for example! You have to work very hard, make phone calls, show up, smile, be polite, pull your tights up, get the stain off your shirt, just trying to get a theater space; why all the chit-chat yick-yack? Why waste my time your time their time with the chit-chat yick-yack? So I don't really *do* that; I don't really subscribe to that as a way of doing business in the theater.

However, in this case I have decided to make just a small exception, because in this case, I was informed by a friend of mine who is very well-versed in show business that the *image* that led me into the next piece that I would like to present to you is kind of south of the Mason/Dixon line in terms of making any sense whatsoever, and so she suggested that I step forward and talk about it just a little bit. So I am doing that.

See, usually, I really trust my image life. That's something I've learned to do: I trust it. If I think something is funny, I genuinely believe that I can walk you right down the corridor and open the door through which this thing is just hysterically funny, and I trust that. For example, one time I just wanted to stand in silence next to a vacuum cleaner. So I pursued that. And another time I just got this urge to sing: 'Oklahoma, where the bears go leaping through the trees!' or whatever it is, and I did that. And that also was very enjoyable and lucrative.

But in this case she did insist, my show business friend, that my next image was in desperate need of some annotation, and I guess at this point I may as well go ahead and tell you that the image in question is a message that was left on my answering machine and, although it is clearly a wrong number, it completely changed my life! So, I guess what I'll do is just go ahead and play that for you without the further chit-chat and yick-yack; I'll play it for you and we can discuss it in a second. Here it is:

(PERFORMER dredges up a tape player and places it on top of the piano, readies herself and turns it on. After a piercing beep, a nasal and imperious voice rises out of the machine; PERFORMER has obviously been listening to this message for months as though it were an enshrined symphony; she mimes and mimics each inflection in a manner that demonstrates her obsessive attention to its every detail.)

RECORDED VOICE: 'This is Bonnie Josephs. Mrs. *Lehrer* just *called* me and she said that she received a note from *Mr.* Lehrer in which *he* said that her check for the half of the insurance payments was, quote: LOST IN THE MAIL. Endquote. That cannot *be*, because, as *I* recall, I *hand*-delivered Mrs. Lehrer's check for the insurance to YOU, and YOU have acknowledged that YOU sent it on to the insurance company along with *Mr.* Lehrer's check. Will you please call *me* or my associate *Rosemary* tomorrow, *um*, or as soon as you get this message, to discuss this peculiar message or note from Mr. Lehrer. Thank you.'

(Sound of caller hanging up; another piercing beep. PERFORMER *turns machine off.)*

PERFORMER: Alright! Well, now, I find that message so compelling! I have listened to it upward of a hundred and eighty times! I know every word, line, tone, and inflection of this message, and I have left it on every functioning answering machine in New York City. Let's face it: if you know me, you got this message on your answering machine at some point. I find it so fascinating. Because I see in it an entire human landscape. You know I said this to my friend; she said, 'There ain't no landscape . . .' But there is! And I would like to walk you through it, as I offered to do for her, like a boardwalk on Coney Island, showing you, piece by piece, the incredible seething humanity within this message.

Alright! So the first part of the message is what I like to call the 'meet 'em – greet 'em – win 'em – pin 'em' part of the message. You know, you can't tell the players without a scorecard, you know what I mean? You meet the people right here in the first part. Here it is. *(starts tape)*

RECORDED VOICE: 'This is Bonnie Josephs. Mrs. *Lehrer* just *called* me and she said that she received a note from *Mr.* Lehrer –' *(turns off tape)*

PERFORMER: Alright! Right there – a whole cast of people, isn't there? Okay, we have Mr. and Mrs. Lehrer, don't we? Now I don't know if they're separated, divorced . . . clearly, they're not speaking – they have this woman as their interlocutor, don't they? Alright. After listening fifty times, I realized that the third person, the caller, Bonnie Josephs, was Mrs. Lehrer's attorney-at-law. And then we have the fourth person, the wild card, okay. Me. Alright, me. Okay. And after listening a while longer, I realized that she thought that I was Mr. Lehrer's counsel. Now I don't know how many people in this room have ever called me, but if you ever have, you realize that my out-going message sounds nothing like an insurance company, or lawyer's office, or anything of the sort.

Now the next thing she says is: '... in which *he* said ...' I've never heard anything like that! Kind of like being on a boat in a storm without a port of call ... it's kind of vertiginous ... sort of like barfing over the side of the boat ... like *bleh* or some-thing, here, listen: *(plays the message)* 'In which *he* said ...'

(She stops tape and leans over an imaginary boat; tosses her cookies.)

Okay, now we're coming up on what I like to call the 'certified letter' part of the message. Because what is the point of a certi-fied letter? It is to quote, to excerpt, to be specific, to cover your ass; to say what you're going to say, say it, and then say that you've said it, right? This is the certified letter part – the QUOTE and ENDQUOTE and be specific and cover your ass, right here: *(Tape resumes.)*

RECORDED VOICE: '... that her check for the half of the insur-ance payments was, quote: LOST IN THE MAIL. Endquote.'

(Stops tape.)

PERFORMER: Fine. Quote, endquote and everything else. Now her next statement is only three words – but it is a killer!

(Tape resumes.)

RECORDED VOICE: 'That cannot *be*...' *(Stops tape.)*

PERFORMER: Alright! Ladies and gentlemen, when you get to be my age, you realize that *anything* can be! And that's the way it is!

Alright, now, we are coming up on what I call the 'Watergate' part of the message. Those of you who are old enough to remember Watergate remember the kind of language the testi-fying senators used, this sort of chit-chat and yick-yack with 'acknowledgment' and 'recollection.' Those were the big words: *(in a Nixon-esque voice)* 'I don't know, Senator; I can't recall what he acknowledged, but I acknowledge his recollection if he acknowledges my recollection – I don't know, talk to him, Senator. I don't recall.' The kind of chit-chat and yick-yack we get right here. *(starts tape)*

RECORDED VOICE: '... because, as *I* recall, I *hand*-delivered Mrs. Lehrer's check for the insurance to YOU, and YOU have acknowledged that YOU sent it on to the insurance company along with *Mr.* Lehrer's check.' *(stops tape)*

PERFORMER: Okay, so there you have it, and there it is, right there. Now, so far I'm sure you'll agree that this message has just barreled right down the line. It hasn't looked right, it hasn't looked left. It has just moved right down the line. Bingo! The dart of the voice is aimed right at the bullseye of the purpose. Wham! Right?

But, now, as you'll notice, we are coming up on what I like to call the 'leave-taking' part of this message. Everything changes. The voice gets kind of a porous quality; air can get through the voice all of a sudden. It has that kind of fibrillating embarrass ment and tenderness. It's as if she's having trouble winding her-self off of these hideous accusations, and she doesn't quite know how to do that. We hear the first 'um' of the message. We haven't heard an 'er', an 'um' or anything like that ... and she gets all mixed up: is it a message, is it a note? She doesn't know what the hell it is! And all these kinds of discombobula-tions we start to feel here. Listen. *(starts tape)*

RECORDED VOICE: 'Will you please call *me* or my associate *Rosemary* tomorrow, *um*, or as soon as you get this *message*, to discuss this peculiar message or note from Mr. Lehrer.' *(stops tape)*

PERFORMER: See what I mean? It gets kind of a little vulner-able in there. This moves and haunts me, she doesn't know whether it's a note or a message or what the hell she's dealing with. Alright.

Now the last thing she says is thank you. 'Thank you.' 'Thank you.' 'Thank you.' I mean, the way this woman says thank you ... it is so full of bitterness and nihilism: 'Thank you.' 'Thank you.' It's like, 'Blaaaah!' It's like, 'I don't know ... thank you.' There is no *neshuma* in it. 'Thank you.' It's soulless and desic-cated! Okay, the image I get is of standing in the desert next to someone who hates me. And they have a glass of water – there's a tiny bit in it, just this much, and we could share it and be saved; but out of bitterness and nihilism, they dash it on the sand – you hear 'tssssss' *(sizzling sound)*. 'Thank you –

thank you – thank you –' – I can't even *do it. (starts tape)*

RECORDED VOICE: 'Thank you.' *(stops tape)*

PERFORMER: Ugh! *(bends over holding stomach as if in pain from just being punched there)* It's like getting shot in the gut. 'Thank you.' Now, that is incredible, I'm sure you'll agree.

But this friend of mine, she still didn't quite connect, or cathect, or whatever it is today's academics call it, to why I wanted to pursue this incredible material. So she suggested that I go home and make a list of all the salient points in this message that drew me so compulsively to it. And so I did that! And I would like to share the results of that list-making with you, as I did with her. Just a moment, I happen to have the list right here. *(She turns around and picks up a stack of large poster-board cue-cards, and faces the audience.)*

(CARD 1: ANNOYING)

PERFORMER: The first thing I noticed about this message, um, was that it was annoying. I mean, that's pretty clear. It's a very annoying message, let's face it. And it's not even like I got this message at home in a relaxed way: get home from work, take off my jacket or something. No, no no no. I was expecting a business call that day. It was pouring rain, and I had a five-dollar bill; I had to use a pay phone; I had to get change for a five, get five singles; get change for a single; get four quarters; put in a quarter; dial my number; get the machine; punch in the code; rewind the tape and get *that*? I mean that is outrageous! I'm sure you could see why I would find that somewhat annoying.

(Tosses first card, revealing second.)

(CARD 2: PRESUMTUOUS) *[sic]*

Secondly, I felt that it was presumptuous. Alright, it's missing a 'p', I know. I had a college education. It is presumptuous. Not the least of the presumptions it makes is that she was leaving the message on the right number!

(Tosses second card, revealing third.)

(CARD 3: CONVOLUTED)

Thirdly, I felt that the message was somewhat *convoluted*, do you know what I mean? I mean, when you first hear it, it sounds reasonable enough, but actually, it doesn't get anywhere, it's like 'he said' and 'she said' and blah and blah but it doesn't really go anywhere, does it?

(Tosses third card, revealing fourth.)

(CARD 4: DEEPLY COLD AND MEAN)

Fourthly, I felt that it was deeply cold and mean. I really did. I mean, here we have Mr. and Mrs. Lehrer – I don't know if they're separated – something's wrong with these people. Okay, they're divorced, they're not speaking ... Maybe he's an alcoholic, maybe he's a wife-beater ... I don't know what's the matter with these people ... Maybe there's children without a home, here. Worse still, maybe there are cats without a home here – I don't know. But, in any case, there is nothing in this woman's voice that would give you to understand that she is representing as counsel somebody in profound human pain, is there? Not at all.

(CARD 5: REMINISCENT of all the PARADOX and TRAGEDY of the ENTIRE UNIVERSE)

Fifthly, I felt that it was reminiscent of all the paradox and tragedy of the entire universe. Because here we have this woman calling to complain to us about what she perceives to be a very serious lack of communication in the universe, and *she's leaving the message on the wrong number*! I mean, come on now!

(CARD 6: VOICE-TRAPPED-IN-THE-NOSTRILS SYNDROME)

Sixthly, I felt that it suffered from the voice-trapped-in-nostrils syndrome. Do you know what I'm talking about? I mean *(sends voice out through her nostrils) ung-ung-ung-ung*! Truly, if this woman is using any other part of her body beyond her nose for the purveyance of her voice, I could not identify what it is.

(CARD 7: NO PHONE NUMBER)

Seventhly, and for me really most perplexing: she left us no forwarding phone number! How am I supposed to return the favor to this woman? I mean, when you think about it, it's really very tragic. Think of Mrs. Lehrer! This lawyer who can't dial a phone is representing her! I mean, these lawyers make a lot of money. She just paid this attorney six hundred dollars an hour to make phony phone calls to the Upper West Side of Manhattan! That is what went down, here, okay? Great way to make a living if you can get it!

(a short silence)

Well now, this show-biz friend of mine remained unconvinced about the viability of this incredible message as material for performance. So I asked her to do something that, actually, I would like to ask you to do also . . . *(shyly)* and that is, with your permission: could we *recite the entire message out loud together from cue-cards? (tosses previous card, revealing one which reads 'This is Bonnie Josephs')* I would very much like to do that and I'll tell you why: because there's something about group chanting, it's like in *shul*, or in church or something, and everybody says something out loud in unison, and it has that kind of transcendent quality. It's like swimming with the dolphins; you sort of go underneath language and come up on the other side. It's like the ability to see the New York skyline from New Jersey just on the other side. Or something.

So, I would really appreciate your indulgence in this project. Great! Oh, let me tell you before we start that these cards are coded. So if something is underlined, give it a little special emphasis, will you? And if it's written in really big letters, scream it out. And if it's huge just really let yourself go! And if it has dots under it, that's staccato, like in music . . . as in 'he-sent-it-on-to-the-in-su-rance-com-pa-ny'. Staccato. Great. So let's begin, shall we?

(AUDIENCE and PERFORMER in unison)

'This is Bonnie Josephs'
'Mrs. *Leh*rer just *called* me and she said that she received a note from *Mr.* Lehrer'
'In which HE said'
'That her check for the half of the insurance payments was QUOTE'
'LOST IN THE MAIL'
'ENDQUOTE'
'Now that cannot *be*, because as I recall, I hand-delivered Mrs. Lehrer's check for the insurance'

'*To You* and *You* have acknowledged that *you* sent it on to the insurance company along with *Mr.* Lehrer's check'

'Will you please call *me* or my associate *Rosemary* tomorrow UM or as soon as you get this *message*'

'To discuss this peculiar message or note from Mr. Lehrer. Thank You.'

(All cards are now gone. It is clear that PERFORMER is now, both literally and figuratively, out of words. She goes back to tape machine and turns it on. Beep is heard, and RECORDED VOICE is heard one last time repeating the futile message everyone has just recited. PERFORMER now interprets the message physically: pulling up her skirt, lifting her leg over her head, flapping her arms and bucking like a chicken, turning pirouettes, bending over and revealing her buttocks. When the message concludes, there is a silence. PERFORMER's breath is audible. After a considerable interval, she returns to the phone booth and picks up the receiver. A dial tone is heard, followed by digital dialing and a hard busy signal: the old, unharmonized busy signal which was in the key of B-flat. She listens to this rejection neutrally for a while; then, overtaken by the rhythm, the odd lyricism of it, she begins to sway and move to it. She then begins to sing the lovely song 'Summertime' from Porgy and Bess, *using the busy signal as a bass line. She makes her way to the piano and finishes up the song there. Suddenly she remembers the audience, its grace and judgment both, turns to them; turns back to the piano; busy signal continues in silence. Then, rejoining it, PERFORMER attempts to please the audience by playing Mozart to the busy signal, then a pop tune, then jazz, then the pop tune again. At the last, she forgets the audience, returning again to playing and singing 'Summertime'; those haunting chords and the PERFORMER's modest voice, singing the lyrics, are heard over the jabbing busy signal. Lights fade.)*

FINIS

Commentary: *Beauty and the Beat*

A telephone booth, the kind you rarely see today, a wooden box with a swivel glass door, a space you put your whole body into to surround your voice. A piano. And a cascading drape – a net, a veil, a gown, a tent, a waterfall. Deb Margolin's first set of solo performances, *Of All the Nerve*, calls for simple props, around and in which she will incubate the concepts that will inform all her later work to date. She describes these pieces as 'a collection of passions under the aegis of a meditation on the fact that it's just a nerve.' Inspired, in part, by a course in psychophysics she took in college, Deb remembers her professor explaining that there is a blind spot in the back of the eye, a nerveless spot where nothing is processed. When one of the students asked why, then, we don't see a hole in our perceptual fields, the professor responded: 'We're not wired to pick anything up there. So we can't experience the absence of anything.' Margolin, I suspect, never believed him. The persistent faith in her performances is that she can lead us into those black holes, like Ariadne, winding her thread around the labyrinthine circuits of our persistent not-seeing, and make us laugh with the joy of recognizing what is manifestly there to be seen in those places where we are wired to *not pick up anything*. It is this 'nothingness-to-be-seen' that comes into focus when we follow her. The theater theoretician Herbert Blau has written that we go to the theater to pursue our incessant desire to see that which is just beyond the frame. Return again and again without abandoning hope, and Deb Margolin's performances will take you there, where angels fear to tread.

'Don't hate me because I'm beautiful, [pause] find some other reason' is the first line of her solo piece. Reasons she will search for tirelessly, and there will be many, but the most important insight she will offer us is that there are none without need. 'Oh, nothin' happens in *any of them*,' her Chelsea diner waitress suddenly realizes as she's describing her first experience at a Samuel Beckett play. Then she just accepts that and goes on sweeping and narrating her story, punctuated by frequent interruptions by call-out orderers, all of whom are rejected for one reason or another, mostly because they don't love language sufficiently to please this waitress, who has no patience with people who are too sloppy to make distinctions between synecdoche and metonymy.

Ah, the beauty of her beats. Like Wayne Shorter, whom Margolin's jazz musician proclaims 'touches every corner of the time,' Margolin caresses every whispering moment of the world and teases it gently in her fondling embrace. Her voice in my ear. Her fingers on my pianos. I am loathe to give her over to you. Like the jazz musician, fired because he couldn't keep a beat, the sound and rhythm of Margolin's words make me feel 'like something inevitable is coming toward me and I can't get out of the way. You know I don't even want to ... I get excited that's all. By the beauty of the beat.' And yes, it is easy to misspell 'scared' when you're in the company of something/someone almost too 'sacred' to touch.

In these first monologues, Margolin is variously: a woman who preaches to the masses on the modern problem of loneliness but is never so lonely (as) herself; a daughter who finds her mother in the love that kills her; a deep-process ganglion nerve cell in some guy's brain; a waitress with the style of an over-wrought and under-employed literary theorist schlepping Chelsea coffee; a woman obsessed with a wrong number who transforms it into the world and all it has lost; and, of course, always the jazz musician, keeping time, making time, beating out his rhythms on whatever surface can hear and hold them.

'Time is not a thing,' wrote Martin Heidegger. And indeed it is not. Though its 'thingness' seeps into the daily rhythms of our lives and coaxes us to believe that we can start, stop, delay, anticipate, suspend, prolong, attenuate, perpetuate, or traverse it. But if *Of All the Nerve*, a set of performances that covers so much ground and raises so many questions, can be forced into a unified thematic, one would have to reach for the most encompassing abstraction: Time. Margolin's nerve cell monologue is perhaps the least 'accessible' of these pieces precisely because it seeks to represent the state of raw, unprocessed time picking up every sensation that passes through the mind's body. This is what each of us might look/feel like were we to lack the nerve. Margolin becomes that nerve for us, and of all her nerves, this is perhaps the one with the most direct, and therefore *least* 'recognizable,' content. Creating the illusion of an unfiltered mechanism – with feelings and thought processes of its own – 'Nerve Cell Monologue' is a visceral trip through a body *by* a body that is blissfully unaware of its own fleeting, vanishing, transience. The 'nerve' does it all for him. He can be named Evan Essent, because he is *not the nerve*. This monologue may function as a metaphor for the way in which Margolin, as performer, carries us, as readers/spectators, through her piercing, probing words. 'Treading the boards,' the old theatrical cliché, takes on heightened meanings in such contexts.

Traveling: nerves firing, brushing soft hairs, speeding down the spine, neck, chest, thigh, ankles, lingering then speeding up. Airports, depots, train stations, trailers for sale or rent. Loneliness and public transportation systems. Strangers on a train. 'Luscious litanies of train stops' become for her biblical, sacred, genealogical, beautiful beat beat beatings of a voice whose repetitions can elicit a dance, if only one can keep time. Light years go by as Margolin takes the LL train crosstown and changes to the number one to Canal Street. A high-school girlfriend runs into her on the street and huskily asks: 'What have you been doing with yourself?' What does one do with oneself? The jazz musician without a beat has the best answer: 'You start with a melody and you do something with it, like, you take it out, you take it apart, you know, then you bring it back to the melody, to die.' The guitarist who fired that guy must have been listening to some really bad music.

It's no wonder that the Chelsea Coffee Waitress evokes Beckett's *Waiting for Godot* nearly square center of this set. 'Did you think my eyes were crossing?' her date asks her. 'No, I think they were waiting for the light,' she answers. In what I find to be Margolin's most hilarious, and therefore most 'tragic,' monologue, she catches herself up short in a moment of anticipation, a moment when she is rushing through time *as if* she indeed has somewhere vital to go. And what she finds is 'destiny,' otherwise known as Bonnie Josephs. A litigator with a mission, a lawyer with a message, a purpose, a 'note' or an 'uhmm,' whose moment of humanity Margolin catches after tirelessly repeating (and making us repeat) her wrong number message. Deb hears both Bonnie's coldness and vulnerability, and insists that we listen to it as well, as many times as it takes to understand that indeed this completely banal (mis)communication encapsulates all the tragedy and paradox of the universe. Not, of course, on its own, but because Margolin's spirit reaches out to the wrong number and to us through it, and turns a simple 'mistake' that most people would simply erase into a fully developed dramatic scene. Then, when she can suck no more juice from the dry voice on the answering machine, she returns to the phone, gets a busy signal, and starts to bop to the beat of its intonation. Then to the piano, where she incorporates the busy signal's rhythm into a jazzy 'Summertime.' And when that diversion wears thin, she keeps looking, waiting, never dulling the moments, endlessly varying them. And the beat goes on pursuing beauty in the most unlikely places. And finding it.

40

Deb Margolin in *970-DEBB*. Photo: © Dona Ann McAdams.

3

❧

970-DEBB

(Stage is lavished with a huge, floozy-like, canopied and caricaturish bed, replete with trapdoor through which two men come and go as needed, stage right. A WOMAN in a pink nightie with feather boa attachment lies reading in bed as audience enter theater and take their seats. Stage left is a small settee, covered in the same fabric as bed duvet. After audience is seated, STAGE MANAGER informs WOMAN, in full view of audience, that it's time for Places, which WOMAN acknowledges warmly. STAGE MANAGER exits. Lights dim, and music begins; WOMAN sings a sad, silly song about saying goodbye, or her inability to do so; her inability to sing is also obvious.)

WOMAN: 970-DEBB! The talk line for the arty kind. 970-D-E-B-B. The extra 'B' is for extra 'buh.' 970-DEBB! It beats a poke in the eye with a sharp stick! 970-DEBB! Where you never have to say goodbye, because you don't even say hello ... well, of course you do in a way but it's not the real thing because you never have to meet people ... because meeting people can be hideous; in fact I find it repulsive! *(WOMAN begins singing again, picking up where she left off.)* But remember! Remember ... *(forgets words)* da da da dum! Have the world overhead and there's *(forgets again)* da da dum! And if I could arrange it, Ah would I care to change it – not me– no way – not me – absolutely not – oh, not me da da da da da da da da da da!

(Phone rings. WOMAN answers, having settled back down in the bed after her exhausting stint as a chanteuse, flung her boa properly around her collarbones and having prepared herself for the demands of telephone sexuality.)

WOMAN: Hello, 970-DEBB. Oh yes, hon, it stands for extra 'buh.' That's right. Do you have a push-button phone? Good! Then press one for *The Tempest*, press two for *As You Like It*, press three for *All's Well That Ends Well*, press four for *Coriolanus*, press five to hear me go to the bathroom. Are you

43

ready to make your selection? Good! Make it . . . *now*! Good. What number did you press? Five. *(disappointed)* To hear me go to the bathroom. Well, to tell you the truth, hon, I really don't have to go right now. I'll tell you what, hon, I'll drink a cup of coffee – why don't you give me a call back in an hour?

(WOMAN hangs up; settles back. Something occurs to her, something joyous and urgent; she snaps her fingers and the lights downstage come up warmly, instantly; she gets out of bed and holds up a magazine picture of a young blonde-haired woman, with diamonds dripping off her, to the audience.)

WOMAN: *(holding magazine cover up next to her own face)* And from her fair and unpolluted flesh, may violets spring! . . . I just paid three dollars for this woman's picture! Come on, take a look at this woman, isn't she something? She is as blonde as the river runs free. Her hair shines and she smiles . . . she can afford the dentist, her teeth are the clean bathtub you put your baby in, and her lips are kind. She has on blue eyeshadow, a kindness to the blue also, like the sky . . . like the sky in May, late May; you know it's not going to snow anymore, and, of course, her eyes are blue, that goes without saying.

Now, this woman, who reminds me of Spalding Gray *(reveals another book from behind the woman's picture)* is dripping . . . *(tosses book)* she's dewy wet with diamonds and kindness . . . there is no difference between her diamonds and her kindness. For some reason, seashells surround her breasts, which are ample, which are generous, which are for the people, all of us, for history, for remembrance! 'Here's pansies, that's for thoughts!' Seashells surround her breasts, seashells and amethysts . . . how well those two go together, I wouldn't have thought of that! in a sort of graduation of value. . . first the seashell, which any child can find, squinting in the summer on the shore while the parents are at tennis, and then the amethyst, still common, but harder to find; children don't find amethysts . . . but women do, for not much money set in so many ways . . . around her breasts, and then the breasts! Christmas! Just look at those breasts! Set like jewels in the ring of seashells and amethysts; a kitchen of possibility!

I love to see candy stores with tons of clear containers in which there are millions of cinnamon hearts, and millions of chocolate horses, and millions of raisinettes . . . there is no scarcity, there's bounty and symmetry; you know that if you take some there are still so many more ... and here, we have shells and breasts and amethysts ... it's like Crabtree and Evelyn, so beautifully packaged! And we have diamonds. Now, the arm we don't see pushing up the breasts is be-ringed with a huge pear-shaped diamond ... a limpid, knife-like, refractionary uterus set in stone. And then the nails: painted natural – painted natural! And on the right ear, the heavy, sweet dia-monding, heavy diamonds pulling on the ear like someone try-ing to speak. Diamonds, leaves and sheaves of diamonds, like writing paper, like a letter full of secrets ... how can love fail? How can love fail? There is no possibility of failure here. A tree can not be right or wrong; a wind, a time of day ... and this woman, neither young nor old: 'I loved Ophelia. Forty thous-and brothers could not with all their quantity of love make up my sum.'

And Spalding Gray! You can't criticize him, really! He too is a time of day, a season, a fact. A fact. Something written on a piece of paper, like: 'The Spanish Armada of 1721 consisted of 86 vessels of varying construction and vintage.' What can you say to that? A fact is opulent, it is protected! It has been verified by a Ph.D. candidate from Stanford University ... And there it is, it has no valence, it is a stable molecule, like the love we feel for this blonde woman, neither young nor old, whose dia-monds are forms of charity and she is a fact, of course. And Spalding Gray: he is immutable! His diamonds are his kind-ness too. He shows his fallibility the way this woman shows her teeth and her diamonds ... it's when you try to hide things that the *60 Minutes* camera crew shows up at your office, isn't that right? See, but this isn't like that. This is all out there: Yes, I'm a WASP, yes, I'm a WASP bastard, yes I'm filthy with dia-monds, yes, yes, yes, smile! Make you feel something, may I please, because I admit the whole thing, I admit it, I'm smiling, my teeth are capped, I'm long, I'm blonde, I'm a WASP, I'm a WASP bastard, my breasts are huge, my hair is fine, I'm a mon-ster in a box, my hair color is a monster in a box, I'm nature in a box, my tits are huge, my diamonds are South African, see it, hear it, no secrets from you, darlings, I love you and I am a fact, panatella and stocking, I am all things considered ... see you in church! See you in the theater! Think of me when you have your first episiotomy. She looks like Spalding Gray to me, this woman; like a fact that no one knows is just a vision.

$\overline{45}$

I live threatened by airbrushes. Airbrushes. Airbrushes keep me in an apartheid township of self-doubt, a ghetto, a possibility. Airbrushes assail my life. When I'm asleep, they brush up the underconscious things as though my life were a floor dirty from a big party, the airbrush against my sleep; my sleep a dustpan; the airbrush, the litter of my underneath life; the things sweep into the dustpan and I wake up clean, like skin after an alcohol treatment. Taut, clean, staving off age like Spalding Gray! Like this woman here. Where is time? Where is time in this photo? She's put away months, years, sexual encounters, the way a secret alcoholic puts away beers. You know, ladies and gentlemen, they pour the beer into an apple juice container and they go back to work, and no one knows! Tropicana, it says. And that's a fact. Tropicana is a fact, folks. Well, it's in the supermarkets, isn't it? Haven't you seen it? There's nothing false about Tropicana! It's airbrushed right smack into the center of my life. And the letters they use – the Tropicana logo – they call that typeface HOBO. The letters are slouchy, they fall inwards like a drunk . . . Hobo, they call it. So this man comes up with his wine cooler, in a fact of waxen Tropicana, and he smiles, like Spalding Gray . . . a twisted, kind smile; and oh, the stories he could tell . . . Who knew there was something wrong? Tropicana? Are you going to blame Tropicana? No. Oh no. Juice is good for nursing mothers.

I loved it when Spalding Gray described being on a beach, not loving his girlfriend, or not enough anyway, or maybe not at all, but who could think about it while he threw up and threw up, while the ocean roared and the airbrush roared, and roars again as he speaks, his girlfriend nags him, he is really talented! Neruda talks about death, about death in the broom; about the tongue of death looking for the dead, about death waiting dressed as an admiral. Well, Spalding has that much power! And so does this woman, she is inevitable! She is inevitable! There is no way around this woman! And who wants to get around her anyway? Not me. Not me, baby, no. She is beautiful, the way getting your period is beautiful.

Letters. I like letters. I don't mean letters like Dear Deborah or Darling Deborah or To whom it may concern. I mean letters: A B C D E F G H I J K L M N O P and all of them. I feel overwhelmed with desire, as if flushed with red wine, by words that employ more letters to create their sounds than are strictly necessary: Yvette Mimieux . . . Mimieux . . . there are a thousand vowels in that syllable . . . a thousand vowels and an x . . . vowels, dripping like diamonds off that syllable, and an x . . . like a chromosome . . . a Barr body . . . a symptom of the feminine . . . an amniocentesis of meaning . . . it excites me: the wealth and sexiness of so many letters to make up such a simple sound: 'euhhh.' Yvette Mim-ieux!

And here, again, I think of Spalding Gray. I think of him, what an incredible storyteller he is! He is really brilliant. He brings incredible detail to bear on a single point! And at the end, after he has drawn pictures, he has screamed, he has sweated, he has acknowledged himself for what he is on beaches, under trees, cowering at the very edges of his life, he just makes a simple point, he thins out his meaning the way hair thins out at the bottom when it needs a good cut, and there it is: 'euhhh'! *Beaujolais nouveau*! There's about forty-five more letters than there needs to be! Stereo speakers of letters, piano keys of letters, look! There are seashells and amethysts around the breasts of those five syllables: *Beaujolais nouveau*! So sexy . . . as immutable as truth . . . as honesty . . .

Just to tell the truth is like quitting smoking. It makes you hyperventilate, it changes your consciousness, it is its own excuse and reward, it cannot be taken away, it cannot be assailed on judgment day. It leaves you deep in conversation with your self while everybody watches. And that is like Spalding Gray. A still photograph of the simple fact of his humanity; that's what he gives you in his work. Or, like this woman right here – stopped. Her smile, it is stopped; her eyes, frozen in beauty.

Think . . . it makes me think about those Japanese ice sculptors. I mean, who sculpts in ice? Somebody not afraid of paradox. Sculpture, the frozen form, that frozen, eternal form, that disappears the minute the sun comes out . . . like a snowman, a meltable form of eternity. Do you see that here in this woman's face? I do . . . and in Spalding Gray's monologues. Not to push the point, but how can I tell you? I am pursued by these images.

For Chrissakes, I am all these people, I am this blonde! Look at me! I am this blonde, I am Spalding Gray! They are screens for the black slide of my lucent ego! See them, see me! Once I took mushrooms, you know, the psychotropic kind. Well, everybody took them, and so did I, and they tasted bad, but everyone was in some pink boudoir of their inner selves, and

47

nothing happened to me. So I just ate fifty thousand more. Then it happened, but wait! I wonder how she felt, this blonde woman, giving back the diamonds, after the photo shoot! They came on slowly, these mushrooms, in waves, like nausea ... Genet talks about nausea, he talks about a nausea of happiness. He talks about raising his crushed farts up to his face with his bare hands. I love Genet. I love his work. You can hear him. There's no airbrush hissing in his work. His language is naked and you can hear his words without the hiss of the airbrush. Steam heat comes to mind, steam heat in the winter makes that hiss ... and the heat airbrushes the cold right out of your lungs and right out of your consciousness. Well, sure, it's winter, but the heat has that airbrush power. And heat is a fact, like Tropicana. Costs a certain amount, but it's good! And it's necessary!

I was out on the beach in the Hamptons when these mushrooms hit. Ooops! You know what? All of a sudden, this entire monologue and situation is starting to sound a fuck of a lot like Spalding Gray! But that is a coincidence! Nature has a limited number of ways of expressing itself! That's why this lady *(picks up magazine)* looks like Spalding, and Spalding looks like me! That's why the Lady is a Tramp! Shoobie-doo!

It hits me on the beach, and for the first time I experienced what trails were, you know what I mean? *(picks up white nightgown)* Trails, the continuous movement of a visual image; you see *(putting on white nightgown)*, not only the illusion of a single image, but the image, the image, the image, wow-wow-wow. A hallucination is more truthful than plain sight because that is the way neurons work, of course, they fire and fire 24 frames a second, but we don't see our own seeing ... unless, of course, you happen to eat fifty thousand mushrooms, and end up like Spalding Gray on a beach in the Hamptons, which makes Cambodia look like Eden, spiritually speaking ... and I am dripping in diamonds of sight. I move my arm and I see it – see it – see it, whoosh-whoosh-whoosh. I bat my eye and I relive-relive-relive the motion of the lid against the cornea ... light-light-light, whoosh-whoosh-whoosh ... Like when you take a nap in the sun and your dreams groan with gold, moan with flickering light, aortas of pumping light ... and I wrote a poem! And it went like this:

My heart, the red horse
Drenched in blood
Racing towards eternity

And when I swim, each stroke is like a luscious summary of an entire ballet, a Balanchine ballet – a condensation of years of poise and coordinated movement – and, coming out of the water, I'm in love with my breasts. *(She holds her breasts.)* There's nothing wrong with them, they swell out from bone and flatness the way life comes from orgasm, the way word flows from thought, diamond from coal, fruit from leaf . . . I approach the man I'm with and I say to him *carpe diem; seize the day; gather ye rosebuds while ye may.* Like the *National Inquirer*, splicing together two separate pictures of two different movie stars so I can accuse them of a lurid affair . . . verbal falsies. I puff 'em up! I pad the truth! Gay deceivers, Amanda Wingfield called it. And that incredible trueness . . . I move my arm and I see it – see it – see it – wah – wah – wah – My breasts were like hers! Time stopped where my breasts bifurcated . . . my breasts, refusing to swell apart . . . they looked like they yearned to be one efflorescence, so close and high did they stay, and I am dripping with diamonds of sight; I move my arm and I see it – see it – see it, whoosh-whoosh-whoosh . . . I move my leg and I see it – see it – see it, wow-wow-wow . . .

Then it's time to go home and so I get on the Long Island Railroad. And you know what? Traveling itself is a kind of hallucination. An illicit, irrational deal where time is exchanged with space and streets and sky and railroad tracks, crack for a dollar, for miles – for towns, any town; traveling itself is a kind of hallucination, much less the actual hallucination that was happening when you see it – see it – see it . . . where you pass tree-tree-tree, you pass bike-lake-tree . . . child-child-child, child-with-tree, tree-with-child, lake-lake, tree-with-sky, tree-with-sky . . . It's like paintings of neural firing, just looking out the window, and they start announcing the stops, and the stops sound like prayers, like Bible recitations, like those chapters that are in the Bible about genealogy: and Noah begot Isaac, and Isaac begot Jacob, and Jacob begot Yahreb, and Yahreb begot Pete, and Pete begot the other guy . . . it's like Bible recitations . . . like facts misplaced in a holy context. And we're moving along and I spoke to someone, and my lips

49

moved a thousand fractions, little twitches of time for each syllable, and I remember Yvette Mim*ieux*! So many letters to make up such a simple *euhhh*, say it – say it – say it: smeared across my teeth, I'm picking letters out of my teeth, and then, all of a sudden, we're in Penn Station, and it echoes, it echoes like infertility . . . nothing-nothing-nothing, whoosh-whoosh-whoosh, and I can't get out – I can't find my way out. *I can't get out!* I see things and see them, I turn my head to look the other way but I don't *see* the other way, I see *my head turning* whoosh-whoosh-whoosh, I see my actions, not their result, I see the act of acting, my actions are airbrushed with this crazy, true thing . . . they kicked Adam and Eve out of Paradise for this kind of self-consciousness, and I CAN'T GET OUT OF PENN STATION! I can't get the fuck out of Penn Station! All of a sudden, I hear click-click-click, and I look, and there's this woman, she's a business woman, she walks like she's all business, like nobody's business. She's got those heels that come to the point with every step: click – click – click, and she's got herself a briefcase, too, and a suit . . . and I'm going to follow her out of here! I'm gonna hitch a ride on her star, I can tell she's leaving, she's one of those women that's always leaving . . . and she's going to save me by knowing how . . . she's going to save me . . . she's going to let my people go! Her shoes click like facts coming in on a teletype machine . . . she's a whole newsroom . . . she knows the way to San Jose.

Now I'm following the sound . . . the blur and echo are airbrushing, but I've got the click, I'm following the sound, it's like click-click-click-click-click-click-click-steps. Steps . . . STEPS! Oh God, a staircase is so incredible . . . so beautiful . . . it's like a hallucination waiting to happen . . . it's an ascension through repetition . . . through receding repetition *I'm up, I'm going up, step step click click click I feel cold light I sense it I'm going up all of a sudden I sense the blue stuff that evening is made of I feel it We're almost out Something is getting louder and softer at the same time I can hear the smell of air and life the whoosh that whoosh of traffic or wind or openness and then*

THERE GOD! We are out! We are OUT! This woman is it! And we are OUT! And we are on the CURB; and this woman is IT – she has freed my people! And we are out of there, and we are on the curb! And she raises her arm to hail a cab; and her arm goes wow-wow-wow see it – see it – see it . . . and I screamed

Oh, my God! She has the same problem I do!

(picks up book and magazine and holds them up to audience) We only really find ourselves in a crisis when we try to hide the truth, isn't that true, ladies and gentlemen? Like this woman here, or like Spalding Gray. It's true he's a WASP from Providence, but that's what this book is about. He's talking about that. He lets you look at that. Or like this woman, right here. Sure. She's a woman. She's a real woman. Her hair is fine her teeth are capped her diamonds are huge and her breasts are South African . . . but it's all out there. There's nothing hidden about it. The Truth sets us free, don't you think, ladies and gentlemen? We only really get ourselves in trouble, when we try to hide the truth. Right?

(PERFORMER returns to bed, climbs up on it; kneels in the center of it, clasping hands together in prayer.)

SUPPLICANT: Now I lay me down to sleep, I pray the Lord my soul to keep. Guide me through the starry night and wake me up at sunshine bright.

Actually, I don't really care what kind of weather it is you wake me up in. I don't know who writes these prayers, the writing is awful. I don't really care what kind of weather it is that you wake me up in. I don't care if it's the kind of weather where the sky is yellow and suppurating and it looks like it has pus in it, or if it's that kind of weather where the sky is slate gray and you can sort of see it's going to snow and you can smell the rust of snow in your nostrils, or if it's that kind of weather where there is no weather because one season is trying to leave and another one's trying to come and in the balance there's nothing; I really don't care what kind of weather you pick, any weather is fine.

Not that I think the weather's trivial, not at all! It's not small talk, really. It's very big talk. I mean, it's like a canopy that we all live under, and it's non-sectarian! There's no such thing as Episcopalian weather, or Catholic weather, or *Yiddish* weather, or Buddhist weather, or Islamic weather, I mean there's just the God-given weather and I appreciate that also!

Listen, I'm sorry I haven't talked to you in a long time. I don't like praying, I'm bad at praying, I'm better on the phone! You know, on the phone you say something and you get a response. Not that I find you unresponsive, it's not that, it's just that . . . talking to you is like talking to someone in the hospital who's in a coma! I mean, you don't know if they hear you or not, they might very well, you just don't know. I mean you don't want to say anything that you don't want them to hear, because they may hear you very well, you just don't know.

And it makes you talk funny. It makes you talk funny to visit someone who's in the hospital who's in a coma. Just like praying makes you talk funny. I mean, you visit someone in the hospital in a coma and you find yourself saying things like: 'Well, she has a neurasthenic icthanoma, it's very common in the ear canal, it's benign and won't metastasize, but the real crisis is, she's wasting sodium, her creatinine and bunn levels are going up and down, we don't know.' No one really talks like that, you know? Like saying, 'Now I lay me down to sleep, I pray the Lord my soul to keep . . .,' nobody really talks like that.

I guess I should tell you a little bit about what I've been doing. I've been swimming a lot. I like swimming, especially in the ocean. You know, when I go in the ocean it makes me feel like I go from someone's lips onto their tongue. And then at night, from the beach, the ocean looks like a big velour skirt, a big black velour skirt, with a little lacy hem of foam. That's really nice. Hey, nice work with the ocean! Thank you for that!

I guess I should also tell you that I've developed a small, localized, limited but very, very intense obsession with Madonna! I wish I could say this was your mother, but it's not! You know, the rock star? Did you see her HBO special? My God, the way she moves! The woman cuts the air like a knife. Her muscles pop under tourniquets of vein, at no expense to her femininity. Now I want that for myself! I want that! See, now I know it's my responsibility to get that, and I *could* get that! I just can't bring myself to go to the gym and push and pump and pull and shove. I mean, I'm conscious at all times that I *lease* this thing *(indicating body)*, I mean at any minute it could go away. I mean, my attitude is: why put in all new fixtures when at any minute the landlord could take away the building?

But Madonna, she doesn't really think that way. I mean she has a personal trainer and she eats macrobiotic foods. Me, I have my mother and I eat Hostess Twinkies and Ding Dong donuts. I mean there's a difference right there.

It's a question of conscience, too. You know, her conscience is like lean and pared down, it's all muscle. Mine isn't like that, mine is clanking and big and it bangs and smacks. I mean, one cannot sing 'La Isla Bonita' with one's conscience clanking and banging like pots and pans. I mean, it just doesn't work.

And ... and ... she's cool the way no Jewish person is cool, do you know what I mean? She's just cool the way no Jewish person is cool. It's a question of *cold* really, actually. You know, when a plane takes off and it flies above the weather and there's raining and blowing and the plane gets high enough and there's just cold! That's what she's like and that's where she operates from. She is the furthest thing from a Jew I have ever seen.

Now I know we're the chosen people, and I feel chosen! I genuinely do! You know what I especially like? Especially I like waiting for the Messiah. You see, these people that think the Messiah has already come, I don't know what they do all day! You see, me, I'm waiting for the Messiah. That is what I'm doing. And I wait downstairs and I wait on the balcony, and I wait by the movie theater, and that's what I do, I wait for the Messiah. But people ...

You know there's this guy walking down the street, he had no shirt on, and he had no shoes on, and he was walking down the street, and he was an elderly gentleman and he was screaming: 'Israel! A peace-loving country! A peace-loving country PISSING ON EVERYBODY!' And then he took another couple of steps and he screamed: 'Israel! A peace-loving country! A peace-loving country PISSING ON EVERYBODY!' And then he put his face in my face and he said: 'HOW'M I DOIN'?'

This combination of Louis Farrakhan and Mayor Koch did not help me very much. Although in retrospect, I guess it makes a lot of sense that these two souls should end up in one body somehow.

Listen, I need to talk to you about something. I need to talk to you about something, I'm a little uncomfortable with the occupation of Gaza. You're Jewish, right? I only talk to Jewish people about this. I'm a little uncomfortable with the occupation of Gaza. Listen, I need Israel. If they march tomorrow looking for Jews, I'm going there. I'd go in a second! I need Israel, you see, but I don't always *like* it ... it's like a little kid and its mother. You know, I'm becoming politically neurotic about this. *(pause)* You're not saying anything! Rilke says the reason you don't say anything is that you're silent because you're listening to us, you're listening. He said in the beginning you talked all the time. He said first you wrote the Old Testament, and then you wrote the New Testament, and then you chatted with Moses and then you spoke to Pharaoh and then you murmured to Jacob wrestling with the angel on the mountain and now you're silent because you're listening to us.

Fuck Rilke!

You know I called up a friend of mine recently to ask him if the human soul was truly immortal. I think you were busy that day or something. I needed to ask and I knew he'd know, because he used to be a priest, but now he just drinks wine and has sex all the time, so I knew he'd know. And I called him and I asked him, 'Is the human soul truly immortal?' And he said,

Sometimes.

(There is a lighting change, and music is heard, softly at first, then building in volume. The PERFORMER *slowly rises from her prayerful position, removes her bedclothing to reveal a bodysuit with pointy breasts and sexy hosiery underneath. As she removes pots and pans from around her ankles, swings them around and tosses them, the music reaches a disco-like beat and crescendo, and two men emerge from the bed to begin a wild, Madonna-like dance. They lift the* PERFORMER, *caress her, toss her about. A wild scene within the bedcovers is a part of this frantic choreography. Finally the music ends, and the silence finds all three dancers on the floor, breathing heavily. After a pause the* PERFORMER *stands, looks at the two supine men, and snaps her fingers. The men instantly rise, lift the* PERFORMER *and carry her to the settee stage left, where she sits in silhouette with her knees bent and the soles of her feet flat on the bench, in the shape of an upper-case N.)*

LETTER N: Pleased to meet you . . . delighted . . . I'm silent N . . . I'm the letter N in the word *condemN* . . . *NNNNN* . . . Jesus! A man said me the other day . . . it was strange . . . First I was floating on the lips of a French woman who was using a lot of plural verbs . . . *PLEUR* . . . *Elles pleur* . . . *ENTS* . . . I was stuck all day between E and T, and wishing they would just phone home . . . when a strange man said me . . . he said me so beautifully: . . . he tongued me . . . He said, This painting of a woman looks like it's all one stroke . . . just one line . . . I feel that I could pick the line up off the canvas at her fingertips and pull till she's completely dislimNed. He was a handsome and sexy man . . . I turned to smoke on his soft palate, perched on the tip of his tongue, and I floated out his nostrils and around the back to where his hair touched his collar. I love that area of a person . . . the Nape of the Neck . . . I spend a lot of time in people's nostrils . . . you know, people with colds, that kind of thing . . . and I figure prominently in the sneeze . . . I come roaring out like one of Bob Fosse's dancers split right down the middle in a crash of jazz . . .

But this man . . . mmmmmmNNNNNNNN . . . I wanted to get him mad enough to curse because I wanted him to say me really sweet . . . so I went through his nostrils into his sinus cavity and created a rite-of-spring sort of disturbance . . . the kind bees make in honeysuckle . . . He was flirting with someone at the museum. And he made this pretentious remark about the nude painting being so *dislimNable* . . . I think he was about to kiss her . . . yeah . . . so he was about to kiss her when I altered his senses completely . . . his eyes filled with water and he said it, O, he said it, O, he said, GODDAM*NNNNNNNNNNNNNNN*!

I flew back to his uvula and shook with the air . . . and the woman left . . . she was too good for him anyway . . . she didn't buy that bullshit about the nude painting being dislimNable . . . well I probably saved him a slap in the face . . .

When I'm silent, I'm undressed, y'know . . . but when I get voiced I get dressed . . . when the going gets tough, the tough get going . . . SOLEM*N* becomes SOLEM*NN*ITY . . . And I go from nude to dressed in an instant . . . I think of that nude woman in the painting . . . I bet she wanted to grab a bathrobe real fast standing nude in front of a lech like that . . .

You know, when letters meet in words it's not a simple thing . . . they are like actors on a stage, trying to create meaNing out of the simple uNits of themselves . . . a word is a whole show . . . and the energy between letters is . . . physical, you know . . . again, like actors on the stage. When you say a word you see it, don't you? . . . you lick it . . . and when you write a word down, you are painting portraits of these actors . . . for example, the word MISOGY*N*IST is like a Chekhov play, because all the letters just stand around wondering how to relate to each other, the Greek roots are sticking out all over the place, and when all is said and done, the meaning is very sad . . .

So. I was in a relationship . . . that didn't work out. You see me at a depressed and unfocused moment in my life, rushing around people's mouths and nostrils . . . I didn't used to do that so much . . . and I . . . I had everything I ever wanted but I didn't know it . . . you may already have heard . . . I was living with silent G. When he's lower case he is so well HuNG, down below the baseline, the floor of the letter, and when he's upper case his form is so beautiful, curving around and back in toward himself like recrimination . . . like remorse . . . like GUILT!

I first met him when we were both in the word IMPUGN, and then we started hanging around together in formal words like CONDIGN . . . words where I was voiced, and cuddled myself on either side of him while he stayed silent . . . women do that shit for men all the time . . .

Then we moved toward a more mutual relationship . . . we were INDIGNANT! both voiced and full of bristle . . . and I was . . . in love, I think . . . and I found I was PREGNANT . . . my body was changing . . . then things deepened . . . we became POIGNANT . . .

I had my baby . . . and I named him ñ . . . and he . . . he went silent again . . . he took a traveling job . . . he's a luG Nut on the wheel of a truck that's moving, moving, moving all night . . . the way he used to move me . . . I feel it when he gets knocked out of aliGNment . . . one of the places where we lived together for so long . . . so long . . .

So what's left for me? The ballet of my upper case, the yoga of my lower case, my little place in the dictionary upstate. Come visit me there, if you want, all unvoiced on the tip of some word. Whoever you are, we'll find a way to be close, or at the very furthest, on either side of a vowel.

Or, if you prefer, just write me a letter . . .

(Two men appear again and, lifting PERFORMER, still in the shape of an N, they carry her gently downstage right. When they place her on her feet there, the opening refrains of the Christmas song 'The First Noel' are heard. As music plays, the men dress PERFORMER in a blonde wig, conservative pink skirt suit with pillbox hat and matching purse. When finished, they recede again and disappear into the bed, leaving PERFORMER swaying gently to music. After the lyrics: 'Born is the King of Is-ra-el!' music fades down.)

LADY: Now this may come as a shock to you, but I am not Christian! No part of me is Christian! But you'd never know it! Appearing Christian has changed my life! This means that people mistake me for a Christian, and actually believe that I am Christian! I look Christian, I act Christian, and I seem Christian, and *farchtik*! What else do circumstances ever require? And I never could have done it without TLC!

TLC is a non-sectarian, unparochial and non-ecumenical equal-opportunity organization that hires the handicapped and is tax-deductible to the fullest extent permitted by the law! TLC, which stands for Trying to Look Christian, was founded by Sammy Davis Junior. Mr. Junior, who was Jewish, believe it or not, and it *is* difficult, founded TLC in an attempt to share his dreams of assimilation with people very much less fortunate than he. TLC has been running on the diesel fuel of donations since 1952, and has helped such very diverse people as Dinah Shore, Sandy Koufax, and the Brooklyn Lubavitcher Rabbi to lead fuller, deeper lives. And these people are even celebrities!

Take me, for example! *Ipse dixit*, I speak for myself! Prior to my affiliation with TLC, nobody asked which church I belonged to, believe you me! Or take Woody Allen, for example! Now to meet Mr. Allen's very special needs, TLC actually formed a casting agency that helped Mr. Allen find the 48 attractive *shiksas* to play the leading ladies in his movies! And this helped him! He did not get stuck with Barbra Streisand, now, believe you me! No people who need people for Mr. Allen!

Redecorating the surface of myself has moved me deeply, thanks to TLC. Prior to my affiliation with TLC, certain of my facial features just bulged like a turnip in a field! And that was hideous, believe you me! But TLC sold me this attractive little nose-nipper and it just fits right over my nose. It's like an aesthetic valium for a face not quite at ease in a Christian world. And I've sold off all my buildings. And my Swiss Bank accounts. And I'm no longer a slumlord or a landlord or even a rich grocer right across the street. And I haven't had a manicure in four weeks. That is so fulfilling, thanks to TLC.

And when I took my Grandma to St. Francis of Assisi Home for the Aged, no one asked to see her baptismal record, believe you me! And it was a nice place! What a lovely place they had! And one old man kept yelling HELP! HELP! But for him that was perfectly normative! I'm sure he said that frequently! And it smelled like urine, but urine is sweet! Like an old melody on a cracked record! And what a beautiful lounge they had over there! It was all windows, you see. Just one big window after the next! Now a window can be seen as just a wound in the wall, can't it? But not these windows, no! Because these were big windows!

And after they strapped my grandma into a wheelchair I wheeled her into her room. She was happy in there! She was happy in there. She talked about her sister, but her sister was dead! And they fed my grandma green grapes. Green grapes! Now eating grapes is like biting into blind eyes . . . cold. Tart. Full of dead visions and fluids. So sweet. So Christian!

And her sister was dead. And I looked out the window, they had great big windows! And there out the window was a little brook! Isn't that attractive? A little brook, running tight and straight, like a perineum between two spread thighs of woods! Like a perineum . . . you know, that clean sweep of tissue that runs from the asshole to the genitals. Perineum, a clean sweep! That is very Christian. And there were two white ducks, swans I think, and I would have liked to see their legs but they were under the surface, and . . . and . . . and a voice came over the loudspeaker and said WE WILL BE HAVING A VALENTINE'S DAY TEA PARTY! BRING YOUR SWEETHEART! BRING YOUR SWEETHEART! But they're dead, you see, the sweethearts are dead! But they had a tea party. They had a tea party! That is very Christian, a tea party, believe you me! It's almost British!

It is a waste of time not to appear Christian. And it's unpopular, too! Now you see, I was in Italy, and if you don't appear Christian in that country, then what the hell have you got? But I did! And I was transfixed! Every two steps, there's a ruin! Now that is very Christian, a ruin! Because you know why? Because when you stand in ruins, when you are surrounded by ancient and crumbling stone, it is very hard to tell where the ruination lies, in you, or in the stone! And as dilemmas go, that is very Christian! Jesus said: 'Raise the stone and there shalt thou find me; Cleave the wood and there I am!' *And that just makes me want to have sex.* Because first of all, why shouldn't I? *This* will outlive me. *That* will outlive me. A 'Have a nice day' button is going to outlive me! And you see, second of all, because sex on a bed of stone is decent and Christian! And I bought a cross in Italy! I have wanted a cross since I first had my bas mitzvah and TLC gave me the emotional purview to buy it! And I did. And I bought that cross and I hung it on a chain. And it was magnificent! I wore a low-cut blouse, and you could see my breasts bursting, and it was magnificent to see, that ancient, crumbling symbol, the ruin, the cross dangling above the twin lions of my life! A tableau vivant of martyrdom right here on my chest! That is incredible thanks to TLC.

And TLC gave me the language that is so very much a part of the Christian appearance:

Our Father who art in Heaven Hallowed be thy name.
Thy Kingdom come,
Thy will be done, on Earth as it is in Heaven.
Give us this day our daily bread
And forgive us our trespasses
As we forgive those who trespass against us.

Whereas my neighbor didn't forgive a trespass! He didn't forgive it at all! He said my dog shit on his lawn and he was going to take legal action! But I act as a Christian! And I said: 'It's not my dog! How do you know it's my dog?' And he said he had videotape of the alleged behavior on the part of the dog! Now videotape is not Christian! Now which Christian is going to go out on the lawn with a camcorder to videotape the defecation of a dog? Jesus said: 'The fowls of the air, and all the beasts that are upon the earth and under the earth, and all the fishes of the sea, these are they which draw you, and the Kingdom of Heaven is within you.' So if my dog shit on his lawn, it was a Christian expression! And I was very irritated!

But one night I became intoxicated and in my desire to conciliate I bought popcorn and a beer! Jesus said: 'Love thy enemies as thyself!' And I did! And I bought popcorn and a beer and I rang his bell! And he came to the door! And he looked for all the world a Christian man in a blue suit, Giorgio Armani. And I said, 'Behold! I have brought popcorn and libation, and I would like to conjoin with you in the Lord to view the videotape of my dog, which you in such kind faith have proffered unto me!' And he said: 'I'll show the movie to your lawyer!' And he slammed the door in my face! Now, no Christians have lawyers, and no Christian lawyers go to the movies. Believe you me!

But I ... *(chuckles)* ... I saw a beggar ... believe you me ... a man with only three teeth ... but they were very white! Very white! And he was talking . . . as I passed him, he was talking . . . as I passed him, he was talking and he said: 'I love my life! I love my life!'

(CD 101.9 smooth jazz radio logo is heard.)

LADY: Could you shut that off, please? *(Music goes off.)* Thank you.

Of all prisons the body is the most beautiful! And we strive as Christians to decorate the body in celebration of that which resides within! That is why bums are not Christian! You look at the body of the bum and you see it for the Riker's Island that it represents! You can hear the spirit looking for release! You can see the soul struggling to unhouse itself. Jesus said, HELP! HELP! He said, OH MY GOD, WHY HAST THOU FORSAKEN ME? Which for Jesus was perfectly normative. I'm sure he said that frequently!

And even the Earth . . . the Earth is like that! I looked out the window, but the snow didn't fit the ground! It was all hiked up in front. It was too short, like a pair of homeless man's pants that he found in the garbage! And it was threadbare in parts, and you could see right through the snow to the skin of the ground. And the lawn just stuck out like a pair of scabby ankles. Now, what kind of snow is that? What kind of snow is that?

(Be cool! CD101.9! Be cool! CD101.9! is heard again, and continues through the end of the play.)

What is this BE COOL? CD 101.9 BE COOL? The Universe is not cool! It's a very warm place, the Universe! The Universe was not created to say BE COOL! *Be cool* is a sleazy byproduct of a great miracle! What is this 101.9? What a stupid number! What a random and arbitrary number, 101.9! What a stupid number! Jesus was on the cross, he was crucified. And his blood ran like rivers under his skin, and he was talking to himself, like a bum! Our deafness made a bum of Him! The Son of God! And was he saying BE COOL? What was he saying to himself? Was he saying BE COOL? Was he saying CD 101.9 up there? No, he was not! No, he was not! He was saying: I love my life! *I love my life.*

(The sounds of saxophone music shoot out into the fading light, which turns to complete darkness.)

FINIS

60

Commentary: *The Girl Can't Help It*

The audacity of this piece. Margolin is very visibly pregnant in this show, playing a call-girl, slipping in and out of a luscious, enormous, cotton-candy-pink bed, hiding two men in a trapdoor beneath its covers, quoting Shakespeare and promising a caller to fulfill his scatological fantasy, but making him wait an hour until she has her cup of coffee. And dancing, dancing, hot and heavy, sweating and surging, bopping and balleting, flying wildly in the face of so many dominant cultural stereotypes about women. Sassy hookers who won't shit on command, pregnant women who flaunt their sexuality, Jewish women passing as *passing* Christians, artists who challenge other artists' work on the basis of ethical issues, icons of the Western dramatic canon sent up like the beauty, horror, and fragility of a hot air balloon swerving through a windstorm.

Perhaps if there is one thing a patriarchal culture can't take, it's a woman who knows what she wants and just *takes* it. And refuses to wait. If waiting was a recurring obsession in *Of All the Nerve*, not waiting is a through-line in *970-DEBB*. Margolin revels in the ecstasy of excess in this piece: the jars and jars of various candies from which one can grab handfuls of treats and never has to worry that they will become empty; the abundant mucus that her body produces during the pregnancy; the grotesque opulence of the model on the magazine cover; the spewing, spilling – doesn't give a damn if no one wants to hear it – diatribe about Spalding Gray's infuriating passivity. All letters lolling around on her tongue exceeding their functions, like boxes of bonbons one can almost imagine the boa-bedecked hooker sucking out of their party-colored papers. Margolin's mouth is an envelope stuffed full of letters, all punctuated, point/counterpointed, by the persistent and inescapable emergence of these words from a body undeniably engorged with impending new life, ripe to bursting, and wholly immersed in the paradox of this ripeness. If one can ring DEBB and opt for *The Tempest*, *As You Like It*, *All's Well That End's Well*, or *Coriolanus* it's a veritable banquet. But there's more. Both 'ripeness' and 'readiness' are 'all' in this piece, *Lear* and *Hamlet* spliced together, the accepting despair of mortality, and the daring, dashing, last stab/grab at the orgiastic plunge into the body erotic. Scarcely ever do we find representations in which it is the pregnant woman's body that holds and makes manifest these timeless paradoxes.

And once again, Margolin takes such timelessness, without

begging 'our' pardon, and gives it time. 'Where is time in this photo?' she demands shaking the cover-girl's image in our faces. The model's image is timeless because it lacks a narrative. Margolin experiences it as an assault on truth, and weaves her own narratives around it to place it back into time. Margolin tells me she's never read Lacan. And I believe her. But I'm not sure why she needs or wants to, except perhaps to find that she is in agreement with him about many things. Most philosophers venture at some point to say what makes 'man' a creature apart from other animals. For Nietzsche, it was promising. For Lacan, the human being distinguished him/herself by being alone in the capacity to lie by telling the truth.

Margolin writes to me about the genesis of her obsession with the cover-girl image:

> walking down Broadway, saw the cover of *Town and Country* magazine, beautiful ageless blonde on the cover, just her head and cleavage, diamond earrings, diamond necklace, perfect teeth, Swiss maybe, the *neutrality*, the country that sat and knitted while Jews were exterminated in Europe. Saw that face and just fucking LOST IT! Ran home and wrote and pounded so furiously the typewriter BROKE, so just pulled the paper out and continued by hand, like someone in a roadside emergency. Ran all the way home with the sudden realization that *we use honesty to hide the truth.* How evil that is. (personal correspondence)

We may laugh when Margolin tells us that her life is threatened by airbrushes, but, indeed, the images of women that the media constantly flaunt are derived from and perpetuate a fascist ideology. Oh, perhaps that's too 'extreme'? Well, this is a performance about extremities and the ways in which they are part of the ordinary fabric of our daily lives. What goes without seeing, without saying, that's the casual violence that *970-DEBB* makes us witness.

What is extraordinary throughout Margolin's work is the persistence of passion and her passionate faith. 'Confession is not morality,' she says, apropos Spalding Gray's monologues about his casual brutality. Morality is about as fashionable as the trick gear Margolin slinks in and out of in her performances. Neither are fearless women. In the 'Now I lay me down to sleep' prayer segment of this performance, Margolin argues with God. She insists on dialogue, not without a hint of trepidation, but nonetheless, she demands a voice that speaks back to her. Citing Rilke *to God*, she says that 'God is silent because he's listening to us.' But even as she says this, she is anticipating an answer. And she won't wait too long for it; if one doesn't come soon she will make up all the voices herself. In this early piece, years before *O Wholly Night* (1996), that later work in which she turns her burning passions toward the subject of faith with focused intensity, she is already 'waiting for the messiah,' and actively so. Faith is something like an hallucination, like the staircase that paralyzes her in Penn Station with the paradox of its architecture, simultaneously infinitely receding and ascending. The truth of hallucinations is more poignant for Margolin than the 'truth of reality,' which is only a ruse to conceal the real. Faith fuels her passions, and thus *970-DEBB* moves through the languages of the body and the bodies of the letters with flagrant disregard for the spurious boundary between the profane and the sacred.

Deb Margolin in *Gestation*. Photo: © *TheaterWeek* 1994.

4

❧

Gestation

(A very pregnant woman, dressed in a hospital gown and wrapped in a sheet, enters from behind a hospital curtain strung across the stage as if separating two parts of a hospital room. She begins to read from an outdated book on childbirth.)

WOMAN: *(reading)* DELIVERY. Having discussed pain relief at length, we can rejoin the parturient in the labor room. By this time she has probably received Demerol and Scopolamine, unless she has chosen psychoprophylaxis, and her husband has been dismissed and sent to the waiting room to join other expectant husbands and their retinues of expectant grandparents and aunts and uncles. The laboring woman is oblivious to all this. She is sleeping soundly between uterine contractions; perhaps snoring. When a contraction comes she wakes, tosses about, moans and, as soon as it subsides, returns to sleep. Her own doctor, the nurses and resident physicians are constantly going in and out of the room. It is likely that the sides of her bed are equipped with movable metal guard rails which are kept raised except during an examination. Analgesia makes one behave as if drunk, and the guard rails protect the patient, restraining her from jumping or falling out of bed if she is momentarily left alone. At frequent intervals a doctor or nurse checks the fetal heart with a stethoscope, noting its rate and regularity. At less frequent intervals a physician determines the extent of labor's progress by rectal or vaginal examination. Now the pains become longer in duration and more frequent, occurring every three or four minutes, and the show becomes bloody. When examination reveals the cervix fully dilated and the baby descended to the vaginal floor, the patient is transferred to the delivery room.

(WOMAN closes book and opens hospital curtain to reveal delivery table, covered in white. She lies down, moans, tosses, snores, tries to sit up, lies back

65

down, snores again, starts laughing as if drunk, half-sits again, lies back down, snores, rises, and finally sits.)

WOMAN: *(staring at audience)* You know, it's the weekend! What are you doing here? There's a new Nick Nolte film just opened up! Why are you people sitting here? I mean, me, I'm behaving as if drunk and am oblivious to all this, but what's your excuse? Oh! You must be that retinue of expectant aunts and uncles, husbands and grandparents in the waiting room! You are sweet! That is so awfully sweet of you to come! Thank you so much, it's the weekend, you could be at the movies!

And don't worry about me! I'm fine! I'm really fine! I love the night! It's night right now, and I like that. I love the night. I know the night like I know nothing else. I haven't slept in 248 nights. I've seen the night without her teeth in. I know what's inside the night ... I've seen the shows *The Joker's Wild*, *The $100,000 Pyramid*. I am not afraid of the night. As a matter of fact, sometimes it seems to me as if the night comes out from between my legs ... as if I labor the night, I push it out ... and then I push out the pink placenta of the dawn, and there you go: another day! You put on your suit and tie and you go to your job, if you still have one.

No, I'm not afraid of the night ... I love the night ... these eight and one-half months that I haven't slept ... each of those nights seem like long novels by inexperienced writers, or like run-on sentences full of mixed metaphors. And yet the night is real regular ... real regular in a jagged and hideous and horrifying kind of way. I can judge the age of the night by the comings and goings of certain events that are very regular. For example, every night at the same time this dog begins to bark as if it's being beaten or as if it's terribly hungry, and this rouses me, and then I hear the garbage cans dancing under the hands of the homeless, and then every night at the same time the guy upstairs gets to fucking his girlfriend, and it makes that kind of rhythmic noise like a clock, and then at the end of this very very predictable extravaganza she screams Oh my God I'm coming Oh my God I'm coming, but I don't really see the point of that. I mean, you don't stick your head out the window of your car and shriek Oh my God I'm driving Oh my God I'm driving. Not that it isn't great to get enthusiastic about what you do, but I mean why state the obvious?

It's easy to judge the whereabouts of the different pieces of the night by the comings and goings of her screaming she's coming and that dog that barks and there are certain trains that only come in the night, you don't hear them during the day.

See, the thing is, my mind and my TV are both on all night, and in the night they become the same, they develop the same strengths and weaknesses. As strengths go, there's something to be said for images that just come and come without regard to quality or value of any kind. And as weaknesses go: you know, recently, Manhattan Cable sent soldiers up to the rooftops of all the buildings to disconnect the cable boxes of those customers receiving cable without paying for it, and then they waited to see who would call them and complain so they could arrest them instantaneously. I discovered this one night, I came home and turned on my TV, and there was nothing on there but *bukisheh-benh*. But I did not call them! I did not call them! No; instead, I propped myself up on pillows and I just stared at the TV screen all night, just as I always do! And I thought about things. I thought about sex. And I thought about typographical errors. For example, at this restaurant I frequented all the time for years, there was this line in the menu that said: 'All of the above served with tempting home fires.' And I thought about this other typographical error from high school, in a history book, in which our country was referred to as 'The Untied States' and in the morning I rose from my bed and I turned on the TV and everything was okay again. And I thought that I had sat out and won this taut and vicious little war with the Cable Company.

But little did I realize that they were secretly incubating the worst terror that they could think of, and this was that they disconnected the box and they rewired it so you could get all the channels, but they just were not where the cable box said they were. So that Channel 2 had people speaking Japanese, Channel 3 was Channel 4, Channel 4 had Spanish soap operas, Channel 5 was completely inchoate and Channel 6 had pictures of jewelry on it while people talked about death and dying in French. You know, every once in a while your friend'll call you up and say, Quick! Turn on Channel 11! John Terwilliger is making a speech!

You know I was crossing the street recently and I could tell I needed to start to walk a little faster as I crossed because the DON'T WALK signs were blinking and the other lights were turning and cars were beginning to slide up the avenue toward me like carbonation up the side of a beverage glass, and it was time to pick up the pace; clearly, it would be okay if I could just PICK UP THE PACE. And I sent a signal to pick up the pace, and the signal went from my thoughts to my spine, and from my spine to my brain, and from my brain to my spine and from my spine to my legs, and ABSOLUTELY NOTHING TRANSPIRED. You know, speaking of his inner life, Neruda said: 'I call for the fireman and the arsonist comes.' It was kind of like that.

So, I spent the first three months of my confinement forging new mental connections between numbers, letters and channels, like someone trying to learn to speak again after a stroke. I discovered ABC TV on Channel J Leased Access. I discovered WOR on Channel 8, I found A & E on MTV and PIX on VH-1. I thought of labeling these things, but I never did. Some channels I never found, and I discovered channels I never knew existed, and which probably didn't. I never found PBS, Channel 13; this left a hole in my life, like brain damage.

TV is the vocabulary of the night, I guess; the way the night speaks to me, those images all pushed up against the dark, and the baby pushed up against the right side, against the bladder, and the night passing by: I labor the night, I know the night like I know nothing else, I'm slow, I've had a stroke called night, Johnny Carson is on where Al Goldstein used to be, and the Joker's Wild, I'm all knocked up, and when they show me those dirty pictures deep in the night, all I can do is giggle and say: O, that silly machine.

(WOMAN seductively sheds her sheet and hospital gown to reveal a skin-tight black spandex dress; dons 4-inch black spike high heels; she approaches audience members directly, as a PROSTITUTE would prospective johns. She rubs her protruding belly seductively throughout.)

It's nice to see you tonight, how're y'all? Ooooh, you look nice to me, all 'o you, you look really nice to me tonight. How ya doin'? Oh, you're lookin' at my dress, you like my dress! Ha ha! Yeah, I like tight things! It fits me like a glove, don't it? Yeah, I like that. Yeah. Oooh. It is a sultry evening tonight. *(to one man in audience)* Hey what're ya doin' here, you wanna party? I've got a lovely place right over here, you can see it from here! *(looking down at pregnant belly)* You're worried about him? Oh, don't! He is very discreet and he loves meeting new people! Yeah, it's right over here! You can see it from here! So if you'd like to party, you happen to be here, and you look very nice to me. I'll be right over here. You think about it. *(approaching another man)* How you doin'? You busy? You look wonderful to me tonight! You wanna party? You wanna go out, I have a place right over here! You can see it from here! *(touching stomach)* Listen, don't worry about him! Ménage à trois! I'm gonna name him John after you, if you're nice to me! You busy, you wanna party? I got a place right here! *(to first prospective john)* Did you change your mind, I see you lookin' at me? Well, I'll be here!

(WOMAN reluctantly leaves prospects, dons lab coat and glasses, approaches a podium in very official manner; transforming into GENETICS LECTURER.)

GENETICS LECTURER: Would anyone like some apple juice? Some apple juice? Good. That's what it's there for! Good! If you'd like some refreshments, please help yourself, because that's what we're here for! Good!

I think we're all here, so let's begin, shall we? Because that's what we've come for! Good! Now! Any genetic counseling must necessarily begin with a discussion of the sperm cell and the egg cells, which are the couriers of chromosomes, which are the purveyors of genes! Which are the main morphological unit of genetic prose, aren't they? Now isn't that a beautiful analogy! In other words, if a baby were a novel, a gene would be a word, wouldn't it? Or perhaps the etymology of a word, and the word would be a toe or finger or some other digit, wouldn't it? Don't you think so? Well, never mind! We can contemplate this analogy a little later further on! Or rather, a little further later on! Well it's easy! It's easy to make a mistake! Ha ha!

Good! Now, girls, as you know, are born with all the eggs they're ever going to produce! Whereas males are continually producing sperm and sperm throughout their adolescent and adult lives, girls come packed for the picnic! Girls are born with all their eggs in one basket! Not that you have to have kids! You don't! It's just an option! Look don't ask me! One of our trained technicians would be delighted to help you! When you pick up a baby girl, you are holding the future to your bosom! Because in the armoire of her ovaries is every egg she is ever going to produce. And we don't even think about it!

Now let's discuss menstruation, shall we? Because that's what we're here for! Now menstruation is a kind of *Folies Bergères*, isn't it? It's a sort of circus juggling act in fancy-pants underwear, isn't it? Because every month the follicle MATURES, and then you get your PERIOD, and it MATURES, and you get your PERIOD, and it MATURES and you get your PERIOD, don't you? Now I've brought along a visual aid to help you understand this a little bit better!

(GENETICS LECTURER goes over to podium and picks up three juggling balls, and does a clumsy two-up one-down juggle while repeating:)

The follicle MATURES, you get your PERIOD, follicle MATURES, you get your PERIOD, follicle MATURES, you get your PERIOD!

(LECTURER fails to catch balls on the last throw, and they drop to the floor disgraced.)

LECTURER: *(continuing)* Let's look in depth a little more at this phenomenon, shall we? Every month, on a miraculous negative feedback system, the brain produces a chemical called FSH . . . Follicle Stimulating Hormone! And this causes the follicle to make the egg mature and mature and ripen and ripen! And when the chemical level gets high enough in the brain, then the brain sends a signal to the pituitary gland. And the pituitary gland releases a hormone called Follicle Stimulating Hormone Releasing Factor, or FSHRF! And then this information gets down to the follicle, and it causes the egg to BURST THROUGH the skin of the ovary in a triumphant and violent action known as ovulation! And when it BURSTS THROUGH the skin of the ovary, it leaves behind a scar called the CORPUS LUTEUM! *(to a man in audience)* Did you know, sir, that every time you ovulate, it leaves behind a scar? Because that's what corpus luteum means: white body! The scar! Like a ghost! Scars are like ghosts, aren't they, haunting the surface of the body to remind us of events from the past! Isn't that true? Like celestial spirits wandering the surface of the body! And then the corpus luteum produces a chemical called Luteinizing Hormone, or LH, while the egg promenades down the Fallopian tube like a society woman! Now if the egg is not fertilized, the level of progesterone gets so high in the brain that the brain just clicks off! Like at a gas pump when the tank is full and the car just clicks off! And then you get your period, because your body just says: well, forget it!

But if the egg gets fertilized, that's a different story. Now you know, the sperm line up like mooses in a field! Because the sperm are very small compared to the egg! Now the egg is big! It is behemoth. It is be*she*moth! And the sperm line up like men at a stag party looking across at Tuesday Weld. And then the cream of the crop, pardon the expression, charge forward and plunge themselves at the egg. Because the egg is very aloof! The egg acts like it doesn't even care, like this:

(LECTURER goes over to wall and stands nonchalantly, chewing gum, wiggling her leg, not unlike the PROSTITUTE in the previous section.)

But the sperm secrete a special substance that melts the defenses of the egg! That wines and dines the egg with flowers and candy! And finally the egg drops her defenses, and when she does, one of the sperms rushes in, and then the doors of the egg slam shut and there's a hush! Like a car accident! A silence! And then comes the royal wedding. Like Prince Charles and Lady Di! Because then the sperm and the egg united begin to march down the Fallopian tube toward the grand altar of the uterus! *(to audience member)* Would you be kind enough to demonstrate this with me?

(LECTURER takes audience member and commences a brief, pompous promenade across the stage; then releases audience member to return to seat.)

And when they arrive at the uterus, the corpus luteum caters the whole affair! With entrées and hors d'oeuvres in the lining of the uterus, which is called the endometrium! And then, after everyone has eaten and the guests have gone home, it's time to implant. Which is something like looking for an apartment in New York, isn't it? You have to pound the pavement, don't you? How 'bout over here? Nah, bad block! Down by the cervix? No, it's inconvenient to my job. How 'bout by the bladder? Sure! Right here! And then they dig in ... UNH! And after it digs in, then the cells begin to replicate: HOW YOU DOIN', SEE YOU AROUND, HOW YOU DOIN', SEE YOU AROUND, HOW YOU DOIN', SEE YOU AROUND until the egg becomes a zygote!

Now, let's step back for a moment and get the picture, because that is what we're here for. Now the egg, which has become a zygote, and has dug in, is in the body of a living, breathing woman. Now as soon as it digs in, this same woman may begin to weep, wheeze, gag, gasp, sneeze, vomit, sleep, vomit, sneeze, gag, gasp, weep and wheeze. Which does not lead to sleep, ladies and gentlemen, no! Where does it lead? It leads right into the center of the night.

(LECTURER returns to birthing table, once again becoming the semi-conscious laboring woman, snoring and laughing as before; then sits up and says:)

You know, it's one thing not to sleep for the night; it's another thing not to sleep for 248 nights in a row. I've noticed that people in the day do not acknowledge the night. The night is like a sick relative or a poor relation. To me, the day and night have come to seem like the left and right hemispheres of a brain that's been cut down the center, so the words have no pictures and the pictures have no words. And you would think that the people who program late-night TV would have some compassion and pity for people who are so alienated from the normal circadian rhythms of daily life that they never sleep! You would think they would show us some interesting and decent television programs, like Shakespeare plays or sex, active sex or something! But no, what do we get, we get *The Joker's Wild*, we get *The Match Game* with Gene Rayburn! *Get Smart*, or the *Donna Reed Show*, this is what we get! It's kind of like the homeless situation; being homeless is very exhausting, it requires a great deal of energy, going from house to house and weather to weather; you'd think that at these soup kitchens they'd give them filet mignon and caviar and broccoli and cauliflower, and all they really get is shit from a can.

(LECTURER gets off birthing table, takes off lab coat, and appears again as PROSTITUTE.)

WOMAN: Are you quite certain that absolutely no one in this room would like to party? Because I have a place right here, you can see it! *(touching belly, referring to fetus)* He is wonderful, he just really enjoys rocking rhythms and things, he's a wonderful person! Anybody? Right over here!

Awright, well I don't even care really, I don't care! I mean, what is it, this? *(holding belly)* Is it THIS that bothers you? Well if you can't deal with this I don't know how you're going to deal with life's BIG problems! I mean, what do you think sex brings? This! That's what sex brings! I mean, seriously! You know I used to be so busy I had to make overlapping appointments and hope somebody got diarrhea, and now everybody's lined up marchin' to Delores! Fine! I don't care! Go ahead! I'm busy anyway! *(to fetus)* C'mon! C'mon sweetie! Fine, I don't even care. C'mon we'll go home and watch some television . . . *(to audience)* I'd rather watch TV alone than look at it over your shoulder anyway!

(She turns away from audience. Blue television lights replace more surgical ones; as she talks to her unborn child, she puts on a bathrobe, slippers, and a wig with curlers in it.)

WOMAN: *(to fetus)* C'mon sweetie! Sweetie, I'll eat some pizza, I promise you I'll eat some pizza, I know you like it, c'mon sweetie, *The Joker's Wild*'s on, I know you enjoy that music, it's three chords, but boy do they jam. And after that, sweetie, we can watch *Nightwatch* tonight, I think that guy Charlie Rose is doin' it, yeah. It'll be fun. Alright sweetie.

(She pulls a string, and a diaphanous, television-screenesque scrim falls from the ceiling.)

I'm gonna get some pizza. I'm gonna order it, sweetie.

(TV switches on; WOMAN becomes characters on late-night television, as seen behind scrim: characters from the B-movie The Girls at the Office, *Gold Bond Medicated Powder commercials,* The Joker's Wild, *etc. Channel switches are audible. WOMAN plays both parts in dialogues.)*

Greg, it's been lovely!
Yes. So lovely.
Well, I better be going. I need my beauty sleep.
No. Stay.
Oh, Greg. It's late. I'll see you again.
What's wrong with now?
Greg, I really like you. Let's not rush it.
Rush it? Rush it? We've had our evening, now let's finish it.
What? What do you mean?
I mean when I take a woman to dinner I like to finish the evening in a certain way.
Oh! So you paid for the dinner and now you expect something?

I don't rush around wining and dining people for nothing.

(CHANNEL SWITCH)

Gold Bond Medicated Powder! It accomplishes three functions:
It dries;
It absorbs; and it
Gets rid of moisture!

(CHANNEL SWITCH)

I wasn't thinking of a secretarial job. Perhaps something with a bit more responsibility. And money.
The jobs we were interviewing people for were secretarial . . .
Would you like to see me later?

(CHANNEL SWITCH)

Gold Bond Medicated Powder!
Down here we have the heat, which is hot!
And the humidity, which is high!
That's why I'm goin' with the Gold Bond Medicated Powder!

(CHANNEL SWITCH)

Why don't you just give me a hundred-dollar bill! At least that would have been honest!

(CHANNEL SWITCH)

Gold Bond Medicated Powder!
I drive a truck, and the heat is hot.
And the sweat sticks to your back,
and it sticks to your chest, and it
sticks to your stick!
That's why I'm goin' with the Gold Bond Medicated Powder!

(CHANNEL SWITCH)

(singing) Duh duh duh duh duh DUNH! Hey, welcome to *The Joker's Wild*! Let's meet our two contestants, John Jehosephat and Jack Bukishehbenh! Mr. Bukishehbenh, Mr. Jehosephat's our reigning champion so you're going to have to sit tight for just a moment! Mr. Jehosephat, welcome back sir, how you doing? Tell us, what is it you do sir? I can't hear you sir!

Awright, keep it to yourself! Mr. Bukishehbenh ... he's from South Benh! And what do you do, sir? You're a tree surgeon! Isn't that interesting! Okay! So you both know how we play our game, you spin for the value of each correct answer, winner chooses the category, the first one to reach $300 will join us in the winner's circle! Okay, John! You're our defending champion, are you ready? You stand by, Mr. Bukishehbenh! Okay, your category? ARMS AND THE MAN! Good! We'll be right back!

(CHANNEL SWITCH)

Gold Bond Medicated Powder!
I bowl! And the heat is hot!
And the sweat gets under my watch
and then I get the pimples up there under the watch!
That's why I'm goin' with the Gold Bond Medicated Powder!

(CHANNEL SWITCH)

(in a rage) I would prefer an assassin's bullet! To this besmirchment of my reputation!
What can you take from a man? You can take his name!
I would prefer an assassin's bullet!

(CHANNEL SWITCH)

Gold Bond Medicated Powder!
I bowl! And the heat is hot!
And the sweat gets up all the way up there under the watch,
and you get the pimples up there under the watch.
That's why I'm going with the Gold Bond ...

(CHANNEL SWITCH)

Okay, we're back! Here we go, with our defending champion John Bukishehbenh, and your category again, sir? ARMS AND THE MAN! Each correct answer is worth duhduhduh! Okay, here we go, fingers on the buttons! ARMS AND THE MAN!

How many arms does a man have? ENH!
What is a man-at-arms? ENH!
Where do men get arms? ENH!

Who wrote *A Farewell to Arms?* ENH!
Which amendment treats a man's right to bear arms? ENH!
Would Joan Armatrading date a man? ENH!

Okay! And, SPIN the wheel! Joker, joker, JOKER!

(CHANNEL SWITCH)

(Throughout the ensuing monologue, delivered in an ominous monotone, WOMAN is engaged in preparing the birthing table, taking off all remaining clothing, smoothing cloths, and lying down for birth.)

Good evening, and welcome to *The Passage of Time*, with our two experts, Mr. Shock and Mr. Sheback. Gentlemen, time has alternately been described as the murderer of all men, the fickle finger of fate and as the ultimate mercy of Eternity, gentlemen, today time has a special valence for Americans as our sons and daughters sit looking at their watches waiting for jobs to become available once again and for breathable oxygen, gentlemen, and as rapes and murders occur in three-second intervals, gentlemen, what are your views on the passage of time, if we could look at you as ecological experts on the evolution and life forms of a particular river, gentlemen, this river being time, gentlemen, what are your observations, is time passing any differently now then it did, say, 15 minutes ago, or 15 years ago, or 15 centuries ago, gentlemen, was there even time 15 millennia ago, gentlemen, what is your opinion . . .

(Lighting abruptly switches to DELIVERY ROOM; WOMAN is supine, on her side, thrashing; voice of FETUS is heard, coming from WOMAN's mouth; WOMAN is now like someone speaking in tongues, or someone possessed.)

Mommy mommy mommy mommy OOPS mommy OOPS mommy mommy mommy mommy gonna STAMP on your cervix mommy STRETCH on your cervix mommy STUFF on your cervix mommy mommy mommy mommy OOPS mommy mommy mommy so big to be so small so small to be so big mommy LIGHT! Mommy I like LIGHT! Mommy take back off from on your dress mommy take back off from on your dress mommy LIGHT! Mommy something went up my eyes mommy something white went all the way up my eyes mommy More! Mommy More! Mommy More Park Sausages Mom! Mommy pins mommy little pins are pointing at me mommy

PIZZA! Mommy pizza like before! Mommy pizza! Mommy little pins are pointing at me that made me mommy mommy when you eat mommy drumbeat of your body mommy drumbeat in your body mommy when you eat water comes down between the drumbeats of your body mommy pizza! Mommy pizza like before! Mommy can you see me I don't see you yet mommy do you see me Mommy nice mommy warm Mommy no! Mommy no! Mommy SQUEEZE!

(A tape of WOMAN's voice is now heard, reading from the same childbirth book as in the very first scene. During it, WOMAN herself lies, quietly thrashing, on the birthing table.)

VOICE: THE DELIVERY ROOM. A delivery room looks like a small operating room. It contains a complicated-looking anesthesia machine full of knobs and different-colored cylinders of various ancsthetic gases. There is also an instrument table draped with sterile throws. An infant resuscitation machine is off in one corner. The personnel are capped, masked and sterilely gowned and gloved. Until recently, few patients ever saw all this; but now in the era of psychological pain relief and conduction anesthesia, many laboring women see the entire birth process. The woman is transferred to the delivery table, a very broad type of operating table equipped with legholders which, when she lies on her back, hold her legs wide apart. Her wrists arc strapped to the side of the table to prevent her from fingering the sterile drapes when they are applied. If the membranes are intact, the doctor ruptures them with a clamp or hook. At this stage, unless the patient has received epidural or spinal anesthesia, the baby's head pressing on the tissues of the lower vagina and bowel make her bear down involuntarily with a reflex desire to expel the offending mass.

(Voice of FETUS can again be heard, under calm voice narrating events in the delivery room.)

FETUS: Mommy push mommy squeeze mommy squeeze . . .

VOICE: With each labor pain, because of the powerful force generated by the contraction of the large, muscular uterus, aided by the mother's vigorous straining, the baby descends lower and lower and soon its scalp appears at the entrance to the vagina.

FETUS: ... Mommy squeeze! Mommy stop! Mommy no! Mommy stop! Mommy MOVE! Mommy move! Mommy can't you see my Mommy's pregnant MOVE! Mommy move! Mommy stop! Mommy no! Mommy squeeze! Mommy my head is cold! Mommy stop! Mommy stop! Mommy my head is cold! Mommy touch! Mommy squeeze!

(Over these last prayers, a tape of a crying newborn is heard, voice of FETUS continues softly beneath crying; lights fade.)

FINIS

Commentary: *There's a Party Going on in Here*

Gold Bond Medicated Powder has a toll-free number: 1-800-745-2429. It must be something like a 1-900 number, only it's free. Maybe it's kind of like a sex line for people who need to talk about their jock itch, pimples under their watchbands, heat rash between thighs that rub together. Maybe I can talk Deb into ringing them up with our questions and comments. 'The Heat is Hot!' the Gold Bond actor repeats. Deb describes this as 'a humiliating tautology – a phylum of hopelessness in that phrase the level of which [she] has never encountered before or since.' *Gestation* extends the work of *970-DEBB*. Now in a very advanced stage of her pregnancy, Margolin encounters the anti-evolutionary effect of conception: 'From the moment of conception I wanted sex. All I thought about. It was so bad, so desperate. I'd have to go into bathrooms and alleyways. It was involuntary. Must be the hormones. No one ever told me I'd think of nothing but sex after sex took its due effect; Darwinian thinking cannot possibly account for this kind of endless randy and orgasmic desperation *after conception.*'

Her genetics lecturer in this performance explains that the ovum is 'aloof' like a whore hanging on a lamppost, attempting to lure her clients without moving, while the sperm are all lined up like moose in the wild, poised to spring into action and may the fastest man win. Margolin devises new metaphors to send-up this biological model which has been accredited to gender, creating a symmetry between masculinity and activity and femininity and passivity. The word 'gestation' shares etymological roots with 'gestic' – 'pertaining to movement of the body, especially in dancing,' and with 'gesticula-tion' – 'a deliberate and vigorous motion of the body.' All three words derive from *gest* (to bear). But the latter two are active and connote grace, discipline, vigor, and agency. Gestation, peculiarly alone, has come to signify a passive state, an inertia, an endurance. This perfomance takes up, once again, the notion of a time in a woman's life when she is presumed to be waiting – a time without a narrative. And of course pregnancy *is* usually represented as something that happens *to* a woman (she doesn't knock, she gets knocked up). At the opening of this performance, Margolin reads from a manual on pregnancy from a section that describes what might be expected to occur just prior to and during the delivery. The pregnant woman is described as the *object* of this process, and, moreover, virtually oblivious to what her body is doing – she moans, snores, twists, turns, wheezes, snores, expands, contracts, and pushes – all while anesthetized and restrained, surrounded by a retinue of expectant others. Her 'gesticulations' are carefully monitored and kept out of view, following, perhaps, Lord Chatham's social proprietary note: *Above all things avoid any gesticulations of the body.* Pregnancy has long been understood as a period of *confinement,* a time for restraint. Margolin experiences her bondage as being mastered by Gold Bond, a crude sadist who assaults her senses during her prolonged insomnia. But by performing this confinement, Margolin, in what by now has become a signature gesture, confronts her audience with looking at that which is not to be seen. Refusing to be alone, she has a party going on in her body, and everyone is invited. Slipping off the delivery table and out of her hospital gown, she walks toward the audience wearing a skin-tight black dress, caressing her belly, tempting them to come on over to her place – it's right around the corner, you can see it from here. She gets no takers. A whore put out of business by being knocked up, her come-on effects multiple transgressions: having sex with a pregnant woman is a ménage à trois she suggests. What? The idea isn't so appealing when you think of the third person as one already inside the woman's body? Her place is really close, if you look hard you can see it from where she's standing. Oh, no one wants to change places with her? Western civilizations would not have endeavored so hard to represent pregnant women as docile, passive, reverential vessels, were it not for the obvious fact that they are *not.* 'Oh, my god, I'm coming,' Margolin's upstairs neighbor screams nightly, punctuating *The Joker's Wild, The Girls at the Office,* and those endless Gold Bond Medicated Powder commercials. 'Why state the obvious?' Margolin retorts in response. What Deb Margolin considers the 'obvious' is more like the transitive

79

verb 'obviate' – to dispose of effectively, anticipate so as to render unnecessary. Virgins turned whores, or whores turned virgins? Feminist theoreticians have written volumes about the patriarchal double-bind that insists upon women occupying both categories at once *while* demanding that they remain exclusive. Anticipating this division, she obviates it. She's going to have it both ways *inclusively* and invite everyone to this party.

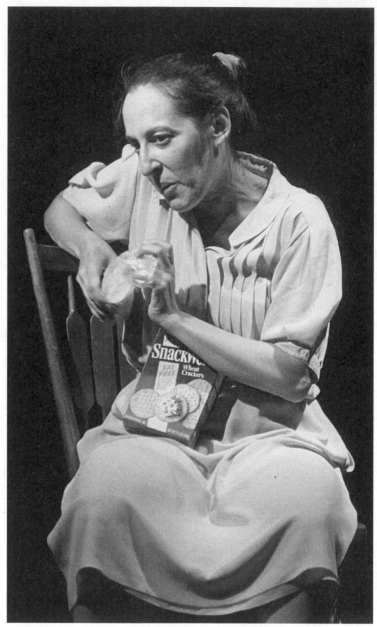

Deb Margolin in *Of Mice, Bugs and Women*. Photo: © Dona Ann McAdams.

5

Of Mice, Bugs and Women

(Of Mice, Bugs and Women *is performed on a set which features, stage right, a kitchen table with tablecloth; on this table are an ashtray with matches in it, a coffee cup, a box of Cheese Nips and a glass with red wine in it. Two chairs are at the table: one of them is austere and wooden, with arms; the other is more luxurious, sensuous. A window frame, dressed with curtains, hangs from the ceiling, all the way stage right, next to the table; it is the window referred to by both the EXTERMINATOR and the CHARACTER CUT FROM THE NOVEL. Upstage left is a piano bench or table with various children's toys on it; the entire stage picture coheres into a homey atmosphere upstage, and downstage a blank, open playing space. Between the four monologues, as well as at the very beginning of the play, the buzzing of an insect, the semiotic bee, is heard. Costume changes between characters take place in complete darkness while the sound of this bee is heard; when the lights come up on the next character, the costume worn by the preceding character is visible, quickly discarded, on the floor. The stage floor is littered with costume pieces by show's end. The performer works around them.*

Some final blocking notes: Except for his initial swatting of a fly that lands on the kitchen table, the EXTERMINATOR uses the empty front playing space for his monologue. The NOVELIST sits in the austere wooden chair, placed at the downstage right corner of the kitchen table; the CHARACTER CUT FROM THE NOVEL sits in the sensuous chair, at the upstage left corner of the table, placing her nearly dead-center stage. The final, more naturalistic monologue, in which the PERFORMER sheds character, takes place all over the stage and encompasses all aspects, symbolic and naturalistic, of the stage setting.)

(Sound of insect buzzing; EXTERMINATOR knocks on door offstage.)

    EXTERMINATOR: Hello! Exterminator! Exterminator!

(Enters)

Alright, I got it! I got it! *(pulls out fly swatter, looks for insect, swats. Sound of buzzing off.)*

Hello, exterminator! Tell me about your problem! And yes, I'm still the exterminator! Still on the job! You know, people think because it's ex-terminator that I no longer have the job, but I'm still on the job! Exterminator! See it's Latin! EX is from the Latin! Anybody here take Latin? Anybody! Anybody! See, ex is Latin for out! It means out! Like EX-IT means you go OUT of IT! Or like EX LAX means it gets the shit OUT! Or like EX-TERMINATOR! OUT of people like me, they make a TERMINATOR! Exterminator! Now! Tell me about your problem!

Now! A woman I service on the East Side got them big thick roaches! Waterbugs! You know she actually tried to kill them by stamping on them, covering 'em up with oaktag! She'd herd 'em all up, put oaktag cardboard over 'em, and jump! Took two hours a shot! Now! Tell me about your problem! You know, bugs! I'm a bugs man and a mouse man! Bugs and mice are different! Okay! What's the difference between a bug and a mouse? Right! A mouse is a little bit bigger than a bug but there's another important difference! What is it? Anybody! What is it? It's *motivation*! *Motivation*! Because a bug just tries to survive, whereas a mouse is burdened with an actual *will to live*! Will to live! Separates the bugs from the mice! Will to live! See a bug... alright, now what is a bug? Okay, it's an insect... maybe it has wings or whatever, but it's no falcon! *And you, senator, are no Jack Kennedy!* Haha! That was very good when he said that! Haha! Whereas a mouse has no wings, but flight is its middle name! It flees! It flees! Silently! See, what's the most devastating thing about a mousetrap? Anybody! Anybody! It's the *noise* it makes! Because it's attention! Mice don't want no attention! Bugs don't mind! I saw a mouse once, brown. Lived at the apartment of one of my clients. Lived there so long it was listed in the phone book! Tried everything. Tried everything with this mouse. One day, mouse left. My client was going to work, fumbling with her keys. The mouse ran out of her house and under the door into her neighbor's house. Disappeared all at once, just like that. Gal called me up the next day, said she missed the mouse! Said she didn't have no *closure* with the mouse! Made me come back and look for it! Crazy gal! Crazy gal!

Whereas the bugs won't move when they've got it good!

84

Now! Tell me about your problem. Now, bugs swarm around the dead! Mice don't swarm around the dead! Saw a frog once, dead! Dead, it looked like a bearskin rug! Dead before it had a chance, flattened by a guy walking to the swimpool! It looked like a fossil! Fossils are funny! Okay, what is a fossil? Anybody! Anybody! Fossil's an impression! You know, not the creature itself, but the impression it makes on a soft surface! These impressions of the dead last for years! Centuries! Impression of the dead! Anybody! Impressions of the dead! So there's this dead frog, you know, and it's like Tavern on the Green for the flies! Now, this young frog's mother did not intend for her baby to lie squashed under a bunch of bugs like the buffet table at a bar mitzvah. But you take a mouse! A mouse won't do that! Mouse won't do that! Mouse won't get all gussied up to come out and eat barbecue from the dead! Why? Because it's *publicity*, you see! Publicity! A mouse don't want no publicity! Like a criminal, or a celebrity on vacation! Mouse is private! Quiet! Good neighbor, see!

Saddest mouse I ever seen in Port Authority! They beep me, tell me Port Authority! I go over there, second floor up the escalator, there's a mouse in the candy corn! Ploughing with its feet in the candy corn, it can't even eat cause it can't walk, can't walk cause it can't get no traction, like a treadmill! Treadmill of death in the candy corn! Couldn't breath too good in there either! Flailing its legs, wagging its tail, trying to move, scared. I get it out for them, they reopen the store, don't clean up or nothin', little kid comes in, what does he want, he wants candy corn, mother buys him candy corn, he's eating it. I show him the mouse, he falls in love with it. Had little orange crumbs on it. Killed it with the spray gun.

Tell me about your problem! See! I know a lady got porcupines! Porcupines, they eat houses! Lady's got porcupines lunching on her house, see! So what does she do? She buys a gun, right? She puts on a hat, lies down on the ground near the floorboards, starts shooting! But she shot a mouse! Because the porcupine's too smart for that! The porcupines, they loaded their guts with wood, laid down, waited it out, like at McDonald's! Kid hid in the dishwasher till it was all over, see! Twenty-three people dead, kid hid in the dishwasher! Kid hid in the dishwasher! Wouldn't come out! Didn't know it was over, wouldn't come out! Wouldn't come out till the cops drug him out!

It's against company policy! See, I'm not allowed to kill anything myself, see! With my own hands, see! It's against company policy, see! I just create an atmosphere, see, where they just drop dead! Or an environment! I create an environment! But I don't do it myself, see! I'm an operative! And I got a radio, see! A radio! Someone got bugs, they can reach me! Call the front office, they send me right out! To the exact place and everything!

One lady calls me up for a bee! Christ I got stories! She calls me up for a bee! See, she's sitting there in a bathing suit with a cup of coffee, and there's a bee caught between the screen and the blinds! Buzzing deep! She's aging! I see her, a young woman! This is the best moment of her life, see, she's been swimming, she's got coffee, she's strong, see, but she's listening to this bee! She's at the top of the V! See your life is an upside down V! Everyone's is! Everyone's is! And you reach the top of the V at, let's say, 29! And you perch up there in a little outfit with a cup of coffee, see! And you know that's the best it's gonna get! See! And how long it goes on like that depends on how long you can sit with your ass perched on a spike that sharp! Anybody! Anybody!

So she's listening to the bee! See, it was gonna die anyway! The buzz was low! See, when the buzz is high it's got a will to live! Well, not a will to live, but it's trying to survive! It's conserving energy, which is a bee's form of hope, see! But when the buzz is low, it's weak and angry! And that's a bad combination, weak and angry! Can't conserve! Can't conserve! It's death in a matter of minutes, see! So here was this beautiful gal! And her life was at its best moment! See, I could tell! I could tell! Swimming! Coffee! Summer! Bathing suit! Enough money to call a man to kill a bee! Listening to a bee trying to die at four o'clock in the afternoon in the summer! So I said, tell me about your problem! And while she was telling me, the bee died. I'm like a psychiatrist or something! That's what they do!

One guy's got ants! He lays on the windowsill 'cause he got nowhere else to sleep! And red ants ate him alive, so he calls me.

See, psychologically she knew! She knew! She knew she was at the top of the V, she was balanced at the top, and the bee was on the way down! That's what was upsetting her! They were heading in opposite directions, and she couldn't take it! See that's I-ronny! See, when something is sitting over here, and the other thing's going in the opposite direction, it's I-ronical!

Got to have a stomach for it! Like doctors, military men! They got a stomach for it! She got no stomach for it!

See, then you got lightning bugs! They're nice, right, everyone likes 'em, right? Little kids and so forth, right? But they're not all they're cracked up to be! Okay, what is a lightning bug? Anybody! It's little flashes of light all night! What mosquitoes do with sound they do with light! They whine all night with light! Meaio, meaio! *(sound of insect buzzing)* Alright, I got it! I got it!

(Lights out, then lights up on NOVELIST.)

NOVELIST: Planes and flies. All night long, I've got these planes and flies. They've got us right on the flight pattern here, so I'm sorry about the flies, the planes I can't do anything about. Well I can't do anything about the flies either, but people don't know that, my friends all say: spray this! Spray that! I'm not going to spray these things, I mean, God knows what they have in them? I heard about this ultrasonic device that emits a high-pitched sound above the spectrum of human perception, and this sound supposedly gets rid of both bugs and rodents. They all just line up at the front door of your home with their things in a little scarf tied to a stick, and try to emigrate as quickly as possible to a better life, that's the impression they try to give you, they're selling it in one of these catalogs. So you buy one, you think it's okay; you plug it in, your mice and bugs leave, your house looks great, you're throwing dinner parties left and right, and the next thing you know you're jumping out the window! And you say to yourself: *now why am I doing this?* And it's from listening for three months to the shrieking of this machine you didn't even think you heard!

You know they have us right on the flight pattern here. I'm not even going to go to the airport anymore, I'll just take my luggage and go up to the roof, they can pick me up there, it's right on the way. All night, these planes. It's like having your ear to a huge stomach in the throes of a terrible hunger; they sound like pangs to me, these planes. No wonder I can't sleep. Plus alcohol. I always think if I have a glass or two of wine it'll help me sleep, but it never does. Oh, I fall asleep . . . but then I wake up like a dog on a leash on a sidewalk in the summer whose master just jerked him to attention. I've got sweat in a circle around my lips.

Anyway, that's just the way I write. It's just that way, always has been. I'm having a fuck of a time.

Well it's incredibly hard! Writing's so hard, it's amazing I get anything done. Terribly hard. Terribly hard to get anything done. I wake up, and out the curtains through the window I see the mountain, and that draws me outside onto the porch, and once I'm out there I like to smoke a cigarette, and after I smoke I get hungry, so I come inside and eat; then of course after I eat I need to go back out and smoke a cigarette, then after I smoke I feel like lying down, and once I'm lying down I go back to sleep again. And this palindromic series of events follows me in cycles many times throughout the day; it's terribly hard to get anything done at all.

You know, 34 years ago I sat down and I wrote the first industrial novel since the post-industrial era, and it was terribly hard. And I thought it was hard because it was my first novel, but every novel has come equally hard, and hard in the same way.

See I'm not an intellectual really, I'm just a good listener. I don't sleep well. I get up at night and I hear people talking; sometimes it's my neighbors, sometimes it's voices in my head. And I listen and I write down what I hear, that's all; plots invent themselves out of voices. And I insist on politeness from my characters. I want to get to know them. I don't like it when real or imaginary people get to telling me their whole life story when I don't even know them. It's false intimacy, I hate it. I once moved into a building and said hello to a good-looking young lawyer type who lived in the apartment below me. Next day we happened to get on the same subway car and he ended up telling me about his 16-year-old daughter, he's divorced of course, and how he took her with him on a Club Med vacation, and how she happened to walk in on him screwing a girl about her own age. Now did I need to hear that? Did I? Now every time I think about the American Bar Association I think of statutory rape at the Club Med.

Same with my characters. I have to get to know them. I need to listen to them, chat with them for months before I'm ready for stories like that. I had one gal who wouldn't wait. Little college gal from the Jersey shore. Not only wanted to tell me everything about herself that first night I imagined her, but also demanded to know everything about me: why I dye my hair, how my boobs got the way they are, why I always write about dissatisfied men instead of dissatisfied women. My politics. Why I fantasize about being a teenager when I have sex . . . the whole works. Well, none of her beeswax! It's interesting. . . I wanted to know all that stuff about my mother . . . that must be why she ran away from me so much and hated me so often . . . It's like some natural principle . . . whatever you did to drive your parents crazy, there's someone waiting in the wings to do that to you . . . even if you have to invent them. I had a dream about this college girl. She was a lit major with a minor in theater, by the way. *(munching)* Mmm. These things are delicious! And it says here: No Cholesterol. *(turning package)* Oh, but there's fat! Eighty grams of fat! Imagine that! No cholesterol but a thousand blobs of fat! Fat and cholesterol are like Sacco and Vanzetti, everybody knows that. So in the dream this little lit major said: *I spin with my planet in deft, senseless earnest.*

She was quoting a poem. I thought the line was vacuous and stupid, I'm opinionated, I admit that. She defended the line, thought it was resonant and meaningful. When I woke up I realized maybe there's something to it; I mean, we are all spinning all the time, and that's probably very debilitating in its way: I mean, our TV dinners are spinning, our books are spinning, our papers are spinning, our clothes, our literary agents are spinning. I mean, you get on a plane and fly across the country; when you get off the plane you're exhausted when all you did was sit there for six hours; the involuntary movement was exhausting. Maybe that's why we're all so inexplicably blank and tired all the time.

I couldn't stand that college girl character. She was smarter than I am and I don't suffer geniuses gladly. . . so I dropped her from the novel. Couldn't enjoy her, didn't want to listen anymore. It's so funny. . . that's what my mother did to me, only she wasn't a writer, she was my mother. Although the point could be made that we write our kids . . . instead of ink you use DNA, but the channeling aspect is the same. *(munching)* These things are delicious!

(eating) You know what these things remind me of? Those Bongos . . . no . . . the Condos . . . Conchos . . You know, those cheese things that have the *peanut butter* stuffed up them! Combos! The Combos! Those say no cholesterol too! I was in the library working, and there were these two boys in there

eating the Combos . . . I loved those boys! They were about 14 or 15, wearing hats . . . one of them had a baseball cap on backwards, the other had a rag tied around his head . . . these headdresses were acts of rebellion, intelligent friendly rebellion . . . and they were laughing and laughing . . . so I stopped what I was doing and started eavesdropping . . . turned out they were talking about how when the atom bomb fell, it landed on this one particular girl! The first boy said: 'The Atom Bomb landed on this one girl! It was really funny! She went splat! Parts of her body were spread out for ten miles! Her hands were all cut off and everything! It was gross!' And they laughed hysterically. So then the other boy said: 'I heard when you get shot in the head sometimes you don't even know it! I bet she didn't even know it!' And they laughed again, but a little bit different. Then the first boy said: 'Have you seen my sister? She has never cut her hair and it's four feet long, and she has a little triangle missing from her nose! My dad was giving her the beat and she fell and chipped a part of her nose! If you look you can see a triangle missing!' And they laughed again.

I love these adolescent kids . . . I love the way they take the gruesome things they hear about and merge them with the details of daily life, and then laugh! That's adolescent humor! *Mythic* humor! Like that story I grew up with about the girl with a beehive hairdo, and then one day she put honey in it and a thousand bees came and stung her to death! Mythic humor! It's a humor whose purpose is to try to understand horror, act real casual about it and establish a big distance from it, all at the same time . . . it was so cute, that gruesome story about the bomb falling on this one girl . . . what a nerd, eh? . . . and then combining that with the story about his sister with the Medusan hair and the Bermuda triangle missing from her nose . . . I loved those boys!

I wrote nonfiction . . . it was beautiful, my nonfiction . . . it was beautiful the way novels are beautiful, because I used images from my own life . . . images I'd saved up from all places: here, there, little bits and chips of poetry I'd been collecting all my life. Makes me think of sea glass . . . you know, that's what they call those smooth, not quite but almost transparent slices of shell you find on the beach . . . they're clear-colored, or nearly green, and smooth from who knows what years of compression and abrasion at the whims of the tide . . .

sea glass. I collected that too, sea glass, found hundreds of pieces on thousands of sleazy beaches up and down the world, saved them up and finally put the pieces in a big glass jar with water. I loved the sound the pieces made as they clicked, they looked like trash, like beautiful pieces of a shattered ... something, only smooth from centuries of abrasion ... or like the glass windows people put up in the bathroom to keep people from looking in.

That's what these images were like, but I don't have any more images. They're all gone, I used them up, tossed them into fountains of other purposes, gave them away ... people wondered why my work was beautiful. I'm out of them now, all I do is listen. So as you're leaving please speak extra loudly. I've got my notebook and pen out; this is how I make my living now.

(Buzzing insect sound, lights out, then up on CHARACTER CUT FROM THE NOVEL)

CHARACTER CUT FROM THE NOVEL: You're looking at me like there's something wrong with me. Something, like you're thinking, there's something 'unnatural' about me and there is. See, I was in a novel, but I got axed. I'm out. I'm not in the novel, but that doesn't mean I just WENT AWAY. I'm still here, the bitch got up one night with a hangover, she thinks all writers are supposed to have a hangover. And she axed me. She's a fucking bitch. See I was in a sketch. She did a lot of *sketches*, you know, character sketches, like the way the great painters did pencil sketches of the famous paintings before they painted them. Kind of like a prenuptial agreement between the oil and the canvas. In the movies, that's called a *treatment*, but I think that's really stupid. To me a treatment is something you take for a disease. All these words. People just litter the streets with words. Like *sides*. When you're supposed to audition, and they give you the lines in advance, those are called sides, but to me sides are what you take in an argument. My character used to audition a lot on the college campus, and she always thought the word was – *sighs* – like *(sigh)*. So there's some big symbolism right there! And all these words! All of this is just words! Like this dress! This table, this chair, my arms. Words. All this is just a bunch of words! You heard that bee before. That's a fear she gave me. Of *bees*. Writers are our mothers, they give us fears, phobias. Like, this one 'sketch' she wrote me was about how afraid I am of bees. She wrote me a dream where this bee keeps painting itself bigger and bigger with strokes to its underbelly, first it became the size of a sparrow, and it goes stroke for stroke bigger till it's the size of a duck, the hum getting louder and louder, and finally I turn in the dream to the main character of the novel, a man who I'm supposed to want very badly, although he did nothing for me, he's a middle-aged married man with three kids and all of a sudden he realizes his life is still unlived, and his son is a pig, his daughter's a jerk, and I forget the third kid, and his wife's gone to fat and wears cold cream and curlers, so that's not very interesting anymore, so we fall hot and mad for each other, we meet at a college campus, mine of course, and we have an affair, although he *bored* me and I *horrified* him, so when she saw that, she axed me and gave him an African-American woman, which is more interesting but a lot less likely given what a racist sexist jerk he was. So anyway: in the dream this bee is getting larger and larger, the hum's getting deeper and deeper, and I turn to him and say WHAT IS THAT, and he says: I believe they call it DEFERENCE. And then I wake up. So there was some more big symbolism, my fear of bees is my fear of subservience, I guess. Well I mean she wrote me a college education as a lit major and I fucking well intend to *use* it! Although I never understood what the word POSTMODERN means, and now that I've been axed from the novel, there's no one I can ask, thank you very much.

So I'm out and about. A mutant. I've got a character and no ongoing circumstances. So I sit. I sit at this table. This is where she left me. It's nice, this table, I'm here a lot. To my right is a window, and there's a tree out this window, a young tree, and I'm on the second floor, and from this height, all you can see of this young tree is four feet of skinny bark, like the back of a young immigrant worker, shirtless; you can't see the roots at the bottom, or the leaves at the top, just the work in progress of ascension, of going up to offer leaves. That's where the window catches the tree. I like that. That's like me. I liked the way she did that. That's reasonable symbolism. The only problem is, the tree is still in the novel, and the window too, and the table, and the chair, and the main character with the wife in curlers, so everyone's just fine except for you know who. Sitting here in a black floral dress. Twenty-nine years old. I've been 29 for 44 years; it's starting to bore me. Like Cher. She's been 29 for 44 years too, but at least she has a bank account and a boyfriend.

So fuck O fuck O fuck these women writers, man. I prefer men: Hemingway, Faulkner, Milan Kundera, John Updike, Saul Bellow, Camille Paglia. I mean, this woman . . . the woman who wrote this novel I was cut from, she's not stupid! She's very bright! She teaches literature at a college in Connecticut, although that doesn't necessarily show how smart she is . . . but she can't plot! She can't deal with the plot . . . there's NO PLOT! I mean, she *had* a plot, in a way, but she seemed scared of it . . . like the way she put me up all scared of the bee . . . waiting to be stung by it . . . so instead of a story there's just a bunch of disorganized anecdotes . . . some of which are beautiful! She writes beautifully! She's got an ear for dialogue . . . like the way people don't always respond directly to what's said to them, but instead respond several lines later, so it's like music. There's asking and answering but not directly, like life. Like that! She's good with that. But where's the plot? It's going along and all of a sudden you have to hear about her drug problem and her mother and her trip to Peru! See I don't care about Peru! Just tell the story! Just tell the story! But no! She can't! Almost an apology, she has to apologize for having a story by developing some crippling, vision-obscuring problem! See, it's women! The problem is Women! Women! Having a story, it's too scary for them, it's too scary, it's like throwing a spear at an animal and having it hit, it's violent in some way, it's terminal, it *ends*! Stories end! So instead they throw the spear, and then, afraid it's going to hit the good heart that they aimed it at, they run after it, *catch* it; the animal shrugs its shoulders and walks away, and then what? Where do you go from there? To *Peru*! Or get a drug problem. Or talk about your mother. Or, no, you know what it's like? It's like they write themselves roles as Greek heroines, walking in white togas, but they write themselves togas that are too long and they're walking along having deep philosophical conversations and they start to trip on them and fall, or, *I don't know!* I don't know what it's like! I'm not the writer! See that's why I like Camille Paglia! He says that women are fundamentally inferior, and that the reason nature rendered them fundamentally inferior is so that men will find them sexy and we can perpetuate the race! And I like that! That makes sense to me! I mean, here I am, so fundamentally inferior that

93

I can't keep my ass in a plotless grade-B third-rate novel, but am I sexy up here, or what?

But she did write me some nice moments, and those are for keeps, like when you don't win the grand prize on *Wheel of Fortune* but you get to keep the cash and prizes from the first few games, right? She wrote me some nice moments. She wrote me this dress, and I like it. She wrote me on the verge of smoking, and I like that: here are the cigarettes, and here are the matches, O! I like that. I'm always about to light a cigarette, it's so lovely. Frozen, like a painting. And she wrote me two scenes that I love, that you can probably see in me, just looking at me. I'll tell you about those.

In the first one, I'm much younger, like 14. See, right now I'm 29. But then I was 14, and I'm living in this development complex. That sounds paradoxical, doesn't it: Development complex. I mean, you can't develop so well if you have a complex . . . witness the main character, the businessman with the curlers wife . . . but anyway. I'm this teenager, with an awkward body but a beautiful face; my body, if I recall it . . . my legs were like thick sticks, the baby fat refusing to come off the ankles, the legs resisting womanliness; and the hips and chest just the opposite, refusing to put *on* flesh, again resisting womanliness, but the face is all woman, all woman waiting to happen; a face that looks licked by candlelight all the time, with downy hair above the upper lip, blond, and hair that falls from the top of my head like 'hopes in a spell of sadness.' And I'm gawky and everything, but one summer they notice it, the boys, they notice my face, as if a shroud just fell away, which it did, and she goes on real nice about how beauty reveals itself in a single month, or in a single moment; how suddenly beauty is present in a new way. And that one summer, every night in August, that summer I turned 14, I allowed the boys in the complex to push me up against the metal fence by the tennis courts and *put my lipstick on me* . . . they take the top off the lipstick . . . it's gloss really . . . and then fight for who can turn the bottom and raise up the stick of colored gloss . . . they do it so slowly . . . it comes up above the metal rim, faint pink and glowing, and they take turns in the twilight growing dark, putting my lips on me . . . they apply it tenderly so as not to crush the stick . . . they laugh softly . . . we smell each other's breath . . . I open my mouth slightly . . . I tighten the lower lip to make it easier, but the upper lip I leave slack . . . it sits so soft above my two front teeth like a silk blouse above cleavage . . . and the boy who does the upper lip leans in close and works like Picasso . . . sketching an image . . . chest to chest . . . an image of desire . . . and the sky goes from blue to deep blue to black . . . and there's gruff laughter and talk but the work is gentle . . . and we do this every night in August that summer I turned 14 . . . and every time we hear sirens we imagine the police are coming for us . . . that we've been found out . . . we feel so dangerous . . . and when I leave these lovemaking sessions there's lipstick on my chin, in the crack between my teeth . . . above my upper lip . . . I look like I've been necking furiously, making out passionately, and yet I leave that summer without so much as a single, simple kiss. Nice, eh?

The second nice bit she did for me was . . . right here, at this table by the window with the young tree in it. This one is my last image from that fucking bitch. It's nice. It's a still image; just sound, no movement. Here's the background: I'm 29. I've just been swimming like a hundred laps in a nearby pool, tight at first, then loosening 'like a dress that's come unzipped,' and I'm in motion, all breath, and above me clouds churn 'like muscles in use!' But it doesn't rain, and I finish, and I get out, dripping water like power, I dress quickly, go home, sit down at the table by the window with the young tree. Coffee, I have hot black coffee, and in my body pure white joy. I've got a beautiful body by this time, it's perfect in fact, and of course I'm about to light a cigarette. And inside me is health, silence. So here's the image: me at the table, perfect; in fact, somehow, at the very needle's edge of my perfection, at the height of my power as a physical and sexual being. But: there's a *bee*, buzzing behind the blind, caught between the screen and the blind, and I'm afraid of bees, like I told you before, I'm afraid because I've NEVER BEEN STUNG, and I'm waiting to be stung, because I'm 29 and it's never happened. I've never felt that pain, never been surprised in that way by a creature I've frightened enough to commit suicide in order to hurt me for a moment, and it's bound to happen, and each day that passes and it hasn't happened, I feel more bound to the event, to how inevitable it is. So there's just me: still, beautiful, at my height, like when you throw a ball straight up in the air and it goes as far as it can go, there's a moment when it just hangs there, perfectly still, before it falls back down again; that's my moment. And there's the bee, furious and mixed up behind the blind, and my fear of it, I guess it represents the inevitable fall, I don't know, but there's just perfection and fear in one still image, and O God O Christ O God: I wish she could just have told the story.

(Lights down, and back up. Floor is now littered with costumes; a definite unit of dramatic material has been completed. This fourth monologue, SECAUCUS, NEW JERSEY, in a break from the character-driven nature of the past three, is done more naturalistically, and seems to represent an unlayered look at the life of the actress who yearned to become the three characters that preceded.)

PERFORMER: At 1:20 in the morning on December 20th the year of 1991 I had a kid.

And I still have him, and it's almost three years later. This is the most shocking thing in the world that I have ever done or will do. It is bizarre, ridiculous, otherworldly and completely banal. It is exhausting, demented, exhilarating, refreshing, depressing, wretched and queer. *And no one talks about it.*

I have had vomit on my shirt, poop on my pant-legs and spit-out carrots in my hair for two years, and NO ONE TALKS ABOUT IT. Now in a world where there are race riots and ethnic cleansing, where there are guns in the schools and asbestos in the synagogue bathroom and vice versa, having a kid doesn't seem too important, so NO ONE TALKS ABOUT IT. Everyone has kids, so no one talks about it. Very few people in the performance community have kids, so there's not much talk about it.

So, screw it! I'm not going to talk about it either! I feel alienated enough! I feel often enough like my behavior is odd in some way or like I don't blend in properly in some respect! Although I'm sure no one notices! So I'm not going out on a limb to discuss these things! I'm not going to talk about my theory that Dr. Lamaze was either a sexual sadist or a serial killer. I'm not going to talk about how laboring made me weep tears of oil during which I saw Jesus Christ and understood exactly how inconvenient the crucifixion must have been insofar as the thorns and nails were painful but the worst pain was the deep, unrequited love he felt for the people who were killing him, and he shrieked for help while the nurses gossiped in the hallway! Or how he cried out for God his father whose answer either never came or was inaudible; a lot of angry people speak too softly, it's called passive aggression!

I'm not going to talk about how the tender flowers that grew up between my nerves took a shock-bath in ice water and couldn't move anymore, couldn't signal anymore; or how I sat for half a year with the beige curtains drawn and the sunlight coming through them like weak coffee while I curled up there with a hole in my abdomen the size of the Delaware Water Gap as this tiny predator yanked and gnawed and bit on my boobies 15, 16, 17 times a day! Or how it became clearer and clearer with each passing moment that the child I had borne was a precise clone of his father in every respect, from his appearance to his mood to his sense of humor to the shape of his peepee like as if I had nothing whatsoever to do with his composition.

Obviously this is not what people talk about. So I'm not going to discuss it.

No, no. I think instead what I would like to talk about is how funny it is that all of a sudden, as soon as my kid was born, my sense of vision had no meaning! And I am a very visual person, not because I am an artist, but because I'm an atheist. I believe what I see, that's my religious belief. Like, I never saw a snake talking to some naked gal in a garden who then gave a piece of fruit to some bumbling guy and they ended up getting dressed, leaving that municipality and opening up a bodega or a farm or something. So I'm not so sure I believe that story! Whereas sometimes what you do see is so breathtaking that it's hard not to take it spiritually! I'm a visual person!

So it was so shocking when all of a sudden, I mutated from being a visually clutchy person to being someone who never used their eyes. My eyes became vestigial. I broke up with my eyes. There was no big scene, it happened quite suddenly. Suddenly it was my *ears* bringing in the critical information.

It began in the hospital with Bobby McFerrin on the headphones; the dirty, restless river for my eyes, but for my larger being, Bobby McFerrin stinging my soul through the headphones, singing I'M MAD O MAD! I'M ANGRY, ANGRY. And I just cried until they threw me out of that hospital. I came home, I came up the stairs.

Then there were thuds and gurgling. And there was crying, and within the crying, there were different cries: there was the crackling cry, like a knife; a cry of dumb need that didn't even know what it wanted; there was the soft, social cry to be held; the long insistent, articulate cry of hunger; the short attenuated shrieks for diaper work, and the little croaks that were just games with sound.

(Each toy or device that follows is demonstrated by the actor. Toys and music boxes are set on stage on a table, and miked for sound.)

Then came the toy and TV cacophony. First, the tender little toy Dad brought for him, a little clown that plays 'Put on a Happy Face,' which actually seemed to amuse the little tyke. Then came the white bear that played 'Love Me Tender,' while the animal moves its head like a junkie nodding out in an alleyway. Then came the croaking frog, then he learned to sit up.

Now once you can sit up, you're master of the Universe because it frees your hands! Your hands are free! The world around you is like Mission Control! So then comes the trainsound toy, so digital, precise and mournful, the bells and whistles, and track sounds, and then the animal-identification toy, screaming WHAT AM I? and urging the listener to match the gobble sound with the picture of the turkey, etc. WHAT AM I? WHAT AM I? And then you can combine them! Wind 'em both up and play 'Put on a Happy Face' with 'Love Me Tender', or have the sounds of the train with the shriek of ontological confusion: WHAT AM I? WHAT AM I? I mean, which of us hasn't asked ourselves that question down at the train station from time to time, ladies and gentlemen?

Then pretty soon the TV starts vomiting purple sound into my life, with this low-I.Q. goody-goody dinosaur named Barney singing 'I love you! You love me! We're a happy family! With a great big hug and a kiss from me to you! Won't you say you love me too!' You could check right into a clinic with those lyrics! It brings up everything that went wrong! Everything that didn't happen in your childhood! You need a doctor!

Then the child hates getting his diaper changed so in order to do it, you have to get this SINGING TOOTHBRUSH! It's the only thing that works! You let him hold the fucking thing and press the button while you hose down his ass. Now if you ever wish someone was dead, you just invite him or her over to your house and you play them this song as many times as you can:

I'M YOUR FRIEND BRUSHY BRUSHY! I KEEP YOUR TEETH SHINY AND BRIGHT! PLEASE BRUSH WITH ME EVERY DAY, MORNING NOON AND NIGHT!

Now if your will to go on living is THE SLIGHTEST BIT TENUOUS, this will DEFINITELY finish you off! And, depending on whether he's made number one or number two, and how efficient you are at cleaning it up, you may have to listen to this song between 15 and 30 times per diaper change!

Then the song from the Shari Lewis show that brings existentialism into the realm of Dr. Jack Kevorkian.

THIS IS THE SONG THAT DOESN'T END! IT JUST GOES ON AND ON MY FRIEND! SOME PEOPLE STARTED SINGIN' IT NOT KNOWING WHAT IT WAS! AND THEY'LL CONTINUE SINGING IT FOREVER JUST BECAUSE . . .

Now the thing I forgot to mention is that not only all this noise came in and collapsed in the center of my life, but at the same time I moved from West 76th Street on the island of Manhattan in New York City to SECAUCUS, NEW JERSEY! Now, SECAUCUS, NEW JERSEY! Think about it! It's something you used to make FUN OF and all of a sudden it's where your MAIL GETS DELIVERED, much less your child, the stigma of it! So instead of the familiar and comforting sounds of rapes and murders and car alarms I now have mahjongg, karaoke and car alarms.

There's something very weird about Secaucus. Okay, it smells, but that's not it. The fact is, it's a swamp that got turned into a bunch of outlet centers. Secaucus is known for its outlet centers, and although it's just a swamp, people come here from very far away to buy things. But it's just a swamp and some alleged stores. And they call these stores OUTLET CENTERS. I find that so interesting. And although I have lived in Secaucus among these alleged outlet centers for three years, I've never seen a single center. You go looking for them, there are just these huge flat tracts of cement, with an occasional flattop building with a sign. It's just a scam built on a swamp! There aren't any of these stores! Although once I found one, because a Volkswagen Farvernugen full of Hasidim pulled up and asked me where Harvé Benard was, they said it was a fashion outlet center. And I know there's a flattop building with a sign, so I pointed them that way. Then I went there myself, and it was a big room with a rack full of hideous mustard-colored plaid wool blazers and a man in a top hat talking on the phone. I don't know. They used to slaughter pigs here in Secaucus; now the main business is these outlet centers.

And there are highways. The whole town is highways. You have a feeling here the only thing that isn't a highway is your bathroom. This cab driver told me he moonlights as a toxic-waste disposal contractor man, he works putting toxic waste under the highways, they figure it's safe there because you drive right by, that's why the highways are always under construction, they're busy putting plutonium under them. And you wonder why you get so burned out by a traffic jam! You were being nuked there for half an hour while you listened to Lite FM!

Anyway, in the middle of these toxic roadways and bogus stores with hideous merchandise is this development complex where I live. It's called Harmon Cove. Harmon Cove! Isn't that a beautiful name? Harmon Cove! It implies music and resonance, gentle sailboats on a calm, clean tide! Harmon Cove! And it looks nice! Very nice! There's a pool, and some trees, and lots of different kinds of birds, and the landscaping is very meticulous, they sprinkle water all the time, even in the rain! Plenty of animals here! Unidentifiable rodents, as if all the gerbils escaped and mated with the water rats! And there are squirrels wandering around in a daze as if they just got back from Vietnam and can't find the Benefits Office! And supposedly benign snakes that grow to the size and thickness of your arm and sun themselves on top of the carefully carved bushes! And wild boars and mystical animals that wash up dead on the banks of the Hackensack River, which is a river to the same extent that these stretches of cement are outlet centers! It's very nice! Really, in a way! And precisely because it *is* so lovely, every plane taking off from the Tri-State area flies directly over us! Little Harmon Cove! Wave if you ever take the red-eye! Since it's impossible to sleep with all that horrific, crashing din that sounds like the living apocalypse, I'm sure I'll be awake to wave back!

And the library! The Secaucus library! What a living testament to the value of erudition! First of all it's attached to the firehouse, so if your work ever gets the better of you you can run across and slide down a pole! I went there one Thursday to try to find a certain John Donne poem called 'The Funeral.' It's a beautiful poem, full of strength and posture; I needed a copy of it to put in the program of some show I was directing. I drove over there, parked across from red engine Number 12 and went in. Now for openers it's the only library I ever went in that has MUZAK blasting! I get through the door, I hear WALK ON BY! DUH DUH DUH ... DUH DUH DUH! WALK ON BY! FOOLISH PRIDE! I WILL NEVER GET OVER LOSIN YOU! AND SO IF I SEEM! BROKEN AND BLUE! WALK ON BY! DUH DUH ... etc. Now this is the fucking library! And people are standing around drinking iced tea! All I saw was a bunch of newspapers lying around and a few copies of *Valley of the Dolls* and a notice about how senior citizens can get free Xeroxes on Wednesdays. So I said to the guy: Where is the poetry section? So he takes a sip, he was busy describing how he got stung by a bee on Saturday, and he says, Whatcha looking for, young lady? So I let that go, and I said: John Donne. So he thinks a second and he says: John Donne *what?* Eh, Pete? Ha Ha!

Now you're probably thinking I'm too snooty; that in reflecting on the snobbery of others, I've taken on an arrogance of my own. But I tried! I really tried! When we first moved to Secaucus, I made a real effort! I met my upstairs neighbor out by the mailbox, and WAS I CORDIAL! I fucking was! and she introduced me to her dog Jellybean and she said 'LOOK! JELLYBEAN GOT A LETTER!' And she opened up a card, and made me hold the dog while she read him his Christmas card, and then she said: 'Everyone knows Jellybean. Even the mailman Earl knows Jellybean!' And the mailman for some reason rolls back his eyes and goes into a trance-like state, and he says: 'OH YES! I KNOW JELLYBEAN!' Couple days later I notice that her license plate says JELLY B! I mean what the hell is going to happen when that dog kicks the bucket? The sight of her car is going to shatter her composure!

But that's not the point! The point is that the first meeting went okay! I did very well! I mean, I played my part, I smiled, I held the dog, I read the card, I acknowledged the mailman, etcetera, but not two weeks later I blew the whole gig because I had been pulling up weeds in the front, and all of a sudden I felt something creeping on my thigh inside my pantleg, and I couldn't reach it and I thought it was a bee and I came tearing around the side of the house, kicked open the door with my foot and pulled down my pants but unfortunately my underpants came down too and my entire tushy and all its complements were hanging out there when Jellybean and the mother, the son and the father come up the stairs and see my whole predicament. So what can I tell you. We're on sitcom territory here, right?

They have a newspaper out here called the *Secaucus Reporter*. It comes out once a week whether it needs to or not, there's a limited amount of news over here. But it's free, they deliver it! And each resident gets about eight or ten copies, so it comes in handy if you're moving, you can wrap your glassware! It is a fine specimen of modern journalism! Whereas they can't get the movie times right at the local theaters, and once I had to watch *Rock-A-Doodle* because I was an hour and twenty minutes late for the adult feature, they certainly have drawn a bead on what matters in the news! For example, this compelling headline.

NO GO ON BASEMENT SWAP *(holds up paper)*

This is a real scoop! I read it with such interest! It is a ground-breaking article concerning certain shocking shenanigans going on with regard to Mayor Anthony Just's basement! Just listen:

THE BOARD OF ADJUSTMENT VOTED TO DISAPPROVE A THIRD VARIANCE ON MAYOR ANTHONY JUST'S HOME THIS WEEK, AMID BUFFETING RUMOR, SPECULATION AND QUESTIONS ABOUT PAST PRACTICES.

WHILE MAYOR JUST AND HIS SON SAID A SWAP OF BASEMENT ROOMS FOR AN OUTSIDE BUILDING HAD BEEN DONE IN GOOD FAITH, SOME BOARD MEMBERS BELIEVED IT WAS A VIOLATION.

THE HOUSE MAYOR JUST PURCHASED IN 1963 WAS BUILT ON AN UNDERSIZED LOT, BUT IT HAD A FINISHED BASEMENT IN WHICH MAYOR JUST'S SISTER LIVED!

A little Jane Eyre twist right there!

Here finally is a story worth following! This arresting piece of journalism was written by staff reporter Joe Hallivan. He is a very gifted man who I'm sure lives somewhere here in Harmon Cove, perhaps in someone's basement.

So you can see clearly that Harmon Cove is an incredible place, a little haven in the filthy mist at the elbow of New York and New Jersey. The women here are incredible, too! There's a pool, and they come to the pool with diamonds, waterproof outline lipstick and gold chains BUILT INTO THEIR BATHING SUITS! In other words, the gold chains are part of the suit! The bra straps, the bikini G-strings! They have children but they wouldn't be caught dead with them! And they play tennis all day, which keeps them fit! These are healthy women! I am the only unhealthy example in the entire community. My gold collection is limited to the L'Chaim pin I found on Yom Kippur at the Beth Emeth Synagogue in New Rochelle 20 years ago, and I consistently commit the *faux pas* of being seen with my child not only on weekends but on the weekdays as well.

So, since I have no gold and my neighbor saw my ass, I walk my child alone. It's pretty here! We walk alone every morning, he in his stroller and me pushing him along. He only knows two letters of the alphabet: the letter B, because his name is Bennett, and the letter O, because it 'goes around and around.' And, as with all pieces of his knowledge, he likes to chant them out loud, as if they were a pin that could somehow pop the bubble of all human knowledge and open up the world! So we plod down the sidewalk, the child screaming B-O! B-O! B-O! most of the way, which I'm sure doesn't make me seem too attractive to the neighbors, and I try to act like I don't see anyone, since each person I ignore spares them the trouble of ignoring me, and these people have enough to do, God knows!

And yet, it haunts me . . . Who are we at the moment we choose to ignore the presence of another human being? Who are we at that moment? I was walking Bennett, okay he's screaming B-O! B-O! And my watch has stopped, and it's important! It's important for me to know what time it is because I have to get him in position every day to see the 3:45 train go by, it's critical! It makes his day! Life with a child is a critical mass of routines and, if you miss one, you pay later! So I see this woman coming towards us, okay, she's one of those in-crowd kitty-cool gold-lamé life-is-gay tennis players, but . . . she has a watch! We're all human beings, we'll all be dead in 50 years, and we all measure the element that ages and kills us with the same chronometer! Okay, hers was gold and mine was stainless steel, had vomit in it and had ceased to function, but that's a technicality! It's all the same! So we're going by, Bennett's with the B-O! B-O! And I said to her, excuse me! Could you please tell me what time it is? And she . . . I can't even do it! She . . . she waved me away as if I was a bunch of bugs! You know those frantic clusters of summer gnats you encounter sometimes moving in a wild cloud around each other? She turned her head as if me and my kid constituted one of those blobs of bugs and waved her hands like this, as if to totally disperse us so she could get by! And she kept on walking.

Now look! We may not be the most appealing people! But this woman LITERALLY WOULD NOT GIVE US THE TIME OF DAY! Literally would not!

So anyway, we're out on one of these cordial morning jaunts when all of a sudden I hear a man's voice say:

I DON'T KNOW HOW YOU DO IT.

I was shocked, I mean, someone spoke to me, so I whirl my head around, and there's this guy. He's about 5 foot 10 inches, paunchy, light brown hair, fuzzy blue eyes, broken blood vessels in the nose, like he drinks too much and used to be good-looking. So I said: I beg your pardon? and he says again:

I DON'T KNOW HOW YOU DO IT.

So I said, DO IT? And he says, I DON'T KNOW HOW ANY OF YOU WOMEN DO IT! YOU COOK, YOU CLEAN, YOU TAKE CARE OF KIDS DAY AFTER DAY! So I said, Well, I don't cook or clean, and he says again: I DON'T SEE HOW YOU WOMEN DO IT! I'M A FEMINIST! YES SIR I AM! I STUDY FEMINISM! I STUDY FEMINISM IN A CLASS! AND FOR MILLIONS OF YEARS WOMEN HAVE DONE IT! AND I'M A FEMINIST! AND CAN YOU BELIEVE IT! AND WHEN THE TEACHER HAD TO BE ABSENT FOR A MONTH TO GET A HYSTERECTOMY, SHE ASKED ME TO TAKE OVER THE CLASS! I TOOK OVER! AND CAN YOU BELIEVE IT? YOU WOMEN ARE INCREDIBLE! I DON'T KNOW HOW YOU DO IT!

So I said thank you. And I walked away.

And then came the summer, my second summer at Harmon Cove. And the pool opened, and then came the exquisite, elongated, sensuous sessions between my body and the cool clean painted blue of that pool: afternoons clawing at that body of water like one might the body of a lover in a cheap motel; in the mornings, throwing myself in and clinging to that cold the way a sleeper in the middle of a beautiful dream clings to sleep; and then, in the evenings, my eyes clawing at the jagged edges of the rising moon, my fingers clawing at the edges of the pool, swimming back and forth and back and forth till they threw me out and locked the gate.

So then one day I'm walking my child after a particularly sensuous morning swim, when all of a sudden I hear, from behind me:

I DON'T KNOW HOW YOU WOMEN DO IT!

And I turn around, and it's the same guy! Launching the same rap! And of course at the same moment I realize he says this same thing to every woman he sees, and doesn't even remember the particular woman to whom he says it: a kind of social promiscuity, a new kind of sexism, even, ladies! So I said, DO IT? And he says: I DON'T KNOW HOW YOU WOMEN DO IT! YOU COOK, YOU CLEAN AND TAKE CARE OF KIDS DAY AFTER DAY! So I said, I don't cook or clean, and he said: I'M A FEMINIST, I STUDY FEMINISM! YES SIR I DO! AND WHEN THE TEACHER HAD TO GET A LAPAROSCOPY, SHE ASKED *ME* TO TAKE OVER THE CLASS FOR HER! I DON'T KNOW HOW YOU WOMEN DO IT!

Now this whole thing was getting very tightly on my nerves. I mean, first of all, a disquisition on feminist thinking from a paunchy pixillated white man at nine a.m. of the clock on a Wednesday morning was NOT my idea of what I had in mind for myself socially. So I said to him, Look! There are seven hundred and seventeen women living in this complex who would be *very glad* to clear this mystery up for you with hands-on training! I mean, it was a disgrace! This man was walking around with NOTHING TO DO! So he says: OH! ALLOW ME TO INTRODUCE MYSELF! MY NAME IS TIMMY 'THE TIN-MAN' TARANTELLA! So I said, How do you do? or something. And he says, What do you do? And I said, Cook, clean and take care of babies! So he says, How 'bout coming out for karaoke in the Harman Cove Clubhouse this Friday! You deserve the rest! Take the night off! You can do something! You can do something! Want to be in it? C'mon! Give it a try! So I said, Well, as a matter of fact, I am a performance artist, and maybe I can do a little something. I mean, after the knife fight that broke out during my show at Café Bustelo, I figure a little upper-middle-class hostility isn't much to cope with. So he says GREAT! And he gives me this flyer, look! I kept it! Here it is! It says:

THE RECREATION BOARD
PROUDLY PRESENTS
THE HARMON COVE VARIETY SHOW
CO-HOSTS TIMMY 'THE TIN-MAN' TARANTELLA
AND RHONDA B. REISBAUM

Scheduled to Appear: The No Tones! Mick & Co.!

The Harmon Cove Boy Toys! The Vinnettes

Whitey!

AND FEATURING SPECIAL GUEST STAR
MAYOR ANTHONY JUST!

I thought I was going to die! A chance to dance karaoke with the guy who locked his sister in the basement!

And more Guest Stars and Surprises!
Call Tom or Anthony if you want to be on the bill!
THIS IS THE NIGHT YOUR STAR CAN SHINE!
TELL THE BABYSITTER YOU'LL BE LATE!

See, there's that nice, feminist touch I've come to expect from the Tin-Man! And it finishes up,

STAG OR DRAG – YOU'LL HAVE THE
BEST TIME IN YOUR LIFE

Isn't it interesting, Stag or drag, those are the only choices?
Anyway, I went to karaoke that night in the clubhouse. I was afraid but I went. I went forward with my knees knocking. I got dressed. I put on make-up. Who knew what I would find there at the clubhouse!

(Lighting change: disco lights up, general wash down. Disco music up.)

When I arrived, boy, what a thrill! They sure knew how to do it up! The place looked great! And everyone was there ... Oh, Jeez, there's Timmy the Tin-Man dancing with Rhonda B. Reisbaum! And there's Mayor Just and his son dancing with the woman from the basement! And there's Whitey up on the dais ... he must be the DJ for tonight ... Oh! And there's the woman who waved me away as if I were a bunch of bugs! HI! HON! *(waving frantically)* HI!

Then the performances began! Boy that Vinny sure can sing! And those Vinnettes! What backup! And there go the Harmon Cove Boy Toys! They really are on top of things! Rhonda looks so stunning in that silverleaf bathing suit! And that Whitey! He's got a voice like Sinatra ...

Then all of a sudden it was my turn. I could feel the lights come up on me. Everyone was looking at me. I knew it was my turn to ... I was supposed to perform ... to perform ... but I just ... I just ...

(Fade up. 'I'm Mad O Mad ... I'm Angry, Angry ...')

FINIS

Commentary: *A Little Night Music*

Of Mice, Bugs and Women is a triptych, or as Margolin says, a 'rickety quartet.' In the transition from the triptych to the 'Secaucus' monologue, Margolin has to coach her audience to hold their applause. The show is not over. As she changes out of the short, tight, flashy red dress that her character wears at the end of the triptych and into her 'Payless' shoes and a tacky polyester overall that gives her room for getting pregnant or carrying a gun, she draws an invisible line with her toe and steps back and forth across it repeatedly, chanting: Life/Art, Life/Art, Life/Art. One of the distinguishing characteristics of performance art, as opposed to 'theater,' is the way in which the former muddies the distinction between life and art. When Deb visits my class to give a lecture on her work, one of my students asks me after she leaves: 'Is she really *like that all the time*, or was she performing?' Despite the fact that Margolin's lecture contained a lucid and cogent explanation of the ways in which we are all *always already* 'performing,' there remains, as Herb Blau so eloquently put it: 'a crucial particle of difference ... between just breathing, eating, sleeping, loving and *performing* those functions of just living; that is, with more or less deliberation' (1987, p. 161). What most performance artists do *not* do is create the illusion of reality as do playwrights whose work takes place in the genre of dramatic realism. Perhaps performance artists could be said to reverse this formula, creating the reality of illusion.

Of Mice, Bugs and Women does mark a significant shift in Margolin's style as a performance artist. Here we have three fully developed characters, for whom she creates a referential context that appears to extend outside of or beyond their moments on stage. Her perpetually 29-year-old character cut out of the novel may have a 'character with no ongoing circumstances,' but she *is* a character, and in fact does have 'ongoing circumstances,' albeit negative ones frozen in time. Alternating between despairing and reveling in the fact of her timelessness, she lacks a narrative that is *given* to her, but she creates her own narrative out of that very lack. In a sense, she is smarter than the writer who axed her because she asked too many questions and was too smart for the author who doesn't 'suffer geniuses gladly.' It is Margolin's genius to give depth, intellectual acumen, and indeed philosophical profundity to a character who is overtly marked as vapid, narcissistic, and lacking in agency. This, indeed, is what makes *Of Mice, Bugs and Women* particularly compelling. Margolin doesn't laugh *at* these characters whom one might easily find to be humorous objects; she laughs *with* them, and finds ways to identify with them. She even goes so far as to admit that she makes *herself* up by creating them. The Exterminator: a man who takes his work very seriously. Not merely efficient, he is obsessed with understanding the differences between the insects and rodents whose lives are in his hands. Well, not really in his hands *per se*, as he points out to us: it's against company policy for him to actually touch these creatures; he merely creates an atmosphere where they drop dead. As a character, the exterminator makes us laugh, but Margolin doesn't let us off with a light, comfortable glance into his world. For he is, also, a character who thinks deeply and poignantly about these mice and bugs, almost humanizing them, before he annihilates them. As in all of her work, Margolin wants to know how it is possible for people to commit the intimate, banal, casual daily acts of violence – how these realities pass as illusions. Like the woman in Secaucus who dismisses her and her child with a sweep of her hand as if they are gnats swarming under a lamppost. Margolin wants to know: 'Who are we at the moment we ignore the presence of another human being?' The exterminator's reference to 'creating an atmosphere in which they just drop dead' resonates powerfully with a post-Holocaust awareness. We might like to think that such massive extermination, on a scale that is quite literally incomprehensible, can only be understood through some recourse to a notion of 'depersonalization' or 'dehumanization.' We would like to think that unthinkable cruelties can only be performed if one's *own* humanity is somehow cut off, shut down, or missing. But that's the easy answer, and Margolin doesn't rest with it. Her exterminator is ultimately most hideous *because* he has studied and understood the differences between the creatures he kills. The persistent humming of the insect struggling to die in the night runs throughout the triptych, overlapping and connecting its parts, like a soundtrack that is not exactly a backdrop, but an intricate night music that functions as a through-line for all these characters who share the inability to rest, to sleep, but from Margolin's perspective, there is always the rub, for perchance they may dream, and dream of each other.

While these three characters in the triptych form a theatrical piece that appears to depart from the cloudy division of life and art, Margolin brings *Of Mice, Bugs and Women* back to a performative mode with the addition of the 'Secaucus' monologue. She reports her relief when a critic noticed that 'Secaucus' was not merely tacked on, but a crucial epilogue of sorts to the triptych, a piece that explained where the prior three monologues originated. On the one hand, 'Secaucus' is a monologue that addresses Margolin's own life transition: 'In two weeks, I went from being a hip and single if fat and pregnant swinging chick on the Upper West Side of the cultural urban center of the world to a married matron with a baby living in a flooded swamp that used to be a pig farm.' In itself, this would be more than enough to yield dramatic material for a twenty-minute monologue. But 'Secaucus' performs much more than its content. For it is in this piece that Margolin reinserts herself into the narrative of her characters in the triptych. Closing up the distance between herself and her 'realized characters,' she realizes that *no one* is in a position to judge others; and yet everyone is responsible for who we all become and what action we take in the world. All of us can, and do, find our lives suddenly and inexplicably altered, and in the presence of people with whom easy identifications are not possible. Margolin cannot find a way to 'fit' into the community that she has nonetheless chosen. She cannot change *into* them, nor does she desire to do so. Instead, she accepts the pain of their rejection, the humiliation of their refusal to recognize her own humanity in her differences from them. And she turns them into works of art, *without* denying their lives. So she goes to the karaoke party, and when the spotlight comes on her, she dances her differences, but fully in their midst.

Deb Margolin in *Carthieves! Joyrides!* Photo: © Tom Brazil.

6

Carthieves! Joyrides!

(Carthieves! Joyrides! *has been performed both with and without a set of any kind. The set designed for it at Here Theater featured the simulacrum of a car, with the back seat raked so as to be visible to the audience and to provide a second vertical performance level. The car was placed stage left, and was angled inward toward center. The rear of the car was a platform strong enough for the performer to stand on. A hula hoop functioned as a steering wheel. Although it is not noted in the text, the reader should be aware that between each of the vignettes constituting* Carthieves! Joyrides!, *a certain very pleasant, easy-listening light jazz piece plays, and the performer drives the 'car' with the hula hoop. After some moments of this music, a strong, smooth male radio voice says: 'OKAY! You're listening to the WAVE, 98.7, Los Angeles, and that was ...' followed by the sound of radio static. The spectator never ascertains the name or title of the composition.)*

My teeth have rotted. Now this is a dreadful thing. I mean, my teeth have just completely rotted in my head. Okay, my teeth were never terrific but all of a sudden the empire just collapsed and this has been so disappointing, like a solid working-class neighborhood that suddenly went to seed with no sociological explanation. It's horrifying because your teeth are just so close to your mortality. Where else does bone show in the human body but when you smile? So I've been trying to deal with this, and in the process I remembered that I once went to this New-Age dentist who asked me actually to fill out a questionnaire that said something like: well, how do you *feel* about your teeth? And I remember shocking myself at that dentist's office by writing that they reminded me of tombstones in a graveyard. Now, I had no idea I was going to say that. It wasn't like I had been consciously incubating that image or anything, but there you have it. And here I am with these teeth that have just rotted. So now I have to have all this hideous and repulsive dental work done and the place I've been going to get this work done is called the Belville Dental Associates.

Let me just say that the Belville Dental Associates is inconveniently located in a place so far west it might as well be Los Angeles. And I think it's also interesting to note about the Belville that it is situated right at an official United States Duck Crossing. It's a narrow, two-lane, busy thoroughfare there, right through the center of town, and the soulless motorists are forced by the sheer volume of this living poultry to wait and honk, while the ducks line up with great precision and infinitesimal slowness from tallest to shortest. There are some two or three hundred of them and the measuring takes quite some time, and then they line up and they begin this agonizingly slow peregrination across the boulevard, and every once in a while the matriarch will stop to pluck a flea from the animal behind her and then they'll continue. So at the Belville Dental Associates, in addition to the hideous drills and other sadistic instruments, you also hear the honking of both the geese and the motorists, lined up in a parody of perpendiculars, and these are the sounds that attend you at the Belville Dental Associates.

Now this clinic is presided over by these two repulsive people, the Shattners: Dr. Shattner and his wife Chimera or Cholera or something like that. Now Cholera (she's the receptionist) is an unbearably skinny woman who wears waist belts so tight they make her wheeze, and she's got the charcoal/raccoon thing going on around her eyes, you know. And she talks a good deal about what a sensitive person she is and she says things like 'I'm a people person,' and 'I hear ya' and stuff like that quite a bit. Her husband, Dr. Shattner, is a deeply homicidal and creepy man. He's no taller than a child really, and he speaks very quietly and with great politeness which masks a ludicrous and almost palpable violence. Now this is a man with both a DDS and an MBA, but obviously the MBA won out because he doesn't practice, which from what I understand is for the best. Instead his role is to torment the patients for money, which he does very assiduously. You see him with a calculator and a thing like a phone operator coming around his mouth, and he's got things around his head, and he's got calculators and recuperators and pushcarts and pullcharts, and he sits in front of a computer with pieces of paper . . . this is what he does. The Shattners never look at each other the whole working day, but you can tell they are operating in a deep and terrifying collusion with one another, and although everyone knows they're married, they call each other *Dr. Shattner* and *Mrs. Shattner*, which is just so infantilizing and makes you feel like you're three years old. Anyway, I used to have a pretty presentable dentist at the Belville Dental Associates by the name of Dr. Lennox, but I think the Shattners gave him the creeps, so he went to ply his repulsive trade at another location, and he left me up to the auspices of one Dr. Thursten. Now his name is Dr. Thursten but I call him Larry, because let me say I'm old enough to be his mother, and also because I don't believe in that crap anyway, where you call them *Dr. Flapdinger* and they call you *Milly* or something like that.

Dr. Thursten is a very interesting man. First of all, he is a very, very large individual, and secondly, he's reckless and he's out of control and he has no idea what you do and do not say to patients and his wife has shingles all the time and his kid has the chicken pox all the time and he has no idea what to say and everything he does hurts. When he walks in it hurts. When he sits down it hurts. And I don't mean it hurts him, I mean it hurts *me*. And the pain that I'm talking about is not physical, it's *ontological*! It goes beyond the moment, this pain. And anyway he is an unbelievable gentleman. Everything about him shocks me and yet somehow he manages to be very very. . . sexy. Now I have done some thinking about what it is about this man. I mean at 380 pounds, at 400 pounds, that desire is a miracle neighboring a nightmare. But what is it? I tried to ask myself what it is about this man I find so alluring, and I've come up with two images. Firstly, he's young but he looks older, and there's something about hidden youth I find alluring . . . like a sheep in wolf's clothing or whatever the opposite of the paradigm is; and secondly, you know what it is? He talks *dental* to you . . . he talks *dirty dental* to you . . . he talks to you as if you were on his level professionally but just had never seen that particular procedure . . . you feel like you've infiltrated some secret club, like you've *passed* in some way. He has you talking about the *modular* side of the tooth versus the *distal* side . . . about *palatal* injections versus the other kind and so forth. It's like speaking a foreign language, and there's something about speaking a foreign language that's very sexy, you know. It's very transmogrifying.

Anyway I fired his ass peremptorily during our last visit, but before I fired him he said the following unbelievably beautiful thing to me. He said: 'All of dentistry is the study of occlusion.'

Isn't that a beautiful remark? All of dentistry is the study of occlusion! And I remember that I said 'Oh yes it certainly is,' or something like that. And then when I went home I thought about it: what is *occlusion* . . . it's that way that things have of touching other things, of abutting other things, of pushing against them, of keeping them in their place, and therefore within their function, through *touch*. The *bite* is an example of occlusion . . . the upper teeth bearing down upon the lower and vice versa. And as I thought about this beautiful precept, it occurred to me that perhaps he stated it too modestly; that perhaps in fact the entire *universe* is the study of occlusion, and that I myself would blob infinitely out into that universe were I not occluded by water bottles and tapes, and clocks, and microphones, and cars.

Anyhow, this dentist is completely out of control, it's inexcusable! And he told the following absolutely indefensible joke in the middle of a root canal: *A man and a woman are making out passionately and necking furiously and the woman moans: 'Oh God kiss me where it smells the worst' and so he took her to New Jersey!* He told me this joke as he was injecting anesthesia! And in the middle of the same hideous root canal procedure when he proceeded to inject a supposedly 'inert' substance into a supposedly 'nonvital' tooth, he overshot the mark, and this hot stuff goes up beyond the canal into living ligament, causing me to burst into tears; tears burst forth from my eyes with the force of young people trying to escape a burning nightclub in the South Bronx. And I leapt out of my chair; my hands, in fists, rose up as if weightless, and right at that point, on the muzak track in the dental office, comes on the song: 'All I wanna do is have some fun! I have a feeling I'm not the only one!' I fired his ass peremptorily right then and there.

They call root canal *saving the tooth*. I just hope that when they mention *saving the whales* they are referring to something much more humane and worthwhile.

Now of course the end of any relationship is also a beginning. I mean, it's a platitude already; especially as you end a bad relationship, the work begins: the work of trying to figure out what kept you in the relationship for so long, whether it was five minutes talking to some creep on the subway when you should have walked away and read a magazine, or five years in a bad marriage of one kind or another... whatever. So I'm at it. I'm trying to figure out what kept me going to this dentist for so long. I mean, he clearly has some competence problems. And it's inconveniently located. I have to spend hours and hours alone in the car to get there and hours and hours alone in the car to get back. It's on me, why did I do that? And I'm thinking about it and I realize *I had to spend hours and hours alone in the car to get there and hours and hours alone in the car to get back.*

And I begin to see it. The car. Okay, it's the car, the car. The car.

It's a church. It's a church in there... It's got midnight mass: 8,000 pounds of metal and plastic and destiny. It's where you go to go, just go, just get the fuck out; it's like the afterlife, the judgment day. I get in, and music plays, and I'm alone. There's big wind, a storm; I roll the windows down, it's like my own personal hurricane. And I cry in there. I always cry. I cry because I can. I have feelings, I have fast food feelings, I wolf down my feelings like somebody wolfing down a Burger King punched out on a half hour lunch break. I can feel the raw movement of time, rubbing against my nipples as it passes; time blubbering with life and all its waste products and its night light.

You know, I think cars are unbelievable. Literally. Unbelievable. You get in, you turn a hoo-ha, you press a frufru, and it goes! Now what is that? Who is paying for that, really?

Men say cars are like women, and they're right. Just like women. Me? I'm like the 1995 Riviera. In almost every way. The car is a *Bu*ick, and I'm *Jew*ish.

Look at this silent steel arc. That's my line, too. My first line of defense. Green, curved, lit. That's how I am at parties. See what it says here in the pamphlet: Sleek, comfortable, powerful, quiet, agile, beautiful. And fun. Riviera.

Another car ad drives me absolutely crazy. It's on TV, you only see it late at night, when you're alone, of course you're alone! and you're drunk, or desperate, or you've just failed at something. You see a white yacht, wide and arrogant, effortlessly scuttling an endless ocean; yacht and ocean pushed up against each other, occluding one another like the upper and lower jaws of some great god. A gravelly, experienced male voice says:

What is luxury?

Is it power?

Is it space?

Is it silence?

Yes.

Sherry

I asked her to live with me. I just went right up to her and asked her to live with me. I didn't even know her. She was large and beautiful, and her eyes had charcoal painted all around them. She dressed! She really dressed, made deliberate and incomprehensible choices, she was sort of purple, with toothpicks and feathers coming out of her. Her clothes fit her tight and fearless. Her voice was deep and smooth. She looked as if she never moved, never really had to. I didn't even know her, marched right up to her and said: let's room together. Hey, I didn't know what she was, but I knew it was critical that I find for myself at that point in my life, junior year, liberal arts, NYU, the only person in an entire 15,000 student academic environment who would never ever *judge me*.

That's what I found. That was her. She moved right in. She had perfume bottles, and a glass egg. If you looked into this egg it was like being drunk or slowly going blind ... just a world apart, small world giving big thrills, wordless universe of color and freedom. That was her. I once got stoned, and she was standing there, leaning against the dresser. She never moved the whole time I knew her. I went up to her and said something like: What are you? What the hell are you? She shook her head at this weakness, this obvious weakness that was so like the impatience of a child in the back seat of the car who keeps saying: Are we there yet? Are we there yet?, and she just smiled, and then, emotionally, at least, she got up and walked away.

Turned out she was so intelligent she couldn't even function. That was what it was: her I.Q. was so high it was like a physical weight holding her head down on the pillow. She was asleep through most of our relationship, rising to pee, to eat, or to tell me a scientific theory in exquisite poetic and empirical detail which, when I went to check it further, it turned out she had made the whole thing up. Sometimes 36 hours would go by, and she would wake up and dress to go get dinner on a day she didn't realize had already passed.

When finals time rolled around, her sleeping continued. It was our second year rooming together, just us and the glass egg. It was becoming clear that she was going to flunk out if she didn't wake up, and she was finding that impossible. So I took it upon myself to do a sort of academic Florence Nightingale job on her. I wrote several papers for her, and made up a mnemonic opera to help her remember the facts for her human biology class, since we didn't really look enough alike for me to sweep in and take the test for her. This job really suited me, especially writing papers on subjects I didn't know anything about, since right then I thought I knew everything, and, of course, I did.

There was one paper, though, that I didn't have time to write, some sort of heavy research paper for a lab psych course, so she took an incomplete in that course, and got her diploma pending successful completion of that project, and we spent the summer getting it done. That is to say, I wrote the paper while she sat by my desk. She took the train every day, up to where I lived, by the train tracks near the Hudson River in the Bronx, and I had a typewriter set up in this long green unairconditioned hot smelly fecund hallway. And she sat and dreamed, sang, stared at her hands, and dozed, while I wrote this paper for her, waking her to ask for a question now and then, about a book, or a theory, or offer her lemonade. It sounds strange, but I didn't mind, because the subject matter was so incredibly shimmering. This paper concerned the work of a man named Achter Ahsen, and his postulation of a thing called an EIDETIC IMAGE. Eidetic images are magnificent. Just the word: *eidetic!* a word landing on the mind halfway between *identity* and *pathetic*, and referring, or at least that's what I explained in the paper, to a certain sort of dreamlike mental image that appears to the dreamer on the deepest, most magical, most repeatable level; an image as inevitable as breath or rain; an image that seems painted on velvet, so full of feeling and texture is it. And it's an image with great symbolic importance to the imaginer, and that person can call the image up at will.

Whenever they need it: *poof*! This man Achter Ahsen went on and on about these images, I guess he collected money for studying them or whatnot. And during that summer I analyzed his analysis in depth, and commented at length on its meanings and possible ramifications both to the individual and to the scientific community. I became an expert.

But the real payoff from that summer's work came in the form of the realization that I myself have an eidetic image rattling around my psychic briefcase. It comes to me whenever I call it. In all its beauty and detail. I've had it for years but never named it. This eidetic image has a little story that precedes it, the same little story every time. It's a story about the choice to inhabit a body. First I'm just a spirit without a body, so profoundly easy and inherently intelligent. I float without flying. I have no weight. I lack the torture of an orbit of any kind. There is no gravity, no love, just clean consciousness in a cool medium. And then I'm told about the body, offered the tempting body. I'm told about the deal, the Faustian tradeoff without any evil valence. It's just this: I can come into the body: I can experience desire, lust, be entered. I can eat delicious foods, I can see the curve of the earth, notice where the moon rises drenched like a siren from the ocean, dries off and then lights the waters it rose from. I can lie, steal, hurt people; I can give birth. I can read, think and speak, I can drag raw silk across my eyelids, the whole thing. But: they tell me: I get these things only to lose them, because there's a clock running on it all. It runs on time. I come into things, move through them, lose them. I feel pain, I shrivel, I die. This is a timed experience, they tell me, so different from what I am used to.

And I realize every time at this exact point in the sequence, that this is why I love baseball. It's out of time. Now I have always described my love for baseball in the most spiritual terms; I see now that this is because baseball is timeless. A game can take an hour and a half or a day and a half. A pitch can take forever. They bring a guy in, and he warms up with 10 pitches, and then he throws a ball, and they don't like that, so they send him out in a cart, and they bring another guy in in a cart, and they break for a commercial from Nabisco, and he warms up 10 pitches, and etcetera! In baseball, you win not because you did more in 15 minutes than the other team. You win because you win. Spiritual. Out of time. And I love that. But still: I want the body. I decide to take the body. I want it. I want it. I want my own body.

And so, the deal is made: I give up deathlessness and painlessness. I get the body, diploma of the body, with all the rights and privileges thereunto appertaining. And like a hostage, I am given a sort of drop-off point; arrangements are made for my return to the body.

The eidetic image is of that moment, the return to the body. I see myself from very far off, young and luscious, coming out of a tunnel blasted into a mountain, coming around a curve from inside the mountain, sleeveless white shirt, drenched in youth and desire, in a sleek white car. This car. Christ, this car. It's humming like an angel. It looks something like this *(holds up toy car)* only it has no roof on it; it's a convertible, so from the wide angle, you can look right down into it, like someone up in the gallery watching brain surgery. Cars are all time, don't you think? all about time. Cars move through time the way boats move through water. Cars are beached without currents of time around them. They say when the bomb dropped on Hiroshima, cars stopped moving, because time stopped moving.

The most beautiful part of me is my arm, my left arm. My pitching arm. Dew sits on it. It smells like the sun. The muscle is perfect: long and lean and relaxed and full of power underneath the silken skin.

And so I come. I come home in my sleek white car.

Music plays, and I am a gorgeous young woman.

Ephemeral Music

I only ever heard the tune in the car. It figures this curse got started in California in some town near L.A. that begins with a 'T'... 'Teheran ... 'Telemon ... 'Tikkhamun ... something like that. California, where you order pizza into your car, you just give them the license plate number! California, where they do prostate surgery for you in your car if that's the most convenient place for you to meet them!

Anyway, the tune was schlocky, but who knew? It seemed ... upbeat, vaguely insinuating ... smooth percussion ... moving, moving, moving relentlessly toward its own conclusion. Motion such as this fools you about a lot of things. You think something's rare, delicate and lovely, and in fact what you're noticing about that thing is that it's going by! It's going by you, it'll be gone soon. It'll never come back. That jazzes things up quite a bit . . . like a one-night stand . . .

Every time I turned the ignition, there it was . . . I moved for months to this music, but only in the car . . . I took great pleasure in it, and I wanted to control that pleasure . . . I wanted to bring this music home, dance to it, have coffee to it, play it for my friends, put it on my answering machine, but it wasn't meant to be. Every time they were going to announce the artist and title, the car went under a tunnel, or over a bridge, or someone shrieked or someone honked or there was static interference or something! It occurred to me that I could call up the radio station and SING this tune to them and ask someone to identify it, but it doesn't really have a melody, it's not even remotely lyrical, it's just an aura, a mood. I just couldn't catch up to this music, couldn't own it, couldn't track it down.

Suburban Life

Cars are like the phone, they pull up the way phones just ring, and you don't know who's on the line, who's in the shotgun seat, what they want. You say hello, you look out your window. Someone's on a mission. You answer your door, you say Yes when they ask if it's you. I think it's not without significance that the new directions our phones are supposed to take us in are referred to as a Highway, an Information Highway. Because you travel along, and you show up anywhere. Your image, your voice, your words: Shoot them like a Kleenex into the trashpail of someone else's life. Do Driveby's. Whatever.

Cars invade your privacy at dinnertime, same as the phone. Cars pull up, doors open, and who knows what. Suspense of a very boring, very mortal timbre.

Rick. I ache for Rick. Poor little rich boy stealing cars. Fourteen years old. Suburban lady, runs into her house, leaves groceries and keys in the Pontiac . . . my Rick goes in, makes himself a sandwich, steals the car. Joy ride. Yeah. Joy ride. True joy. True.

They carry him in drunk. There's a dinner party going on, he just stole a car, but all the guests, Republicans, are shielded. Priscilla – she's the live-in help – carries him in, wrestles him down, punches him, kisses him. Punches his skull, kisses his eyelids. Priscilla. She showed us dirty black-and-white out-of-focus photos of people fucking. Except for the growling look on their faces they could have been picking lint out of a carpet. Click of glasses, polite laughter, and, mixed in, the one drunken Republican laugh, skipping on the occasion, the moment, like a flat stone over the sea.

Rick and the lady. Rick stole her car. A joy ride. Finally, some joy in that fucking car.

A car pulls up, they throw Rick out. They screech away.

Rick says: I was French-kissing like a Bitch for seven minutes!

A big dry-cleaner truck pulls up. The dry-cleaner guy gets out. Big stuffed animal. Leaves Priscilla a big huge fat pink stuffed bear. A rose in its paw. He loves her. He loves her out-of-focus black-and-white, he loves her picking lint, he loves her growling. He loves her blur and growl. He loves Priscilla the way I love Rick. Rick stole a car and some kid stole me: they cut me open, took a person out of me. No big deal. Kid was joyriding. I left the keys, the groceries. Some kid took me for a ride.

The exterminator pulls up. Unmarked car, Mom insisted. Nothing at all! It could have been nothing at all! Just a truck. Little 1987 white Ford: nothing at all. Unmarked car. Exterminator. Came to bury Caesar not to praise him. Caesar's a roach, running himself to death inside the clock in Mom's spanking new self-cleaning stainless steel wall-mounted oven. Roach! Roach under glass in suburbia, like an Andy Warhol, as postmodern as a piece of liver draped over a telephone; dying in a clock! That's ridiculous! On display! Near the food! Can't touch it! Hiding and dying in the clock. Turning circles like a chicken on a spit.

Or like the ants in the toilet. The insect karma. See, first I saved an insect in the Sperbers' pool, a dragonfly; its wings grazing the surface of the water, the water bribing it with weight and depth . . . I placed a seedling under it, one of those green things you use to open and stick on your nose, it was struggling, drowning, and escorted it to the side of the pool, deposited on the concrete . . . it shook off my attentions and crept away soggy but free.

Then reversed the karma by flushing these two drowning ants down the toilet. Dad had 'killed' these ants, and dropped them in the toilet; he'd killed them with his bare fingers, a wheedling, rolling gesture I'd seen him do many times: he'd roll UP THROUGH THE FINGER THROUGH THE KNUCKLE TO THE TIP AND UNDER THE NAIL AND FLICK! and then roll UP THROUGH THE FINGER THROUGH THE KNUCKLE TO THE TIP AND UNDER THE NAIL AND FLICK! But let me tell you, they were both still alive when I went to pee ... two strangers from the same species drowning together in a toilet. Plus I gave the ants up; told Dad they were there. If I didn't flush 'em, he would've.

And yet it was Dad who relived, again and again, that image from Ernest Hemingway... one of his big burly butch taciturn classic novels ... of a fire trying to seduce a log, make her give herself to him, to die in his lambent arms, and he's at her, he's at her, he's nibbling her neck, tormenting her with heat, trying to get her to roll over and die her death against his lips, and finally she relents, and she turns over and falls into him, and as she does so, a whole wall of ants, alive on her belly, perishes instantly.

A Chevy pulls up. '76 Chevy. It's his parents'. I love him. His parents and my parents are high-school friends. His wrists are white and straight. They flow into his hands, they become his hands, silently and lethally. Like a woman's; his hands are like a woman's. His fingers are long; the nails are dirty. My parents aren't home. His lips are painful. Painful to think about. I swam away from his lips in the same pool as I saved the dragonfly. It did better than I did, the dragonfly... I drowned against those lips that night ... Dragonfly shook the water off its wings and flew away.

My Mother's Car

My father lured my mother down there on some fake funny premise or other. It was right after the war, you couldn't get a car very easily, you had to put your name on a list and wait until your name was on a shorter list, and hope and wait and listen, and accept any color any model, be willing to accept any car at all.

He lured her downstairs somehow. She dried her hands and came down and there, in the driveway, black as hope and shiny as death, a 1948 spanking new Plymouth, curved, curving from roof to rear like someone's fat ass, making her scream. She screamed with happiness. The unsurprisable matriarch was surprised. And now here, 45 years later, is our new car. It's black also. I'm surprised too. This car isn't curved like that, like someone's ass; it's boxed, like the shape of someone's head. Like a brain's in there. It's a nice car, though not what I expected. It's a '93 Honda Accord EX. Automatic transmission and power this and that, power everything, yet driving it is very physical somehow, you work up a sweat; in fact it's like the Flintstones' car. Just makes me want to blast a hole through the floor, stick my feet through and run for my fucking life.

Set Your Bearings Straight

SET YOUR BEARINGS STRAIGHT it says in the car repair book. It says: The most common forms of adjustment are illustrated on these pages. In all of these, the amount of tension applied on the thrust washer by an adjusting nut is set to the manufacturer's specifications, or according to feel for lack of free play and smooth rotation of the wheel.

Adjustment by feel, although reasonably accurate and practical, should be done only if a torque wrench is not available.

Page 42.

It says: SYMPTOMS OF POWER STEERING TROUBLES: Leaking fluid, hard steering, binding or poor recovery, excessive free play, noise, steering chatter, rattles and complete loss of power.

It says: THE TRANSMISSION is a group of parts that transmits power from the engine to the drive shaft. The power produced by the engine is made up of speed and of TORQUE, which is twisting force. The transmission permits the ratio of speed to torque to be varied. It can reduce the speed to increase the torque, or reduce the torque to increase the speed.

Cars move, and when you ask why, or how, they tell you it's a series of controlled explosions, and that makes so much sense it's worthless. I mean, isn't everything?

The Body

I didn't want to drive. Really didn't want to. Only member of my whole high-school class, whole student body, not desperate, not itching to drive. Cars filled me with terror, too little margin for error, much too little; get it wrong and die.

Plus cars unequivocally acknowledged the body, which for me was unseemly and humiliating. The idea that we need cars because our BODIES must be lugged somewhere. See, the mind, the mind needs nothing; made of air and unearthly wisps of desire and logic, the mind doesn't need a Jeep Cherokee to skim the muddy mountains of springtime. But the BODY. Not only do YOU go to orchestra practice, but your UTERUS goes! Your infected sinuses, impacted bowels; your toenails go! And they can't get there themselves! They are of here, they eat, they shit, they need to be transported! They are mortal, they die; what gets into that car dies, and when it dies, it stinks!

And all this from me, Ms. Achter Ahsen of 1975, Ms. Eidetic Image in a white car, choosing the joys of the body.

She got an A minus on that paper. I think it should have been an A.

Car Show, Car Girl

Welcome! This means welcome to the Tra La Ooh La La Car Show! Although that wasn't really a rhyme! Because it was tra LA and then ooh la LA! So that's just the same word really! It's like 'Carefree Gum is Sugar*less* and it comes in full-size sticks, no *less*'! They're so sloppy, really! And they make so much money! There's no excuse for that really!

The Toyota Motor Corporation is proud to introduce its all new compact/sport/utility Recreational Active Vehicle (RAV4). This car is power itself! It's got a 2.0 liter 16 valve engine with double ended rear suspended dual overhead cam and monocoque body construction, independent suspension and full-time four-wheel drive. Instead of part-time. And that means benefits from the government! Like retirement and social security! This model features 15 by 8's made by Sendel, and they stick out one inch all around with the help of 145/ 50R15 tires. Plus you'll enjoy our Hypertech chip, K&N air filter, Doug Thorley Tri-Y headers, a Pete Gibson three-inch cat-back exhaust system, a Robert Shaw 180-degree thermostat with the noise restrictor removed from the Herman Melville air inlet, Mobile l synthetic oil, March power pulleys, SplitFire plugs, ACCEL external coil/cap/rotor, Ed Moroso wires and some chrome covers with Pippy Edelberg heads and a manifold and cam Turbo City blueprinted throttle body/spacer/ MAP adjuster, an electric fan, Bergen Belsen modified transmission for firmer shifts and kickdown and a Vortech or Whipple supercharger with RU486.

Phew! This is a real hunk! It's a lot of car! You can feel it on the body and smell it in the rear! And you know if you were to ask Luke Shaffer of Chino, California, why he spent the last four years making his '91 Chevy extended-cab daily driver into an awesome custom, he'd tell you he did it so that he could race and have some fun.

And Jesus and his friends, is this car fun! Look at it! Look at the body. It's got a buttoned-down winter boxiness, but it's all brawn underneath. Note the front fender contour, the way it rides high on itself in the back. Acceleration to 60 is superlative in the 3 series, although it takes quite some time! The controls all work with precision. This car never breaks down, it merely ceases to proceed from time to time. In French, that's *De Temps En Temps!* Once when I typed *de temps en temps* I put in an extra 't' so it was *de tempts en tempts!* And this car tempts!

It's got a dark interior. The leatherized custom work is all a sabled silver, and the carpet is ebony and the roof is black and the lights have dark gels over them and the whole thing is black as pitch and you know what, the truth is you can't see a thing! It's got a frail little glovebox door! I knew this man, he died at the racetrack one day! He said You've Got No Business Driving Where You Can't See! He said that! And he was right! And yet in my community they have corners where you have to turn left or right onto a two-way street but cars are parked along the sides so you don't know if another car is coming or not! You have to turn without knowing! You have to glide out into the stream of traffic and hope! If it's night, you just have to try to sense if there are any lights moving toward you, and in the daytime when you can see more it's even scarier, because there are no moving lights there's just prayer! Raw prayer! And kinaesthetic clairvoyance! But that's not what they test you for at the Department of Motor Vehicles in Rutherford, New Jersey, believe you me! And sometimes when I get to those corners I just don't want to go on . . . I think of that: you have no business driving where you can't see! And I just want to stop, turn off the motor, and stay there! Stay on that corner forever, I don't want to turn that corner with such blindness, I don't. I just want to live there. I just want to stay there. I want to wash my clothes in the fire hydrant! And he just died at the racetrack! He had no idea! He went with his wallet, and a green overcoat, and a hat, Russian hat, and he had a horse he liked, and he was smiling, it was a beautiful day, it wasn't cold, it wasn't warm, and that's it! You can't see around that corner either! Fucking joke! Hahahahaha!

At a remarkable $17,970, including destination charge, this RAV4 comes fully equipped with all the standard features we specified so clearly, plus a personal security system including remote keyless, illuminated entry and panic alarm, which is tautological really: *panic alarm*, and integrated fog lamps.

And as H. A. 'Humpy' Wheeler says, if it's not integrated, it's just a bunch of rich Europeans you never heard of!

The Toyota Motor Corporation is proud to present the RAV4. Come see about it! It's an animal! Only you don't have to walk it or scoop the poop or anything. Let us drive you, move you, the new 1995 Toyota RAV4. From the Ford Motor Corporation!

Sex

We're leaning up against a car. A stranger's car. It's eighth street, or fourth street, or some street divisible by two. It's an old car, got no alarm, no blinking red lights, no protection. That's what being old means: fewer defenses. If you lose it, so what. He's got me up against this car, and he's tall, he's so tall, he's so much taller than I am, than the car is; his head is the size and level of the streetlamp, only the light coming out of his head is infra-red: you can *hear* it. Halfway between a mugging and a seduc-tion, this struggle: the metal against my thighs, something under my short skirt, either a hand or a brake. I think of the expression: *shocks and struts*. These are car parts, but I'm not sure what they do. I think shocks are what keep you from bouncing too hard in motion, but struts make me think of peacocks, and of men. And there's the expression: *parking*. They went parking. So old, that expression; so stupid, so innocent. I've got these things in my mind, sitting on the floor of my mind like rotten metal under a riverbed.

The car is warm. Day ended so long ago, but the metal is warm, not with use but with sun; it's high summer midnight, someone has parked this car, and we're up against it, struggling; a Biblical struggle; we look, from high up in that building, like Jacob wrestling the angel God sent to him on a mountain. Only our mountain is a car, old and hot like I am, unlit and still, like he is. Against this car I moan out some delicious, pointless encounter; I love this car; I leave my smell on this car, like a cat; this car held me up bearing down, this old car: I'd never recognize it if I saw it again.

Clark

Clark was killed by a car. He was on our baseball team, the Shalimar Shallies. We were the kind of team with real spirit, and if we couldn't win by normal means we'd win by default. We never lost a game. If we were losing real bad we'd just stop fielding with any energy; if the ball was hit way out past third, possibly even an in-the-park home run, we'd just walk casually to the ball, our arms around one another, talking of Michaelangelo, chatting, laughing, and, the competitive edge thus deftly removed from the game, the other team would become demoralized and quit and we'd win by default. I played first base although I was phobic of flying objects, and I always hit the ball to the same place but no one ever stood there, so at bat I always made it to first base, my fielding position. It came to seem as if I spent my whole childhood at first base, there by the wooden fence with the thorny wild pink roses.

Clark was a beautiful kid. He was skinny and easy and sweet. Hard to get to know. He was Rick's best friend. He had an older brother who used to write love letters to my older sister, that's all I know. He was riding his bicycle on Murray Avenue and the car came and hit him and he flew off his bike like a sudden bird and was pinned to a tree. There's still no bark on the tree he embraced with his death.

We weren't sure if he was dead, and all of us had a weird new feeling; to me it felt like merriment. I remember getting all dressed up. Then a car pulled up, a guy got out. And then the word came, and everyone cried, but I didn't cry. I was so far from crying, so drily, icily, oddly far. It's a death I was too young to cry for. I didn't want anyone to mourn. I just wanted us to fly off our bikes to some point way beyond his death; to some point where his death was as tall and old and unnoticeable as the tree he died against.

A couple of days later his father marched down the hill to the baseball field with Clark's three bats. He gave them to Rick. That was a week before Rick got drunk and took the lady's car on a joyride.

Sherry Again

Years later, we're still roommates, she and I; we've lived together in an apartment the size of a sarcophagus on West 87th Street with a hotplate and without a phone, and in a sixth-floor walkup on 21st Street which a guy lived in and then died in trying to open up a window from the outside, holding onto the wall with his feet and left hand, because he forgot his keys. We decide to take a trip to my Aunt Betty's cottage, and it's in Connecticut somewhere north of Hartford; we both cried the whole time we were there, half from awe and half from boredom, and then, on the way back, the joyride began.

I was driving. With her, I loved to drive. Between the two of us, I was the man, the buck, the fearless one, the one who held doors, shot lions, kept their nails short. Her mind's curves were too voluptuous for speed. I had her dad's old car up to 80 miles an hour, the windows were down, we were laughing and laughing and then, like streetlamps at dusk, red lights popped on the dashboard: HEAT first and GENERATOR next and then SOMETHING ELSE. You could smell the trouble, and then smoke, or steam, or smog or something started pouring out from under the hood. We were laughing hysterically, half out of awe, half out of boredom.

Adventure stows away inside failure. The car failed utterly. We pulled over whence we were, some town between important towns; began with a B, like Butterfield or Bakersville or whatever. We opened up the hood, and it was something out of Dante. Since we were two young girls, two young guys pulled up and offered to help; they got us a tow to a fix-it place. Someone offered us a beer. I was glad to be stopped by HEAT and GENERATOR lights in a weird slow town, but was concerned because the playoff games were in full swing and the Yankees were serious contenders. That was the year of Mr.

October and all that, and that homer of Reggie's that whined like a ravenous mosquito past my left ear in the bleachers and on out into the chilly Bronx night. I said: just take me someplace where I can see the game, and then the two guys who picked us up deposited me in a local bar, surrounded by town natives, all with chins raised and eyes riveted on a wall-mounted TV.

That was when it started with the bartender. He was drawn to me immediately, half out of awe and half out of boredom. He kept hanging around, lurking by, smiling, sort of laughing. Finally began trying to engage me in conversation in the middle of the eighth inning, when I could least afford a lapse of attention. He says: what's your number, and, dropping my eyes to look at him, I noticed that he was staring at me, and so was everyone else, and that there was something devilishly public about this whole routine. So I said: I don't have a number. My car died. I'm here by accident. Not car accident. Fate. I'm here by Fate, which is a synonym for No Reason At All, and I don't have a number, and he says: Well, let me give you mine, and at that moment, in the sweetest unison, EVERY SINGLE PERSON AT THE BAR SHRIEKED OUT:

775-0796.

Bungalow Bar

I wonder how Bungalow Bar ice-cream trucks drive . . . I wonder if they hold the road around curves, if they come with anti-lock brakes, air bags; or if their recreational purpose, or the summer itself, is supposed to be enough to save you.

Everyone has in their memory someone they found sexy before they knew what sexy was. We had Freddy Jablonski, the Bungalow Bar man. Freddy got to our neighborhood at the witching hour of every summer afternoon . . . five o'clock or so . . . when eating ice cream was a struggle . . . dangerously close to dinner time . . . a fight with your mother . . . a struggle with your own conscience . . . we were almost always playing softball on Rick's mom's yard-turned-arena when the bells of his truck landed on our ears like cold rain. Freddy, understanding the role of local politics in successful commerce, often played with us for a while.

It gave us a chance to look at him . . . he was older . . . maybe

20, maybe even 30... sort of a young Marlon Brando type... he was dark, and he smelled of time and power ... his muscles were swollen. He smelled like a man. At the plate, he was laughing, sarcastically gentle ... catching balls, he only used one hand ... he caught balls like a prisoner, one hand pinned behind his back, the power in his legs forcing him to fly almost against his will, as if on the verge of a daring escape.

Two girls loved him, two girls on our street, a virgin and a whore, of course it was like that, he was a man of visible polarities, even to a bunch of 10-year-olds. The virgin was Linda, a girl of good Italian family, quietly beautiful, soft-spoken and sophisticated by virtue of chastity. The whore was Tina, who had sharp eye-teeth and lipskin that folded over them provocatively. Tina: born to carry the flamboyant burden of all women; it wasn't her fault, she was chosen for the job. She wore fishnet stockings to Linda's bobby socks, and pointy falsies to Linda's soft cotton sweaters. They had different approaches: Linda the virgin could be seen every afternoon at her bedroom window, her face like a distant planet, misty and full of reflected light. At bat, Freddy would glance behind him and smile, and she would disappear. Tina's approach was more direct ... she'd get herself all up and sashay down the street and around the corner, shaking her ass like the green race-car flag they put out on the track after they've cleaned up an accident. She'd have her heels and falsies screwed on and her trip down the block was nothing short of a parade for one, a sexual solo. This competition ran like chamber music under the summer, and was laughed about by us without being understood.

One day it all broke, just like in the movies. Sex, violence, tragedy, mystery. Just like Shakespeare. Freddy arrived late and he smelled funny... he was drunk, I think ... and when Tina was halfway around the corner, he jumped the fence and grabbed her ... the sleeves of his uniform almost tore ... his tongue was in her mouth when the distant virgin light appeared in the window... Linda ... Linda ...

He shoved Tina away, jumped the fence again, took a slow, hanging curve pitch from Fatty Arbuckle, the Fernwood pitcher, which he wacked so hard the ball felt pain and it disappeared for five days. Bat in his hand he jumped the fence back to the street again, smashed his headlights with the bat, ran around to the back near the freezer and smashed the tail-lights, pulled open the freezer, yanked all the ice cream out and threw it into the street . . . I remember that image, it looked like a dying man fighting through a snow storm . . . and he took off down the block at 80 miles an hour, and we never saw him again.

The next day an item in the local paper talked about a man named Friechelm having been arrested . . . found speeding in an ice-cream truck, he tore up the summons given him by policemen and then tried to run them over . . . I picture him spending that night in prison, sleepless, his groin aching, some part of his life over forever, some part of his life just begun.

The ball was in the brook a half mile away. We found a duck sitting on it, pretending it was a baby.

Baxter Krueger, Amway Products, the Lamborghini Countach with the Gull-Wing Doors and the Dead Woman

She's telling me all about it, my neighbor, only she won't say what it is yet, but she will soon. But right now she's telling me about Baxter Krueger! He's a marketing genius, and he is very successful, he's a multimillionaire and he owns an island and an isthmus and a Lamborghini Countach car with gull-wing doors! That's the kind of doors that open up instead of out! Up instead of out! Gull-wing doors! The fucking car practically flies, that's Baxter Krueger! And he is accessible! You can see him! You can touch him! He will come to your house to conduct meetings to teach you how to instruct people how to order their toilet paper by computer! Everyone buys toilet paper! So it's recession-proof! So you buy your paper that way, and more importantly, you teach other people how to do it! And every time someone you taught to buy toilet paper by computer buys toilet paper by computer, you get a commission! And every person you taught is called your leg! And under Baxter Krueger's leg are so many people he is a millionaire! And he has that incredible flying kind of a car with wings for doors! And we are right under him, just a few people down, just a few vendors removed, under his leg! He has many legs, actually! We are so close to him, we are, so to speak, between his legs! And lettuce, too, you can buy lettuce, and soon UPS will deliver it, because no one wants to go to the mall anymore, because it's dangerous! Look what happened to that woman, a whole shopping center collapsed on her! And that's the marketing genius of Baxter Krueger! He's a doctor! And he must be a good doctor, too, because he has such a beautiful home, an island and an isthmus, and such a wonderful car, wings for doors, effortless income, he watches golf on TV on Sunday, he accidentally topples a massive pile of unopened checks with his feet as he raises them to rest on the leather ottoman!

And of course all of that, and for some reason I keep remembering the picture on the front page of that day's *New York Times*, of this woman who, on her way to a Bosnian market to buy bread, was hit by sniper fire, and the camera finds her lying dead in the street in her high heels, holding her purse, with her eyes open, looking very casual and relaxed. And that's the revelation: Casualties! Suddenly, a clear etymology for that word, clear like impact! She looks fine, there on the page, lying down in the street; in fact, she looks so unremarkable that, tilting the page upward, she seems to be standing up, leaning against a wall, waiting for a bus. Casualty, that's the word. And so, if I sign up, I will be six layers beneath Baxter Krueger, so close I can touch him, and he will come to my house in his car with the wings.

And this is what I'm left with: Baxter Krueger and the Dead Woman.

Now it's possible to say, hold it! Baxter Krueger is one thing and the dead woman is another, but I think not. I say, no it isn't. I don't mean anything by it and excuse me, but when the world gets looked at, it contains these two truths on the same day: Baxter Krueger and the Dead Woman. Baxter Krueger in all his pomp, coming to your house to teach you how to manufacture money buying dinner napkins over a modem, and this unremarkable village woman murdered on her way to buy bread by someone who didn't even know her.

Two different ways of shopping.

Hope her chariot had wings.

Kathy

My friend Kathy knew how to burp out a song. She could send the notes to whole show tunes out on small belches. Kathy failed her driving test eight times and passed on the ninth because they ran out of room on the piece of paper where they record the results in the file.

When she passed, she took a bunch of us out on a celebratory ride. Stevie Wonder was on the radio, and Kathy was driving, her head turned a full one-eighty to burp out You Are The Sunshine Of My Life. Drove directly into a pothole the depth of a gravesite at 40 mph. The steering wheel came out of its moorings, popped out into her hands ... she turns around and is holding this disenfranchised circle in her hands ... it's no longer connected in any way to the car's direction, or to the fate of the people riding in it, and then she started laughing and just ... threw the wheel out the window!

FINIS

Commentary: *Making Time*

Thinking he could take the world and all its pleasures into his body, Goethe's Faust chose immortality over the body in time. And he lived, lived to be tied to the burning cross of his desires, and to rue the day that he made such a pact with the devil himself. Margolin's eidetic image, in *Carthieves! Joyrides!*, saves her from such a fate. Wanting the body, choosing it again and again with the full knowledge of its blissful bondage, Margolin takes us on a ride in her many-winged chariots. And who would want to get out, or stop, unless it were merely to pause, for some stolen moments of parking?

This performance traffics in the eternity of mortality. It does not promise us the romance of lovers frozen in the Keatsian moment of the always almost but never quite consummated suspenseful pleasures. Rather, *Carthieves! Joyrides!* picks up any hitchhiker who dares enough to risk the pleasurable dangers of going all the way. Not recklessly, but riskfully. Yes, Margolin hesitates at those crossroads where the driver is blind to oncoming traffic; she chafes at the implicitly sadistic logic of constructing a blind spot on a busy thoroughfare, and trembles at the possibility that one false move could be her last. Maybe she momentarily wishes that she could just stay there forever and wash her clothes in the fire hydrant. But finally she opts not to let time pass as she waits securely in her car, but to pass with and through time, to get on board, to go for the ride, accompanied by passengers like her friend Kathy, who hits a giant

133

pothole, finds the steering wheel a suddenly disconnected circle in her hands, and tosses it out the window.

Carthieves, Joyrides! moves through a series of what may seem to be random associations, images, and narratives: her rotting teeth that remind her of 'tombstones in a graveyard'; a 1995 Buick Riviera that reminds her of herself and promises space, power, and silence; her college roommate whose I.Q. was so big she could not lift her head off the pillow; the aleatory pleasures of watching baseball; the poor little rich kid, Rick, who steals an even richer Republican lady's car and is beaten and petted by Priscilla; the mirror-imaged karma of the dragonfly she rescues from the pool and the two stranger ants dying together in a toilet; a childhood friend killed when his bike collided with a tree; a seduction, or a mugging, of metal and flesh; an ice-cream vendor wrenched apart by a teenage virgin and a teenage whore; Baxter Krueger, a man who creates commodities on the Internet and buys people to sell them; a woman casually killed by a sniper's bullet on her way to buy bread. What brings all these seemingly disparate parts into one performance is Margolin's perpetual fascination with the ways in which we make time, even as it seems to be passing by us. Like the cars in this current obsession, which we manufacture to transport our bodies into spaces that our minds might travel alone, Margolin's words are vehicles for transporting us into places that she has been, or desired to be in. Most importantly, places where the 'word' alone will not suffice, but where the word must become flesh.

The motif that returns throughout the performance, its repetition reminding us that what we most desire is often, if not always, that which is just beyond our sight, our hearing, our touch, is the song that plays on the car radio and just as it comes to a close, the driver concentrated, poised, ready and willing to track it down to its origin, loses contact with it as the announcer's voice is distorted by static or drowned out by the sound of car horns. At just that moment when we think we are ready to tap into the origin of things, we find ourselves in a tunnel, or lost in the cacophony of street sounds, our senses overwhelmed by other music that it was not our intention to hear. But again, as always in her work, Margolin is concerned, precisely, with making the most of the present, and with making what is present, the most. Not only can she always find something to do when the time appears to be ripe, while the body of time takes a different turn, but she can also find passion and beauty in the spontaneous, and show us how to make time out of errors. Such is her alchemy: a repulsive and sadistic dentist is transmogrified into a man whose 'dirty dental' talk invites her into his secret world and hence his sensuous side; a delinquent adolescent becomes a boy who can teach us how to seize joy in a banal prank; a college girl overwhelmed and failing is elevated to a goddess deserving worshipful service; an anonymous peasant woman who is merely one of thousands of 'casualties' is celebrated, individualized, and paid homage.

If we wait, in this performance, for Margolin to satisfy her own or our desire to know the title and artist of the song she cannot stop hearing, we will be disappointed. She never finds out herself, and hence we never know. But we misunderstand the very essence of this piece if we wait for such revelations. For the fact that we are here for the ride, and not for its source or destination, is the music this performance plays.

Deb Margolin in *O Wholly Night and Other Jewish Solecisms*. Photo: © Dixie Sheridan.

7

&

O Wholly Night
and Other Jewish Solecisms

(A minimalist stage in low but inviting light contains nothing more than a wooden chair with arms, stage right, a largish and strong table, angled slightly, stage left, and a hat-tree on which is hung an old, tattered, greenish dress, upstage just right of center. ACTRESS enters and comes downstage in warm, welcoming manner.)

ACTRESS. Good evening, and thank you all so very much for coming. It's always an honor and source of excitement to be able to present new work, and I'm extremely grateful for this opportunity. Before I begin this evening's presentation of *O Wholly Night and Other Jewish Solecisms*, I'd like to share with you something which has been both a literal and a figurative symbol of my desire to say the things I'm saying with this piece, and that is *(She walks upstage and gets dress, hanger and all; carries it reverently downstage toward audience.):* this dress. I hope you can see it from out there . . . it's a threadbare and incredibly beautiful garment, and it whispers to me of times long past. It's all silk . . . threadbare and gossamer . . . and all hand-embroidered by some ancient, loving fingers. It's old. You can tell I didn't get this at The Gap. In order to be able to share with you fully the impact of this dress on tonight's work, I need to share with you the story of how this dress came to be in my possession.

While I was growing up, my parents had many friends, and these friends were by and large in couples: there were the Goldbergers, the Sperbers, the Friedmans, the Galkins, the Goldmarks, the Fraidowitzes, the Hermans; if you're here and I've forgotten to mention you, please forgive me; there were so many of you. These people were like extended family to me. Some I got to know well, others not so well, but all these people were in my life, and I revered them the way a runner reveres a

137

brick wall: they were there, and I needed to negotiate my way around or through them.

I found out not so long ago that one half of one of these couples, Mr. Friedman, was seriously ill, in fact terminally so. Mr. Friedman was one of those friends of my parents I didn't know very well. He was a high-powered attorney of some sort, and he had a reputation among the gang for his fierce loyalty and Bolshevik intelligence. But he spoke in a VERY LOUD, BOOMING VOICE which, in the absence of any intimacy with him, I found very frightening when I was a child. I always imagined him to be a man who smoked big cigars all day long, although he never smoked a day in his life. Yet he did die of lung cancer, which gets one to thinking.

Anyway, since Mr. Friedman was terminally ill, I asked my mom and dad to take me to see him, and they immediately agreed. I mean, so often after a person dies, we think to ourselves: now what did his teeth look like when he smiled? How did he hold his hands when he was making a point? And given a choice, I didn't want to be left with those questions. My parents were delighted with my request, and they made the necessary arrangements, and we went over to the Friedmans' house on the appointed evening.

The conversation was ordinary on that occasion, as it so often is in extraordinary circumstances. I believe we discussed the stock market, or how to put things in escrow, or something like that. As we were getting up to leave, I kissed Mr. Friedman on the cheek, and Mrs. Friedman walked us to the door, and as we approached her front door, I noticed her hall closet was open, and hanging from the top of the closet was this dress! This incredible garment from another age, and it took my breath away, and I just stopped walking. Mrs. F saw me looking at the dress, and she came over, and I said: Mrs. Friedman where did you get this incredible dress? And she said: Well, you know, Debbie, this dress has an extraordinary history. It was found under huge boulders in a destroyed synagogue, and the story goes that the woman who owned it, a young immigrant mother, had to abandon her possessions and leave very quickly lest she and her children be decimated by the destruction of the temple ... or something like that, she said something like that, but I did not hear her, so enraptured was I by the garment itself ... I heard it whispering, calling to me

138

susurrantly from another era. Her words melted like snow-flakes on the hot pavement of my awe. Then finally I heard her ask:

Debbie. Would you like to *have* this dress?

And I said yes, I would, I would, yes, I would, yes. And I couldn't help feeling like I had extorted the dress from her with my reverence for it, but I took the dress! And I brought it home *(She walks upstage and hangs the dress back up, touching it briefly and with longing; turns and comes back downstage to audience.)*, and I hung it up. And I would visit it regularly, every few days or so; dust it, brush things away around it; it hung precariously as a spider's web, one sleeve hanging from it like a flower broken off at the stalk by the hands of a careless child. And I knew that the time would come when I would be able to find the right and proper use in my life for this remarkable garment.

So when I was invited to write and perform a piece about Jewish life, about Jewish identity, I knew the dress had found its moment. But I didn't remember the story Mrs. Friedman had told me about it, and I decided to call her and ask for a little refresher on that. So I went to the phone ... dialed her ... *reached* her; her husband had since passed away since she made me the remarkable gift I was calling about, and so after some sorrowful pleasantries (?!) I said: Mrs. Friedman, something wonderful has happened! I've been commissioned by the Jewish Museum to write and perform a piece on Jewish iden-tity, and I'm going to use that exquisite dress that you gave me, but I don't remember the story you told me about its history, and I was wondering if you could take just a moment to remind me of it.

And there was a silence, a very large one. It was stony in tex-ture and cool in temperature, after which Mrs. Friedman said:

Debbie, I never gave you a dress!

And you know me, I wanted to say: My honored lord, you know right well you did, and with them words of so sweet breath composed ... etcetera, etcetera. But I did not digress! My sanity was on the line here! Instead I said: Mrs. Friedman! You gave me that dress, that incredible silk dress, it was ancient and lovely, and you said it had been found under a bunch of rocks or something like that, please, Mrs. Friedman!

And there was another of those cavernous silences, after which Mrs. Friedman said:

Look, Debbie, I never gave you a dress. And if you need a story, MAKE IT UP!

It was thus that I wrung an exasperated benediction for this evening's performance from Mr. Friedman's widow, and it is very much under the auspices of that benediction that tonight's presentation *O Wholly Night and Other Jewish Solecisms* is offered, and I welcome you to it.

This show was originally commissioned by the Jewish Museum as a part of their 'Too Jewish' exhibition, and as I was preparing the piece for that august occasion, I remember feeling some confusion as to where my work fit in to that very edgy, very self-conscious, very... postmodern rubric, because I was never ashamed of being a Jew, never. To me it seemed like a status symbol, a symptom of greatness. I was always told that Jews were the smart ones, the ones with intellect, the ones who read books, the ones who dreamed, and I related to that, and I aspired to it. My parents are the son and daughter of Russian immigrants, come from the areas of Odessa and Babroisk, living in Hartford. My mother's parents were joyous, spoke like Americans, and embroidered their poverty with great good humor. My father's parents spoke with thick accents, and I think they found America harder to take; my grandpa got in fist fights all the time, and grandma was afraid of the telephone. Mom's ancestors were fat, Dad's were skinny. Mom's mother could cook, Dad's couldn't. My parents met in high school, went to their prom with other dates, shared the last dance together and thanked each other for a lovely evening. I found a love poem Dad wrote for Mom, that likens her to the moon, slipping the gown off its shoulders to rise up in cold light to the apex of the sky.

Being a Jew seemed so beautiful to me, as it still does; as a child that beauty was heightened, the way so many aspects of identity seem fantastical. Even the moon seems personal to children. As a young girl, I viewed being Jewish like getting your period: I couldn't wait to come into it! ... adult ... dreamy ... sophisticated ... full of ineffable pain, blood, sex, inevitability... grown-up, like smoking or kissing... cool... a series of exquisite burdens.

This confidence survived the prototypical bumpy moments, such as the time the youngest Stingone child accused me of killing Christ. Her mother apologized on her behalf, and I remember saying:

I'm sure she didn't mean it.

Which to my mind sounded composed and grown-up and detached and forgiving. Of course, five years later, I realized how amateur my remark was, how unequal to the force of history, because she *did* mean it, and I knew it even then: meant it with all her heart; she said it with a gut-wrenching conviction and looked beautiful when she said it, as we all look when we stand up against evil. Yet the confrontation made me love my identity all the more, because the accusation flattered me on some level. I was just a myopic goody-goody who read a lot of books and lived in fear of children half my age if they seemed like bullies, so being accused of murder seemed as fancy as a bowl of fresh clementines to me. Besides, I understood the accusation better then, saw its laughable flaws, since I knew I didn't kill Christ and neither did any of my nerdy little friends; and even if some Jew were proven to have done this hit, it doesn't mean all Jews did it or condoned it; reminding me, as I thought about it still five years later, that the bedrock of racism is generalization.

My love of my identity was tested on a deeper level by the Yiddish Sunday School my parents sent me to, the Sholem Alechem School. They had a very dreary attitude over there, very dreary. Everyone who taught there was clinically depressed; it was one of the entrance criteria. I was four, or five, or six but no more, and they used to show us these two films over and over again. They were both those kinds of films that are scratchy, full of black blobs and white flashes which themselves bespeak the apocalypse, and they were hard to hear and see. One of them was called *The Dead Sea Scrolls*, and the main difficulty with this film, in addition to the word Death being a prominent part of its title, was that it was crushingly, numbingly boring. It was in sort of brown and white, as if the spirit had been sucked out of it, turning the black brown. And it went on and on, and the guy, the narrator, had some kind of thick, insurmountable accent, like Henry Kissinger, that made everything sound like Kaddish. It was an act of penance and contrition to have to sit in a room while this film was shown . . . since it was so long and devastating, you ended up entering your own private world just to survive it, and you actually came to fear its ending and the lights coming back on ... squinting into that fluorescent light, with a scraped, empty mind.

I know nothing about the Dead Sea Scrolls ... I don't know where they were found, what the hell they are, the nature of their historical significance. That film took away any possibility of my ever knowing, it dissolved the part of my mind capable of acknowledging these scrolls on any level, and I'm sure I saw it 45 times.

The other film they showed us at the Yiddish school was a Holocaust film, and it was never boring. In contrast to *The Dead Sea Scrolls*, it was striking and clean. This film also suffered from age spots and other technical problems, but it was arresting, like a high-pitched sound, or like that noise your phone makes when it's off the hook. I believe the film itself was silent ... I have no memory of any voice ... It was visual: naked bodies thrown together like crumpled Kleenexes or other soft garbage ... desiccated babies ... people falling down and being shot, or being shot and falling down ... impossible to tell the order of events, to determine any causality ... the feeling that maybe the film was going *backwards* ... comical, slapstick, Charlie Chaplinesque. Then children my age, kind of like me, only their faces full of some dark music ... trees that looked burnt and embarrassed ... big holes in the ground with very skinny people lined up around them, swaying like reeds ... and always people in lines, waiting ... waiting. Everything seemed italicized: tilted, leaning, thin and heightened in importance, the way letters in italics seem heightened in importance.

After the Holocaust movie, which in contrast to the deceased sea scrolls motion picture was mercifully brief, there was a great deal of talk about how lucky we were, and about how if we're not careful, these things could happen to us. That seemed both believable and ridiculous. I think I remember a baby being thrown up in the air and shot.

This was fine fare for a preschooler, just fine! And although it gave me more or less permanent psychological complications, it certainly had greater social relevance than the Power Rangers of today, who are on TV kicking butt constantly, without the slightest provocation or remorse.

So. I'm here before you, trembling, and I love being a Jew, in this body, wondering, shuddering, trembling with a nearly sexual suspense over what force is going to have the power to separate this body from this soul, my weightless, immortal *neshumah* from its coveted resting place between my two mortal, falling breasts; and I'm allowing myself the many distractions from that question that a full, rich Jewish life offers.

I love being Jewish. I love the edge of it, like a knife; I love the way people misapprehend me. I love the stereotypes: the rich people crosstown, the people who control the media, the Hollywood Mafia, the big noses, big cars, big breasts, big genitals, the people who control the banks, the big money, the hedonists, paganists, orthodontists, Christ killers, certified public accountants ... I love it ... I'm just a nerd with glasses trying to raise two kids in the woods, they make me feel like a rock star with these archetypes!

The thing I love most about being Jewish is waiting for the Messiah! That is what I love the most ... waiting, waiting, like so much of life ... we Jews are waiting for the Messiah. Now many people believe the Messiah has already come, but we Jews are waiting ... I love that the book is still open on the question of the identity of Moshiach ... we Jews are sitting out on the fire escape, having a smoke, noticing who goes by. I've noticed lots of people: Eleanor Roosevelt, George Balanchine, Martin Luther King, Nadine Gordimer, Fred Rogers, Richard Pryor, Cruz Irizarry, the woman who takes care of my kids when I'm working, the UPS man who's so nice about carrying in the boxes and setting them down wherever you need, the sexy guys from the cable company ... it's like a big Halloween party, life is a costume party in which anyone may come forward from behind a mask and reveal themselves as Moshiach. And since you never know who or when, it's best to be as graceful as you can to everyone and to try to dress reasonably. The whole clean underwear syndrome.

I see all the places I've been in my life as variations of the Messiah's waiting-rooms; all the jobs I've had as ways of keeping busy while I wait; so many magazines to read before the Doctor comes.

And I have questions about the Messiah, so many questions. I have style questions: Suit and tie? Jeans and turtleneck? Dress and stockings?

I have method questions: Does the Messiah get it all done in one shot, or are there revisits, Messianic booster shots, if you will? I mean, the thing about Jesus, beautiful as he was, is that the world is still a wreck; a sinking, starlit, putrefying wreck, and I haven't seen him in the local Chinese restaurant in a good long time. Is that wreck still his responsibility, or what? Was he like an auditor or something, who comes, looks, files a report, makes a few corrections himself and then leaves the rest to us to put aright? Is that how it works? Or what? Does he just knock on someone's door one night asking for a glass of schnapps and then the whole thing just turns around, or what?

I have waited all my life for Moshiach. I have waited for Moshiach in the arms of my father, I've waited for Moshiach with my daughter in my arms, falling asleep, losing her wakefulness in my arms the way the sky loses light at dusk, changing colors, announcing its beauty in blue and then pink and then smoke and finally in stars . . . I hear her sleep, the weight of her head changes texture, lying in such lucid repose in this place, this place between my collarbone and my shoulder's end, the place God sculpted out in a woman for the head of a sleeping child . . . We are Messianic in each other, my daughter and I . . . from above her sleep I fall into the rhythm of her breath, I feel the only egoless pride God gave me to feel, and it's fucking perfect . . . her sleep is like Moshiach to me: quiet, effortless, a true relief at the end of a long day. . . as I hold her, I realize with certainty that a part of what defines Messiah for me is relief.

I've waited for Messiah with my grandmother, my mother's mother, the one who could cook, who laughed all the time, who had tears in her eyes every time she moved her hands away from her face after blessing the holiday candles . . . I waited with her in Florida, where else? She had just entered into the beginning phases of negotiation with the *Malach Ha Movis* . . . I've noticed that people who are blessed enough to die of old age die in stages, not all at once. I was a young college graduate when I went down there to spend a few days with her. Nan went down to Florida every winter with my grandfather, and after he died, she kept going anyway, to be with her 'friends.' These were not friends in any sense that I understood; they were people who were for various reasons unable to take offense at her continuous assaults on their appearance or their integrity, either because they were hard of hearing, senile, visually impaired, or just too kind to comprehend that they were being insulted. Nanny was already sort of losing it herself, and I remember she would ask me the same question over and over again, which I never minded. It was like a meditation: I would answer the question every time, trying never to answer completely; to save information for the next time she asked, or to rethink the answer I had just given and amend it to the moment. Her hotel room had two chaste twin beds, and when I arrived late one night, she asked me about my job over twenty times, manifesting her incipient senility, and she tucked me in and kissed me just as she had done when I was a kid. That night I accepted her, new and old, with enormous gratitude, and I waited with her that first night for the Messiah.

The next morning we took the elevator down to the lobby for breakfast, and when the doors opened, she said: 'You see that lady in the red dress?' And I looked up, and there, indeed, three feet from us, was a woman with dark hair in a cherry-colored silk dress, and I said, 'Yes!' and assumed Nan was going to introduce me to her, but Nan shrieked: SHE'S SO CHEAP! SHE HOLDS ON TO A NICKEL TILL IT SCREAMS! THE BUFFALO SCREAMS MURDER! and the woman slunk away. Next Nan led me into a crowd of octogenarians who were huddled in a corner of the lobby in sweaters and galoshes, although at 7:30 in the morning it was already 85 degrees, humid and full of a loud, ugly sunlight that reminded me of Buddy Hackett. A woman waved to her from the other side of the lobby, and Nan waved back, saying in a very loud voice: 'You see that lady? Can you believe she's *younger* than *I* am?' After that she settled into the business of introductions, holding me by the hand, telling the assembled company with great pride that I was a math professor. This was momentarily stunning to me until I realized that it didn't make the slightest difference on some level. And far from a bald-faced lie, it was actually a tender and complex falsehood: part memory (my father is a metallurgy professor); part hope that I would do something creditable, or at least explainable, with my life; and part pure hostility, since arrogance was one of the ways Nan covered her head, her identity, as she went deeper and deeper into her dying, into her preparations for Moshiach. It was almost a form of modesty; it kept her hidden. She wanted to show everyone that we were better than they were, in case they couldn't tell just by looking.

When the introductions were finished, our conversation moved effortlessly on to tumors: where, what kind, the size, spreading or not spreading, operable or inoperable, three months to live or six months, which is better, which is worse; the hospital, the oncologist, was he Jewish or not Jewish, was he Sephardic or Ashkenazi, was he famous or not; then came a sort of folk obituary: first amputations, and who had lost what parts; then we covered whose wife had died, whose brother had keeled over; when they died and of what; was it sudden or not sudden; if they had suffered terribly *azochem vay* or just dropped dead or died in their sleep *baruch hashem*. Throughout this cheerful badinage Nanny continued to hold my hand, and I almost fell asleep in her touch ... she had the most beautiful hands, and that never changed, even on her deathbed. They were beautifully shaped, smallish and strong; the fingers were generous and even, ever so slightly plump. Her nails were lovely and unpresupposing, always clean, with fine, fine lines in them; and the skin on her hands was preternaturally soft, soft like an emotion; so soft it was like touching nothing.

Nan's arrogance reached its operatic peak in the dining room. The minute we entered the place you could feel the energy shift because she already had quite a reputation. She treated the waitstaff like vermin, and they responded in kind. Nan complained about everything they served in a voice that really carried, and they slammed down the food with rage and resentment. This delightful repast was topped off with Nanny stealing her own silverware, my fork and spoon, the salt and pepper shakers, and all the butter pats and sugar packets on the table. She did this at every meal, and since there was no refrigerator in the room, the smell of rancid butter has become one of the defining sensory images of that experience for me.

I remember I went swimming that morning, and then lunch was at 11, and then dinner at 4, and more salt shakers and butter pats, and by 9 o'clock Nanny asked after my job several times, tucked me in, kissed me, sang to me, and I waited with her the second night for the Messiah. The whole week passed in that rhythm, holding Nan's hand, swimming, bearing witness to petty larceny in the dining room, and doing my best to remember certain mathematical principles, such as the mystical constantness of *pi*, the magnificent use of the letter *x* to represent things you're trying to solve for, the unknown, and things like:

The square of the hypotenuse is equal to the sum of the squares of the other two sides.

and stuff like that, since I was afraid that someone was going to want to talk shop with me, and I was a math professor and everything. The days passed with my grandmother in the same way they pass as I take care of my small children: pleasant yet exhausting, lacking differentiation, early meals, early sleep, that sense of waiting. You wait with children for them to grow up, you wait with old people for death. Growing up, dying, these are symptoms of the coming of Moshiach. That Saturday night my hormones got the better of me, and I decided to take a walk and look for some action, so I wandered away from the hotel around 10 o'clock that night, but I ended up just having a cigarette in front of the Miami Hearing Aid Center and crawling into bed long after Nanny. She heard me come in, she opened one eye and said: How's your job?

My grandmother died about six years ago. It was a slow process with many phases; fiercely independent, she finally had to be put in an old-age home, because she was calling Con Edison twelve to fifteen times a day to tell them she had *seen a spark*. This last detail pains me especially, because I'm certain on some level that she had. The day before she died I went to see her, because I was leaving for the West Coast and I knew I'd never see her again. I spent that last day just holding Nan's hand. She was in agony, she wanted to die, she was impatient for salvation. She viewed Messiah at that moment like one of the waitresses in that dining room: slow, incompetent, possibly not even Jewish. I have noticed that old Jewish people seem to think everyone's Jewish. They forget that Jews are .001 per cent of the world population or something like that! You chat with them, and then, especially if they like you, they inevitably, flirtatiously say: 'So you Jewish? You're *not Jewish*???' Nan's eyes were closed most of that last day, and it was through her hand, lying in mine, that we communicated, that we waited together for Moshiach. As I was getting up to leave, I said Nanna ... Nanna ... I wanted you to know something. I'm getting married! And she opened her eyes to me one last time, and she said: Oh! That's too bad!

It's about relief, Moshiach; it has to be. Opening the door for Elijah on Passover was always my job, and it was a relief to me to get up from the table, go to the front door and open it; out there the air was always cool and fragrant, with torn fragments of Spring in it, and stars or rain tangled in my hair, and I

147

was seized with sudden relief, always; and quick, wild thoughts of my future, as if I'd gone to the door to kiss a lover no one knew I had; of my escape, of my greatest triumph and joy. Then I'd shut the door and sit down again among my relatives, as if nothing had happened. That's what death must have felt like when it finally came to my Nanna.

Insomnia is an intense form of Messiah-waiting, I truly believe that. When you can't sleep, it's a form of prayer, it's because you're waiting for the Messiah and you just don't want to miss any possibilities. This is why old people often sleep so badly. I've been sleepless at different points in my life; my two pregnancies were both nine months of non-stop insomnia, and the other points have also been moments of impending change. During one of these bouts, I turned on the TV deep in the night, and there was an infomercial on for the Book of Mormon. It had to be 3 or 4 a.m. Anything is believable at 3 or 4 a.m., which is as it should be. There were two parts to this infomercial, the testimonial part and the dramatization part. First people were depicted talking about the Book of Mormon, and how it had changed their lives, shown them the way; made even death a manageable reality, since it meant only packing up your stuff and moving to a new, Divine neighborhood. This young red-haired woman, a tear in her eye, talked about her beloved grandma, her grandma's illness, etc., and then said: My grandma passed away, and that was very painful, but since I've read the Book of Mormon, I know what life's all about. I'll see her again!

Then there was the film portion, sort of like the Holocaust movie at Sholem Alechem, which featured a very powerful background music, and showed Jesus descending into this community, and everybody stopped what they were doing. You could hear their sleeves hiss as their arms came down to their sides. Then Jesus opened his arms, and slowly people understood his greatness, and then they started coming forward. First this man with a messed-up hand came up and put his hand in Jesus' hand, and Jesus closed his hand around the phthisic hand, went into a trance, opened his hand, and then the messed-up hand was okay. It was beautiful, the way they did it, because the hand wasn't *perfect*, but it was orderly and usable, as it hadn't been before. Then a young woman made her way forward, leading her mother; the mother is obviously blind, and the music is swelling, keening. The mother's eyes are blank, open and unseeing. Jesus takes her in his arms, puts his lovely white hands over her eyes, and then slowly moves them away again, and the music is unbearably beautiful by this time, like peeing after you've had the urge for two hours already, and the woman can see! She can see! And the first thing she sees is Him, this holy presence, this image of astonishing, sacred beauty, the Lord Jesus: and she falls to her knees, and yet Jesus, in an act of divine and profound humility, turns her eyes away from him, physically *moves her face* towards her daughter, as if it were her daughter who should receive the thanks and love that suffused her face as she saw Him for the first time.

And that really got me: the love, power, and humility in one radiant gesture, and the music, and it's 4 or 5 in the morning by now, and I just started bawling. I cried and cried, and finally, I couldn't take it anymore, it just evoked such a yearning inside me; I mean, come on, look! When you have waited for someone with as much passion as I wait for the Messiah, it's very hard to watch someone else getting him! ... kind of like two people who want to be virgins when they get married, and they're really trying to keep their hands to themselves, and they go out one night to see *The Sound of Music* with their purse, but they accidentally wander into a porn movie! ... just an unbearable ache for that communion, which just got into my chest and spread to my soul, so what did I do? I picked up the remote and changed the channel, just clicked the pain away! There on the next channel was something much more manageable: two men were having a gunfight in the desert, and after several rounds were fired and one guy staggered and fell, they too broke for a commercial. This advertisement was for Gold Bond Medicated Powder. Gold Bond Medicated Powder commercials are always aired in the middle of the night because they feature low-budget and humiliating testimonials on behalf of the product. They all have people speaking in Boston accents about banal itches, rashes and pimples that really should be kept to oneself. Tonight's guy is talking about, and I quote, MALE ITCH, and I unquote, and how Gold Bond Medicated Powder was the only thing that brought him any surcease from the constant scratching, anguish, and ensuing social stigma of the itch in his groin area. And at first, I thought to myself: how low can you go? and, isn't he afraid someone he would like to date is going to see this? But as I continued thinking about it, and 5 became 6 o'clock, and I heard the birdsongs that presage the dawn, these two images intertwined: that of Jesus healing that twisted hand, and of Gold Bond Medicated Powder returning this other man's hands to their proper place in his pockets instead of in his crotch, and that image made me cry too. The analogy moved me very deeply. It's about relief, it has to be! There is so much human suffering, and it comes in so many forms; the Messiah I await does not take one person's anguish more seriously than another's. One guy's hand is a mess, the other guy's is stuck in his crotch; so for one man, it's Jesus; for another, it's Gold Bond. A friend of mine told me that, in her Protestant Sunday School, she was taught that Jews didn't accept Jesus as the Messiah because they thought he wasn't good enough. And it's not that, it's really not! It's just that here, as if in an employment agency for workers against human suffering, you just want to interview as many qualified candidates as possible.

We try to see doctors as Messiah, but it never works. Their fallibility is such an issue, their high salaries. Plus I have the distinct impression the Messiah wouldn't take itself as seriously as some of these people seem to.

So we keep looking, we keep interviewing, we keep seeing God all over the place, we Jews. We see Messiah where it's inapplicable, we see Messiah where it's most convenient. There's a very cruel, very beautiful blonde woman in the community I live in; her name is Sue. I once mistakenly called her Ellen; that's the last time she ever spoke to me. Since then she has walked by me as if I were air, birds, smoke or mud. I saw her asleep once, by the pool, on a chaise lounge. She had unfastened her bikini top to get her most even tan. Her daughter, also blonde, was with her, asleep, and Sue had thrown her arm around her daughter, and I thought: so much beauty and indifference, these two, dreaming in the raw sun, asleep past sound or light, so heedless of the Messiah that resided patiently in their beauty. I see Messiah where he refuses to see me: in the tranquility of a young girl whom I saw roll over onto a tiny kitten, killing it instantly with her weight in her sleep, and still sleeping soundly, and waking refreshed; in my father's sense of his heroism, crushing the head of the mouse my mother hated so much, crushing it with a rock in the dark and mustiness of our basement. I see Messiah in a Snickers bar: biting in, negotiating that excruciating texture, the peanuts crushed against my palate, the caramel defining with pain the points of dental decay. I see Messiah where he won't see me.

I was really insulted when the kids who edited my high-school yearbook put the following quote under my picture: 'What matter if it be a fool's paradise? Paradise is paradise, for whosoever owns it!' But you know what? That quote has grown on me. And I on it. I mean, just look at me!

I felt someone push me up against the wall of 600 Third Avenue about 22 years ago. That dates back. I was working for a market research firm to make money during college. My job was to cut names out of the phone book on an elaborately random basis and paste them on a form for future torment by so-called 'interviewers.' There was a whole table of random numbers, and I was to pick every third or fourth random number, turn to that page of the phone book of the city in question, and then, consulting a separate random number chart for the column number, excise a chunk of names and numbers with a razor blade, put glue on the back and slap 'em down. That's probably closer to the way God created the universe than Darwin or Genesis lets on. On my way back from lunch break to this stimulating environment, a man pinned me to the glass wall outside the building. My belly to the wall. I twisted my neck around, and there, behind me, against me, was the frantic face of a young Hasidic man, and his breath, and the smell of his eyes, the criminality of them. I was unable to speak, I was so stunned, so he said: Have sex with me. You've got to have sex with me. Now. You've got to have sex with me right now. I can't ... I will never have sex. No one will marry me. I can't have sex without marriage. You have to have sex with me. I have no prospects. I'll die. You must. Sex. Now. Immediately – and other exhortatory-type phrases like that. He talked so much that I could see he wasn't a rapist, because rapists are terse, aren't they, I mean, why waste time chatting? So my fear lowered, and I just looked at him with many feelings: contempt, pity, revulsion, curiosity, and hey, how ya doin'. And I said the appropriate: no, absolutely not, or whatever, and I went up in the elevator, picked up my razor blade, and slashed strangers for a sanitary napkin study from the Dayton white pages. I was slicing and slicing and thinking about this man. This man with the *payes* and the *tsitsis* and glasses and shoes and top hat and gruff, music-less voice, pushing me against this building, and the nerve of him, etcetera. But none of those feelings had any durability. What stays with me half a life later is what was truly gross about this man. And it wasn't his desire for sex with a stranger. Desire is the force of the world, the life force really. It wasn't his presumption that any non-Hasidic woman was a whore and could be reasonably talked into sex with some weirdo in broad daylight on the sidewalk in front of an office building. It was his loss of faith! It was his loss of faith in Moshiach, damn it! What kind of Jew is this, I ask you? He had lost faith! That was his sin! Now even someone like this man could get some kind of roll in the hay from a consenting, not-yet-deceased adult, I'm sure; and haven't we all had moments when our weight or our complexion made us feel relegated to certain dubious kinds of mating techniques; but this man had permanently, totally lost faith in the Messiah! He had lost faith in Moshiach that brings the touch, the haze, the murmur, the blessed release to even the ugly and the weird! And this loss of faith unleashed a hideous animal from inside the filthy cage of this man, and it's the zoo of the faithless to which my rejection sent this animal back. I should have suggested masturbation, but I just didn't know him well enough.

I should have told him that joke, that beautiful joke about the rabbi who presides over a devout little congregation in a valley, surrounded by majestic mountains. One day rains begin, apocalyptic rains, and the water gets so bad that the rabbi is forced to move from the first floor of his house to the second floor, and as he does so, he sees a boat full of his congregants going by the window, and, seeing their beloved rabbi, they shout: Rabbi! Come with us! The town is flooding! We are moving to higher ground! Come with us, Rabbi! We will take you with us! and the rabbi shakes his head warmly and says, No, no! my faith is in God! I have worn his Tefillin, I have kept his laws of Kashruth, my faith is in the Lord, He shall keep me! And the congregants, weeping, bid the rabbi goodbye, and he them. Then the water gets so bad that the rabbi is forced to move to the third floor of his house, and again, as he does so, a boat filled with various congregants is passing by, and they call to him: Rabbi! Come with us! Let us take you to higher ground, and again, the rabbi answers: My faith is in the Lord, He shall keep me! And good-bye, they say, and goodbye, etcetera. Finally the water gets so bad that the rabbi is forced to stand on the roof of his house, and once again there's a boat of congregants, and once again they say, Rabbi, come with us, and he says No, my faith is in the Lord, goodbye, goodbye, and finally, the water gets so high that the Rabbi drowns! And he is deceased! He goes immediately to Heaven, and he is hopping mad, he's just livid. He demands an audience with God; gets it. God comes in, He says:

Moishe! What is it, Moishe!

And the Rabbi says: How could you do this to me? How? I kept your laws, I wore your Tefillin, I taught Torah to my children and to my children's children as your doctrine commands, how could you do this to me? And God says:

What do you want, Moishe? I sent three boats!

Then you have people who see Messiah where even I, ever vigilant, have not opened my eyes to the possibility. It is one such man I married. Very visionary. What an interesting man. He is very compelling. He's handsome, which is fun; but that's truly a small element. I've known him for 21 years, and yet there are times when he's like that Hasidic man against the wall, only in a revelatory, consensual way. His lips are bowed; his upper lip is God's harp. Our son has those lips, and it's divine, not genetic. I can't stop talking, and my husband never says a word, it's so bizarre, so annoying; he has no idea where his body is in space, steps on things, breaks things, is more verbal about alternate side of the street parking than almost anything else, and yet: I am against that glass wall, panting as if for the first time, seeing his face, hearing his voice, contemplating his essence. It's because he sees Moshiach where I am blind. He's got Messiah by the beard in my sleep, in my blind spots. He asked me to marry him on the second floor of the Riverside Funeral Home on 76th Street and Amsterdam Avenue. We had just buried his mother. I rode in the black car. The wheezing grief of his father, the choked grief of her two sons. It was all sound: Kaddish, the dirt, the motor whispering inside the limousine. I was wearing a long-sleeved dark dress with stockings; I was a stranger to myself in that dress, in such lovely weather, in such an emotional situation with a silent man.

When we returned after the burial, he said: Can I talk to your father? And I said, My father? And he said: I want to marry you. Right away. And I think of the Hasidic man in mirror negative, and I say: Don't you think we should wait until you're thinking more clearly? or something like that. And he says: No, on the contrary. I've never seen anything more clearly, on this day, it makes such sense to me: I must marry you. As soon as possible. Now! And, true to the Hasidic man's vision, his last hope, I threw my arms around this grief-stricken friend and we made out like you can't believe, in the ladies' bathroom of the Riverside Funeral Home, with sounds of crying, giggling and negotiation for coffins going on in waves just outside, just beyond us. Now is Moshiach there, or not? Fifteen months later, December 20th, our son was born. Like I told you, he had that upper lip like his father, and everyone said he was a Christmas baby, which I accept because I must, and before we knew it, it was New Year's Eve, our new, gorgeous, tyrannical baby asleep in the next room, and finally midnight came. I wanted to dance with my husband. He's really handsome. But I didn't know how without waking the baby, and there really wasn't any way, since there are no doors in our house, but Messiah appeared to my baby's father; he turned on the TV. He found a station with hot jazz; we both love jazz; he found first one, then another set of headphones. He plugged both sets of headphones into the TV, put on one, gave me the other. Feeling those phones come round the top of my head like a white horse around the edge of a mountain: the sound of a saxophone, bass, drum, something low and luscious, maybe Lester Young or something: looking up, and there's my husband, and I can tell by his eyes that he hears the same low, lovely thing. So he grabs me and we begin to dance. We hear the same song from two separate sources. A stranger walking in that door would have seen two exhausted lovers swaying together in complete silence. Moshiach, or not?

I don't want to give you the impression that waiting for the Messiah is in my opinion a completely passive experience. I feel continually obliged to facilitate the Coming, to pray for it with my actions, etcetera. I try to be as pleasant as I can in general, and in specific, to be sensitive to the fact that we are all called upon at different times to act as Messianic stand-ins. There are moments that I've had, that everybody's had, when a situation calls for us to sort of rise in some way, to get slightly better than we are by methods having nothing to do with our conscious will, to do just the right thing for a stranger, and then disappear, as the Messiah would do if he or she had the time or knew the address. People have done this for me. Countless times, my solitude or despair has been headed off by strangers whom I've never seen again and to whom I've never had to send a thank-you note. And I've done this for others, I've served as Lamb Chop to the Messiah's Shari Lewis. I was in Hawaii one time, taking a walk. There was this craggy promontory out to the ocean, and I decided to follow it as far as I could. This was my hour to myself; such luxuries have been delimited since I had kids. As I started down this promontory, I saw the shape of a young woman down at the end, saw her from behind, and it looked like she was shrugging her shoulders over and over again. As I approached her, with the white noise of the ocean serving as music, I saw that she wasn't shrugging, she was sobbing, and she was holding something, and as I got right up to where she was, I saw that this something was a baby, really small, newborn baby, and all I could think of was *Billy Joe McAllister jumped off the Tallahassee Bridge* or something like that. I said: What's the matter? And she just really started howling, she told me she just had this baby, and she never should have, all she does is cry, she herself could not stop crying, she doesn't know how to take care of the baby, and the baby won't smile, she said, it's nine weeks old already, and they're supposed to start smiling at four or five weeks, and it's never smiled, and there's something wrong with it, and it's so sad, and she just broke off, consumed with despair, and cried. And I could feel myself being lifted, almost literally: lifted out of myself and into the soiled robes of Moshiach, and I said:

My dear. My dear, dear woman. Look at you! You just had a baby, and look how beautiful you look! I gained fifty pounds! Cars couldn't pass me on the boulevard! Look how luscious you are! And you have plummeting hormones, and yet you still express yourself so clearly! Did you know that your hormone levels are plummeting in a way that makes being premenstrual look like a wrong number on Sunday afternoon? All your experience is meaningless, isn't it, compared to this fucked-up, indescribable miracle! Look what your body has done! You've played God!

You've made life! Of course you're exhausted! And what a beautiful baby! He's lovely! Oh, *she?* She's gorgeous! There's nothing wrong with her! She's as sharp as they come! Look at her eyes! Look at the way they followed that bird! All the way from the sky to its dive to its rising back up with a fish in its mouth, she saw it all! I hope it didn't make a bad impression! She's perfect! What's her name? That's a perfect name! She looks like a Hepsibah! Just like! And don't listen to that shit about the smile! They smile when something's funny! Do you laugh at Jay Leno every night? Of course not. Of course not.

And then I took the baby from her, she let me take the baby, stranger as I was, high over this cliff, this raw, natural gravesite, and I sang: O Wholly Night! The stars were brightly shining! It is the night of our dear Saviour's birth . . . See, I always thought it was O *W*holly Night, with a *W!* That it meant it had to be totally night, truly deeply dark, no trace of the colors and streaks of dusk or dawn before Moshiach would manifest, like a virgin bride who'll only disrobe in the dark. And I sang that song in such a stupid voice, such a stuffed-nose DJ Imus-in-the-Morning voice, that the baby stretched its face into a radiant smile, and I turned the baby's face toward its mother, as if it were she who deserved the first look, the first time the baby's eyes opened to Messiah, and I handed the baby back to her, and I walked away.

Moshiach, or not?

Commentary: *Like a Virgin*

Margolin's alchemical beauty burns brightest in *O Wholly Night*. Before it came to take on its contemporary patriarchal connotations, a virgin was a high priestess of the Temple, a shaman with the power to act as intermediary between humans and the gods, not one who was untouched, but on the contrary, one who touched and was touched by everything, or, simply, a woman – she who was one unto herself. The gift that we receive from Margolin's performances, if we are gracious and bountiful enough to accept it, is the gift of faith, which in her work, to borrow James Baldwin's resonant phrase, is 'the evidence of things not seen.'

Over fifteen years before this performance, Margolin wrote these words:

Christmas 1982

I love God unrequited,
Not with lamentation is
the sweet night won; not with mind,
not with awe, not with mercy.
There sits a Judge
who disdains judgment! I have faith
that runs like water, falls, runs, sounds,
drains down, lies still and clean;
a faith that falls where the Earth
slopes down
and rises in the heat.
Wherever my God is
time too is round, and for God
I have run with my whole soul
the girth of my life
and returned to my bed
with the smell of this night
in my hair.

Solecisms are things misspoken – violations, improprieties, incongruities, mistakes. The 'joke' of *O Wholly Night* is revealed at the end of the performance, when Margolin tells the story of her encounter with the young mother weeping inconsolably on the precipice. Her nine-week-old infant in her arms has not smiled, and Deb takes the child in her arms and sings to her, tunelessly, the well-known Christian hymn, 'O Holy Night.' She sings only the first stanza; the infant smiles, and Margolin, like Christ in the Book of Mormon infomercial, turns the child's face to look at her mother, and walks away. She then explains to us that she always thought the hymn was 'Oh Wholly Night,' that in order for the Messiah to have arrived, the darkness had to be total – 'like a virgin bride who will only disrobe in the dark.' In her solecism, what is 'Holy' becomes that which is 'Wholly.' Her solecism is perhaps better understood as a homophone. For what Margolin hears in this performance, despite how the letters look, are the ways in which things, both noumenal and phenomenal, are at once finitely and eternally conjoined. Listening takes precedence in this performance over the limited understanding that comes from that which is merely to be seen. I think of the stanza that moves me most from 'O Holy Night,' the words that, as a Christian child, moved me to the edge of ecstasy: 'Fall on your knees/

Oh hear the angels' voices/ Oh night divine.' These lines had no determinate context; they were, to an extent, non-denominational, non-secular, non-Christian — with the exception, of course, of the reference to the angels! But it was really the falling, the hearing, and the divinity of the night that left me ecstatic. If we understand the ecstatic denuded, stripped of its associations with mysticism or prophetic exaltation, it becomes no more, nor less, than a state of being delighted by that which surpasses ordinary understanding. Margolin's performances routinely, and *therefore* remarkably, offer us ways into such ecstasy. For 'the world is never too much with [her]' when Margolin performs; rather, like a virgin, she approaches the world and all that is within and beyond it as if she were seeing it for the first time, or sensing it through sensuous pathways that are not the ones every traveler would traverse. Follow her, with her generous, intuitive, humorous grace, and we can find 'love, power, and humility in one radiant gesture,' whether the context is Jesus healing the blind, Gold Bond Medicated Powder soothing an itch, a desperate Hasidic man whose attempted rape she understands as a loss of faith, a child releasing her wakefulness in the hollow of her mother's body, or a woman near death who sees a spark.

O Wholly Night begins with a prelude, the story of Mrs. Friedman's dress: how she gave it to Deb and then forgot that she had given it to her; how Margolin forgot the story Mrs. Friedman told her of the dress's history because she was so enraptured by the exquisite garment's appearance; how Margolin knew when she saw the dress that she had to have it, and that the day would come when the dress would make manifest to her what its purpose would be and why it had so excited her desire; how that day came when she was invited to write a performance based on her Jewish identity; and how she called Mrs. Friedman to try to reconstruct the story of the dress. But Mrs. Friedman not only did not know the story, she also emphatically denied having ever given her the dress.

When does the performance begin? Margolin introduces the monologue of the dress specifically as a *prelude*. 'Before [she] begins the performance of *O Wholly Night*,' she tells us, she first wants to tell us a story that has become for her both a literal and figurative symbol for her desire to say these things this evening. After hearing and seeing the powerfully moving embedded narratives of this performance, we might forget, like Mrs. Friedman, the story of the dress, and how it functions as a prelude. So let us return to it for a moment to end this commentary. Remember that Mrs. Friedman tells

Margolin that she never gave her, not just that dress, but any dress, and that, furthermore, if she needs a story, *make it up*. Margolin does not pursue the 'truth' of this dress's historical accuracy, nor does she make up a story to fill in the gap left by the absence of Mrs. Friedman's memory. Unlike her author in *Of Mice, Bugs and Women*, whom the girl-cut-out-of-the-novel screams at in her frozen frustration: 'O God O Christ O God, I wish she could have just told the story,' Margolin tells us the story, the story of the remembering and the forgetting, the story of having acquired something precious and clinging to it despite the fact that she felt she had extorted it, albeit with reverence. The story of having things handed down and cherished, not in spite of their holes and flaws, but, like the dress, *because* of the beauty in their fragility, their vulnerability. Like the nearly translucent weave of the dress where one can see if one looks closely the threads that were once there but have worn away, leaving in their trace the very fabric that gives the dress its gossamer splendor, Margolin makes that which is 'holy' into a whole. Fittingly, then, she accepts Mrs. Friedman's forgetfulness as a benediction, a prayer in conventional Christian services that usually comes at the end of the ceremony. In *O Wholly Night*, the benediction is a blessing and an invocation, part of her prelude, the end of one story that begets the beginning of infinite others in her worlds without ends.

Deb Margolin and Andy Davis in *Critical Mass*. Photo: © Dona Ann McAdams.

8

❧

Critical Mass: A Dark and Caustic Comedy

(Preset fades down and lights come up on a warmly lit, empty stage. NARRATOR enters and comes center, smiling, acknowledging audience with her eyes.)

NARRATOR: I had just had a kid a couple of years ago and was nursing her in a slouchy armchair in the living room, watching a TV show that was so stupid I would have been humiliated to have been caught watching it. So when someone knocked at the door, my first impulse was to get up, throw the baby in the bassinet, turn off the TV and wave the sound out of the room. Then I went to the door and opened it; standing there in work clothes was a painter, one of a team of workmen who had come to paint the downstairs carport. But the guy was acting weird, he was rolling his eyes, seemed unable to make eye contact, he was sort of laughing but not quite, he had this choked laugh in his throat that he wouldn't let out, but it seemed to cost him quite a bit to keep it in, he was rolling his eyes, I found him utterly bizarre. He had come to tell me that I needed to move my car out of the carport because they were painting and didn't have dropcloths, but it took him like an hour and forty-five minutes to say it due to his sociopathic inability to face me. And I thought: What a loser! What is the matter with this man? Is he schizophrenic? Is he autistic? Couldn't they have sent a more articulate member of their workforce to ask me to move my car? Finally I shut the door and went into the kitchen to find my car keys, and as I looked down at the counter I noticed that my LEFT BREAST had been FULLY EXPOSED to this gentleman for the ENTIRE DURATION OF OUR DISCUSSION. Now that was a *critical* encounter, it seems to me, and a slightly tragic

161

encounter, insofar as I judged this man without important information, I judged him based on limited understanding of his circumstances, and he never saw my forest for my trees, by virtue of having one of those trees in his eye.

(NARRATOR quickly exits.)

(Houselights come back up and pre-show music resumes; it is now as if the play had not yet begun. STAGE MANAGER and PUBLICIST are fussing around. A huge chair, placed house left, has an oversized RESERVED sign on it. STAGE MANAGER comes with spray and a rag and washes it down, scrubbing vigorously.)

PUBLICIST: Not there, not there, not there. Sightlines stink here. He'll walk out. Move it over to the other side. You've got the pole here. Over there *(points house right)*.

(STAGE MANAGER moves chair. PUBLICIST hates it over there.)

PUBLICIST: That's no good, you can hear the cars and the street noise. Back over here!

(STAGE MANAGER moves it back. ACTORS peek out.)

PUBLICIST: Closer.

(STAGE MANAGER adjusts chair.)

PUBLICIST: Back!

(STAGE MANAGER adjusts chair.)

PUBLICIST: Further!

(STAGE MANAGER adjusts chair.)

PUBLICIST: Stop!

(STAGE MANAGER puts chair down. PUBLICIST pushes chair forward so it's blocking the aisle.)

STAGE MANAGER: That's illegal according to the fire department. You can't block the exit aisle.

(STAGE MANAGER moves chair back. PUBLICIST picks up chair and heaves it center stage, places it, walks back, studies chair's position.)

STAGE MANAGER: Are you sure he's coming?
PUBLICIST: I just had dinner with him. He had to stop off at

Duane Reade to fill a prescription.
STAGE MANAGER: What's it for?

(Silence. STAGE MANAGER bursts out laughing, then stops abruptly. Silence.)

STAGE MANAGER: Look, I can't hold them much longer.
PUBLICIST: Tell them you have some technical problem.
STAGE MANAGER: *(to audience)* Ladies and Gentlemen, thank you for your patience. We're experiencing some minor technical difficulties and we'll be starting the show shortly. Thank you.
PUBLICIST: It smells in here.
STAGE MANAGER: I think it smells fine.
PUBLICIST: It smells.
STAGE MANAGER: Look, you have 30 people in a room, someone's going to smell.
PUBLICIST: I can't believe we have oo few people.
STAGE MANAGER: That's your department, isn't it? Publicity?
PUBLICIST: *(turning towards sound)* Maybe that's him! *(It isn't.)*
STAGE MANAGER: If he's not here in two minutes, we're going up anyway.
PUBLICIST: *(disgusted)* Suit yourself.
STAGE MANAGER: What do you call the ego of a surgical instrument? Suture Self! Ha ha ha ha!
PUBLICIST: Has the chair been washed?

(Sound of heartbeat. Lights dim slightly. CRITIC arrives; is led in and fussed over by PUBLICIST, who takes his coat and settles him into his seat center stage in RESERVED chair. CRITIC takes out notebook, pen, flashlight, etc. Lights down as if show were just beginning.)

(Lights up on ACTORS. Two women carry a man across the stage, as if he were one of those rods that tightrope walkers use to balance themselves; then they drop him, and at that instant music starts, and they all start singing, and waving their arms, and then another man enters frantically, half screaming half singing.)

ACTOR: GEGG GEGG GEGG! GEGG GEGG GEGG!
ACTOR #2: I AM BLIND! I CANNOT SEE!

(CRITIC sinks down in his seat. Lights down on show, lights up on CRITIC again, who is shaking his head, and begins writing furiously on his pad. NARRATOR enters into CRITIC's light, studying him with bemusement as

he pans the show he has just seen; light expands to include her as she takes stage.)

(NARRATOR struggles to figure out where to stand; is clearly aware of presence of CRITIC. There is some silence as she positions herself here, and then there, and then finally speaks.)

NARRATOR: I tried to cancel this show three times, but every time I heard the producer's voice I hung up. I mean I'm middle-aged here, I'm tired. I live in some distant and bizarre community in New Jersey, and I swore I'd never live in New Jersey, people ask me where it is and I don't know where it is, except it's far away, and it's cold. And both kids got the chicken pox at once.

(CRITIC has reached into his pocket and pulled out a plastic bag with a nasal spray in it; the crunching of the bag interrupts NARRATOR, who glances over shoulder at CRITIC. Throughout the following, CRITIC is engaged in attempting to spray his nostrils with Dristan nasal spray as quietly as possible.)

NARRATOR: *(struggling to continue)* Still, when you have a booking and no show, the question you have to ask yourself is: What can I not die without having talked about? And it comes to me: criticism. I want to talk about criticism; about the IMPULSE to criticize. I want to examine it, walk around it like a sculpture, see the full circle of it.

(CRITIC takes a snort from his nasal spray bottle, causing the appalled NARRATOR to stop talking and try to fathom the depths of his rudeness and the extent of her predicament. She glances briefly around at him, whips around again as though his image were unbearable, then continues.)

The thing that fired up this interest in criticism was as follows: *(another snort into opposite nostril from CRITIC)* the gal who lives across the street from my mother saw me playing with my two-year-old son on the lawn as she drove around the gentle crescent curve of Mom's street in her messy black Lexus. She pulled up, rolled down the window, looked at my kid and said: Is that your son? And I swelled with sudden pride that comes on like an attack of hives, and I said Yes, yes it is! He's two and a half! And she said: He's beautiful! And I said: Thank you. See, I don't usually say thank you when people tell me my children are beautiful, because it has nothing to do with me, really. It's as if someone said: Isn't the sunset lovely! And I said Thank you. But

164

in this case I said thank you because she took the time to NOTICE and CONSIDER my existence, which had seemed to be a problem for her in the past. So I said: Thank You! And she looked at my son, looked at me, looked back at my son and said: YOU KNOW, GOD IS GOOD! THAT A PERSON WHO LOOKS LIKE YOU COULD HAVE A CHILD WHO LOOKS LIKE THAT!

And I was stunned first, and then profoundly amused. It was as if my immortal soul were being tickled with a feather. And it hasn't stopped. Three years later, I told this woman that she had inspired a whole show by making that remark: God is good, etcetera. She seemed very proud! I told her I hadn't been at all offended, but instead quite inspired, and she responded: THAT'S BECAUSE YOU UNDERSTOOD THE SPIRIT IN WHICH THE REMARK WAS MADE!

But you know what? She was wrong; I don't understand... *(turns and faces CRITIC)* but I'd like to.

(NARRATOR turns and exits quickly, leaving CRITIC alone on stage.)

CRITIC: The four corners, the seats, the dust. The curtain, the guy, the pole, the roaches, the bathroom. I know what's about to happen: lights will go down, Betty found me a seat. They sent me the release. It says: A look at fanaticism as seen through the eyes of the Dalai Lama in the imaginations of Egyptian ad moguls and Indian Men-'o'-War, or something like that, or whatever it says, and I know there'll be an investigation of some kind, and a love of language, and some Biblical references and absurd juxtapositions, and I already feel the night air on my mind, and I wonder what the cab driver is doing right now who is going to drive me home. A review almost exists before it's written, that's the painful thing.

(CRITIC gets up from his chair and is attempting to exit; PUBLICIST intercepts him and brings him back to his center-stage reserved chair, fawning on him and taking his coat as before. Lights down once again on CRITIC, as show begins. As before, a troupe of actors enters in some unfathomable avant-garde configuration; again the words 'gegg gegg gegg' are heard as ACTORS traverse the stage in front of and around CRITIC; one ACTOR intones:)

ACTOR: I am the devil! You are the devil! I am the devil! You are the devil!

(Gegging continues around and in front of CRITIC; finally ACTORS exit, lights come back up on stage; CRITIC has nodded off; he wakes up, gathers himself, remembers what he has just seen and begins writing. NARRATOR has been watching him from offstage; smiling, she once again steps into his privacy, and continues her thoughts.)

NARRATOR: Because we all have the impulse to criticize . . . maybe it's evolutionary . . . maybe because women weren't allowed to carry spears or weapons, they used language, gossip . . . maybe men learned literally to stab each other in the back with those same things . . . I don't know. All I know is, people can't wait to tell you what's wrong with your work, with your soup, with your blouse, with your logic, with your lipstick, with your telephone manner . . . *(actors run in with brushes, combs, lipstick, magnifying mirrors)* Bloomingdales is full of cosmetics ladies *(actors push NARRATOR onto CRITIC's lap and begin fussing and applying)* who can't wait to tell you what's wrong with your pores . . .

BLOOMINGDALES ATTENDANT: Bumps! She's got bumps!

NARRATOR: . . . Your eyebrows, your lips, your whole Gestalt . . .

BLOOMINGDALES ATTENDANTS: Eczema! Seborrhea! Age spots! Laugh lines!

CRITIC: *(from underneath all those people)* There haven't been any laugh lines.

(BLOOMINGDALES ATTENDANTS disperse quickly; a harsh, vaudevillian spotlight has come up on CRITIC and NARRATOR, seated like Edgar Bergen and his ventriloquist's dummy; NARRATOR, completely abashed, stands; spotlight disappears; NARRATOR continues:)

NARRATOR: I also think criticism is a replacement for religion sometimes – a theology of fashion don'ts and dark comparisons . . . people who have given up on the myths of their church, and find an even more intense arrangement of pieties in a quest for 'truth' that takes a critical form. Yet criticism is beyond that . . . it's above and below that . . . criticism is also the contextualization of experience . . . it's the need to say what we see . . . to limn the world in our humanity. My baby daughter was trying to grab a bar of sunlight, and it eluded her touch; the only evidence of herself she could find in her interaction with this beam of light was that she could send the shadow of her hand onto the floor by trying to touch it. We talked about shadows. Then, a week later, she was playing by the wood stove and her face got covered with soot; she chanced upon a mirror, looked in it, raised up her hand, looked in the mirror again, and said:

MOMMY! I LOOK LIKE A SHADOW!

Now *that's* criticism.

(Pause. NARRATOR goes over, turns on worklights, house lights come up.)

NARRATOR: *(to audience)* Well, what do you think so far? Does this make any sense?

(ACTORS come rushing from backstage and take seats in the audience as though they were spectators.)

AUDIENCE MEMBER 1:   Why are you talking so much? Isn't the theater a place for enactments?

NARRATOR: Well, sure. But this is the prologue. I was attempting to set up a context into which you could place the rest of the material.

AUDIENCE MEMBER 1:   Well, let *us* do that! I don't need you to tell me what a show is about! If after an hour I have no idea what a show is about, I'll just go to Starbucks, have coffee and forget it. I think I can be trusted to do that.

AUDIENCE MEMBER 2:   Are there other people in this show, or are you the whole thing?

NARRATOR: There are several other people.

AUDIENCE MEMBER 3:   So where are they?

NARRATOR: They're coming!

AUDIENCE MEMBER 2:   One-person shows are out! People are tired of them!

NARRATOR: I was just trying to contextualize the . . .

AUDIENCE MEMBER 1:   You were just trying to preempt any critical reaction to your work. You were trying to get sympathy: you tried to cancel, you're middle-aged, you live in MauMau New Jersey, etcetera, and then you're trying to tell us why and how to pay attention to the material!

(CRITIC gets up from his chair, glares at AUDIENCE MEMBERS; goes over to work lights, turns them off, sits down; picks up his notebook, sits contemplatively in his own light.)

CRITIC: The best thing is when you learn something. You walk in, you know the text, you know the actors, maybe. You sit down, there's that hush around you, your seat has been washed with spray and a rag, and it says RESERVED, and that's like a character description, you feel reserved, they leave you alone, you're quarantined by your importance; the show starts, and you start writing. You write those things you know will help you remember. Legibility is always a challenge, scrawling in the dark; you try to make sure you don't mistake the inscrutability of your own handwriting for meaninglessness in the work. You try to feel things, notice things, and make the kinds of notes in the dark that'll help you remember. A review almost exists before it's written, that's the painful thing. So you watch, and you already know the text, and you've seen most of the actors in other things, and they look the same, only refigured slightly, like seeing the same flower in a garden and then in a vase and then in the garbage, and then suddenly, you learn something. There's nothing like that. When I have those moments at the theater, it's when I love my job the most, and when I have the strongest impulse to quit.

I had that happen at *Godot*. They assigned me *Godot* at Lincoln Center in 1990. Robin Williams, Steve Martin, wonderful actors, actors without stakes. Free actors. Lights went down, set was wonderful: sand. Lots of sand. That desolate tree, and clear, strong, sad lighting. Lovely. The play was going by me like a song, I knew all the lines and was enjoying the music, when suddenly, in comes F. Murray Abraham as Pozzo and Bill Irwin as Lucky. It was the chair. It was the way he made Lucky prepare his chair. His whole dignity depended upon this business with the chair. His dignity was so brittle; his chair, the way Irwin had to keep opening his folding chair, the vanity of Pozzo, the tragedy of that vanity... the chair. It was all in the chair. Like the critic's chair, right? RESERVED, it always says, and the publicist tries to pick it in advance; to make sure it's clean, and it's center, three rows back, and we fuss if it's not. Pozzo's chair. He would have committed suicide were there no one to set his chair, set it properly, in a way that let him know that he existed and was important. I got up crying, which was stupid, and left the theater in that clichéd, deadline sort of way. Although I was angry for some reason, I wrote a rave review.

NARRATOR: *(entering again into the CRITIC's light and sitting down with him at the edge of his chair)* I think it's a substitute for touch, sometimes, criticism: for the desire to touch something, to eat it, to not be separate from it. You can't eat a play; you can't kiss the eyelids of a piece of music. Language is a substitute for touch. And touching language is critical language.

And bad criticism is when you get angry that you can't eat it, or make love to it or stick your tongue in its mouth or put it up your nose and smell it, so instead you try to make it smaller, or make it go away, because unrequited desire is an unbearable burden sometimes. It's terrifying sometimes.

So let's say you approach beauty trembling, and with passable strength and good intentions, but some knife that hails from your own rage or disappointment somersaults through the ages of your life and ends up in your hand just as you go to caress the face of an old friend with a soft, empty palm. It's tragic, really. I mean, what do you think? I think criticism is a reflex, an organic impulse, like eating or sex or smiling.

And don't you think it's also possible that the impulse to praise comes from the same source as the impulse to criticize? Because that's what I have ... a longing to tell people how FABULOUS they are. I yearn to do it; I feel caged if I can't. I don't care who it is. As long as I'm not expecting my period and the person isn't Adolf Eichmann, I can find something ... some beauty, some improvement, some grace to enjoy, and I will mention it! Often! And with conviction and clarity! Now I am fully aware that my impulse to praise probably comes from the exact same source as the impulse to criticize, but still, when all is said and done, who would you rather spend time with?

(Enter CRITICAL LADY; she approaches CRITIC and NARRATOR.)

CRITICAL LADY: Is that your son?
NARRATOR: *(touches CRITIC's head as if he were her son)* Yes. Yes, it is. He's two and a half.
CRITICAL LADY: He's ... beautiful.
NARRATOR: Oh ... thank you.
CRITICAL LADY: You know, God is good! That a person who looks like *you* could have a child who looks like *that*.
NARRATOR: Oh ... thank you.

(CRITICAL LADY exits. CRITIC and NARRATOR make full eye contact. CRITIC still has his head in NARRATOR's hands from previous filial scene.)

169

CRITIC: What kind of language did you say was critical language?
NARRATOR: Touching language.

(NARRATOR exits, EDITOR enters.)

CRITIC: Who's the PR guy on that?
EDITOR: Delaney. It's Delaney.
CRITIC: Okay.
EDITOR: They'll have you booked for the preview, so you'll have 24 to get it figured out, and they'll open, and we'll print Friday.
CRITIC: Is there singing in this thing?
EDITOR: What?
CRITIC: Is there singing in this thing? I can't *bear* the singing.
EDITOR: I dunno.

(Cocktail jazz with voice suddenly comes up. Lights down on CRITIC; up on TRISH and CASS at a cocktail/dinner party.)

TRISH: Hey, Cass. How are you?
CASS: Good. I'm good. How are you?
TRISH: I'm good.
CASS: Good.
TRISH: I'm suicidal, but in a really good way.
CASS: Good.
TRISH: Everywhere I go I feel like I should be somewhere else.
CASS: That's okay.
TRISH: You think it's okay? That's good.
CASS: I feel that way too. Wherever I am, I'm looking for where I should be.
TRISH: You feel that way too?
CASS: Yeah.
TRISH: Yeah, it's good. It really hurts, but in a good way.
CASS: Yeah. *(putting her hand on TRISH's rear end)* Trish, your rear end is really flaccid!
TRISH: Christ, yes. Thank you . . . yes it is.
CASS: And your arms. Like when you gesticulate, they wobble.
TRISH: *(laughing a little)* In art and in life! Hahaha!
JOHN: Hey, Cassie!
CASS: John!
TRISH: You have that shocking vertical line on your brow, Cass. Your makeup accentuates that incredible line, it looks like

an exclamation point, and your eye is the dot at the bottom, only the dot is too large for the line, like a bad typeface.

JOHN: Cassie, I can't believe you're here! You look ten years older than when I saw you last March!

CASS: Time flies!

JOHN: *(putting his hand on her neck)* Come, let me get you a drink. Jesus, your skin is both dry and clammy at the same time. Quite a trick, Cass.

CASS: Have you been able to get an erection since I last saw you, John? That impotence must have made you feel dreadful!

JOHN: Well ...

CASS: Because your penis isn't that large to begin with!

JOHN: Too true. *(puts his hand on Cass's stomach)* But it looks like you've met someone better!

CASS: What do you mean?

JOHN: Well, you're obviously pregnant ... about ... four months?

CASS: No ... why?

JOHN: Because your stomach was just sticking straight out like that, and it's usually a sure bet.

CASS: Don't make any bets, John! You'll need your money for your old age!

PETER: *(entering scene)* ... which doesn't seem terribly far away for you, John!

JOHN: Yo, buddy! Great to see you!

PETER: Thanks, you too.

JOHN: No, you *TWO*! Looks like you've doubled in size, Peter.

PETER: Sure, thanks!

JOHN: Mostly in your legs! They look like redwood tree trunks!

PETER: Yeah, I noticed Trish has fat legs too, with veins in them!

CASS: She sure does. You know, Peter, you sort of smell bad.

PETER: Aw, I'm sorry.

JOHN: 'Ts okay. No biggie.

PETER: Terrific.

CASS: Trish was just saying that wherever she is she feels she should be somewhere else.

PETER: Me too.

JOHN: You too, Peter?

PETER: You trying to start something with me, John?
JOHN: Hell no, Pete.
TRISH: I would like to have sex.
CASS: Calm down, Trish.
TRISH: That's where I wish I was.
JOHN: *Were.* It's SUBJUNCTIVE.
TRISH: Why?
JOHN: Wishing is subjunctive.
TRISH: Why? Why is it subjunctive?
JOHN: Because it's not real!
TRISH: It *is.*
JOHN: It's not happening, it's hypothetical.
PETER: A wish. It's a wish, a postulation.
TRISH: Why is my having sex such a postulation?
PETER: Just *look* at you!
ALL: *(except TRISH)* Hahahahahahahahahahahahaha!
TRISH: I'm sure someone has already said that.
ALL: *(stop laughing abruptly)*

(TRISH has begun to cry.)

PETER: She's crying!
JOHN: That's a shame!
PETER: Don't cry, Trish!
CASS: She can cry, Peter.
JOHN: What's wrong, Trish?
TRISH: I don't . . . I don't know where to go.
CASS: But your haircut is great!
PETER: It does look good. It frames her face better.
CASS: Yeah.
JOHN: Because before, the hair just kind of hung down, and
it made her face look longer.
CASS: Yeah, and she was going through such a hard time!
PETER: *(getting excited)* . . . which just made her whole face
look . . . twisted!
ANITA: Yes! And with the hair hanging down, and the bee's
nests and the crow's feet and the horehounds and who the hell
knows what all else, it was hideous!
PETER: Horrendous!
CASS: Atrocious!
JOHN: Ugly! Ugly!
CASS: Halloween!

172

PETER: All Saints Day!
JOHN: Mischief night!
CASS: Birth of Christ!
JOHN: Ascension!

(VOICES rise in cacophony until blackout; small, haunting light up on NARRATOR, stage left, who sits among live flowers, pawing and destroying them.)

NARRATOR: How unbearable beauty is, how perfectly unbearable, how it falls down into the soul with such a tiny, hollow thunk! It hurts, like chest pain, it hurts like lightning, it goes small, beauty, we need it small. Beauty needs silence, it wants everything, beauty: an aneurysm, a point of life-threatening explosion in one tiny place, one unaffordable place, like the heart or brain, beauty, unbearable beauty, go small. We fuck ourselves with beauty, it's a moment, maybe, where a guy catches a ball meant to sail by him and into oblivion, a moment when a child in a sweet high voice like water says more than he means or could possibly know, it's a tree hussied into radiance by Autumn, and the clean, pointed anguish of brevity, beauty, fuck beauty; beauty serves me like a waitress who wants to be an actress, beauty is polite but nothing more, I ask her, Can I see you? Where do you live, can I call you? Can I see you? It's what we lose when we die, and we die so much; beauty, as luscious and beatified as the word Fuck: Fuck, fuck me; beauty beauty on TV beauty on *Baywatch* beauty in the new moon slamdunked into darkness beauty all over the surfaces of windows and mirrors, trapped in the lenses of telescopes, on the hands of sculptors and nurses, beauty, beauty, I make snuff movies and you're always the star: beauty.

(Lights crossfade down on NARRATOR and up on CRITIC, who is standing by his chair.)

CRITIC: Who the hell knows why people write? Do they write because they have to write? The way people have sex for fun? I was reading *The Times'* Neediest Cases. This woman's taking care of seven people, she's destitute, she said: the girls, they like to have fun; and then gesturing toward her teenaged daughter's three-month-old son, said: There's her fun. Artists are like that. They bring their progeny into the world with no more sense of responsibility than a teenage welfare mother. They

173

move toward intimacy without contraception, and we all pay! We all come, we all watch, we compile, we walk down the street, we ossify into historians.

Then they had that guy with AIDS here come and poke himself with a crown of thorns. Is danger art? Is that the same fucking thing? I could drive drunk and review that! So there's this man with the religious props, and he's bleeding, and he has AIDS, and they're telling the press not to freak out, not to wax controversial. Athey, he was. Don or Ron or something, and he bled himself, and they gave us warnings, I remember, disclaimers, waivers, and he declaimed, the poor man! And he hung himself on a cross or something, and he bled. I reviewed that presentation, but the review existed before I wrote it, it was two thousand years old, that review, it's a valid image but it's yesterday's news, it's happened before, we've already cried about it.

(CRITICAL LADY enters, approaches CRITIC.)

WOMAN: Come to church.
CRITIC: No thanks.
WOMAN: You haven't been in so long.
CRITIC: Please. I have to work.
WOMAN: It'll be nice, you haven't seen Phyllis, or Mrs. McCarthy, they've been asking about you, and Mrs. Farrell's daughter, whatsername, will be there . . .
CRITIC: I really have no . . .
WOMAN: Sweetie, why won't you come? It can be so fulfilling to be with . . .
CRITIC: I feel fulfilled. My work is very satisfying. And I'm allergic to whatever it is they burn in there. I get asthma the minute we walk in. It's unhealthy for me to go there.
WOMAN: Okay, dear.
CRITIC: He says MY-rad! I can't stand his sermons! It drives me crazy that instead of saying 'myriad,' he says MY-rad! Drives me crazy. And he uses that word a lot, it's his favorite word.
WOMAN: Okay dear. *(exits)*

(NARRATOR enters; CRITIC is writing in his chair.)

NARRATOR: Love makes me clumsy. I can't explain the mechanism by which that happens, but it happens powerfully and inevitably. It can be love for a man, a woman, a friend, an

174

idea, a dog, a cat, a small farm animal; it doesn't matter. Falling in love makes me clumsy. I lose boundary, I lose judgment. Once love made me yearn to be taller; I don't know who I thought I was; I stood up on a tall chair that was missing a leg, an old, tired amputee, this tall chair, which abandoned me violently and instantly in defense of its own instability. Once in Europe I fell into a huge hole in an old floor because love made me hurry, I was running and running when really love, like desperate hunger that makes you eat too fast, wants a crazy, sexual slowness. Once I dropped a whole tray of dishes as I brought it toward a woman I suddenly realized I would always love beyond any sense of myself. Once my mother asked me to carry the Thanksgiving turkey on a tray, and in my longing for her unattainable affection I dropped the turkey and it hissed and slid all the way across the dining-room floor and finally shipwrecked on the living-room carpet. Whenever I fall in love, I'm always asked within two weeks by concerned friends whether the new relationship is abusive, because I always have cuts, bruises, stitches, contusions, abrasions on my legs, and often my hands. The bruise on my leg from falling into the European hole has left a permanent indentation on my left calf in the shape of Israel. Whenever there's conflict in the Middle East, I look to my left leg. But I'm not into abuse, I'm in love, and love just makes me clumsy. *(NARRATOR is now standing near CRITIC, eyeing him peripherally.)* If you don't like my work, don't forget that I'm in love.

(NARRATOR runs over and turns on work lights; house lights come up as well.)

NARRATOR: *(to audience)* Well, how's it going? Isn't this a delightful presentation?

(ACTORS once again rush out from backstage and into the audience.)

AUDIENCE MEMBER 1: Well, you raised a lot of questions, and you didn't answer them.
AUDIENCE MEMBER 2: What questions?
AUDIENCE MEMBER 1: Like: Is criticism a kind of religion? Is it a substitute for touch?
NARRATOR: Well, we haven't finished yet.
AUDIENCE MEMBER 1: Well do you address these questions further? Do you answer them?

NARRATOR: Well ... no. No we don't.

AUDIENCE MEMBER 1: Then why raise them?

NARRATOR: Well ... the Bible raises more questions than it answers ... should it not have been written?

AUDIENCE MEMBER 3: You have some nerve comparing this show to the Bible! This show is no Bible!

NARRATOR: I wasn't comparing this show to the Bible.

AUDIENCE MEMBER 2: I liked it when those people were insulting each other!

AUDIENCE MEMBER 1: It was mildly amusing.

AUDIENCE MEMBER 2: How long did it take you people to do this?

AUDIENCE MEMBER 4: Weren't you insulted when she said God is Good? How come you act like it was just an amusing anecdote?

AUDIENCE MEMBER 1: What was with that chanting about Beauty?

AUDIENCE MEMBER 2: It was about fear of beauty. Like the way women get harassed in the street.

AUDIENCE MEMBER 4: It had nothing to do with women getting harassed in the street. This is the least political show I've seen downtown in five years.

AUDIENCE MEMBER 3: How come the critic is a man?

(CRITIC stands up, angry and confused.)

NARRATOR: *(to CRITIC)* Sit down! *(CRITIC sits down.)*

AUDIENCE MEMBER 1: Let's just get on with it.

(Houselights down. CRITIC is onstage, in his chair. A light is on him; EDITOR enters stage right.)

EDITOR: I wancha to go over and see that Christmas Pageant at the high school.

CRITIC: What?

EDITOR: We're doing a feature ... I wancha over at the Christmas Pageant on the lawn at the high school. It's tomorrow at 8 pm.

CRITIC: Are these actors?

EDITOR: Call the Superintendant's Office and ask. I think it's just a bunch of people from town.

CRITIC: What am I, some third stringer? I'm going to review a Nativity Pageant on someone's front lawn?

EDITOR: We're doing a feature. It's a human interest.

CRITIC: Put it in Chronicles, then.

EDITOR: That's the wrong Book of the Bible.

(Heavenly music is heard. Lights up on JOSEPH with walking stick, and MARY huddled together.)

MARY: Please, Joseph, do not trouble; although I am tired, my spirit is at profound rest, and I feel o'erwhelmed in a translucent peace, a divine peace such as ne'er I have felt before.

JOSEPH: Most dear and sacred Mary, it shall be as the angel told it to me: that which is conceived in thee is of the Holy Ghost, and it shall be as the angel says, that you shall bring forth a son, for he shall save people from their sins. We must find a place, here in Bethlehem, and there shall we lay you down.

MARY: Trouble not for me, beloved; I am full of a pellucid strength, and can go on. I have seen in a dream a white horse, running riderless through purple light, running alone and gentle in its passionate freedom; that is thee, Joseph, my husband.

JOSEPH: Is the time nigh?

MARY: It is nigh.

JOSEPH: I shall ring the doorbell for shelter.

MARY: Do not ring the doorbell.

JOSEPH: I shall, my bride; thou art conceived of the Holy Ghost a son: and we shall call it Emanuel, which being interpreted is, God with us.

MARY: I do not fancy that name.

JOSEPH: What is wrong with it?

MARY: They shall always call him Manny.

JOSEPH: What is wrong with Manny?

MARY: How would you like a daughter named Womany?

JOSEPH: His name matters not; we shall call him something else. Now sit down, dear; I shall ring the bell of this person.

MARY: I do not wish to impose.

JOSEPH: Do not attempt to be so selfless in your labor, my beloved. Begin your Lamaze exercises; I shall ring the bell.

MARY: Beloved husband, I am in such excruciating pain that these exercises seem quite stupid. I cannot believe we paid 14 sheep to study a technique as irrelevant to actual human experience as breathing during labor. It is as if long swords or fingernails of fire were being raked over my abdomen by demons,

177

who relent and let me rest briefly, only out of a cruel desire to rip from me a moment later my sweet relief.

JOSEPH: Do as nature bids thee; I'll find us a place.

(JOSEPH rings doorbell. American Gothic couple comes to the door.)

JOSEPH: My wife is heavy with child and fain would lie down. Canst give us shelter this night, for soon she shall bring forth a child, conceived in Holiness and shrouded in Grace.

WOMAN: I've got my in-laws staying here.

MAN: You can go in the manger.

WOMAN: Put your parents in the manger.

MAN: I'm not putting my parents in the manger.

WOMAN: Why not? They wouldn't even notice.

MAN: They would notice.

WOMAN: They didn't notice my haircut.

MAN: My mother said your face didn't look as long and sallow as it had. That's the haircut.

JOSEPH: We shall gratefully accept this manger, and there shall my wife lay her down.

(Scene changes: Soft light: A radiant MARY holding newborn, exquisite baby boy. Animals. A slow aggregation of WISE MEN with canes, and citizens in wonder; slow and beautiful, like a ballet in moonlight. ANGELS hover.)

WISE MAN 1: Thou art sacred, Mary, Mother of our Lord; most sacred; this gold and frankincense and myrrh are but symbols of thy beauty, thy strength, thy fertility.

WISE MAN 2: A stab of joy awakened our souls through the light of the star that bespaketh thy labor.

(WOMAN steps forward, in full raiment and cowl.)

WOMAN: *(bowing deeply before MARY, staring at the child in amazement, bowing again)* Is that thy son, thy first-born son?

MARY: Aye, 'tis, my lady.

WOMAN: He is . . . he is so very beautiful.

MARY: Thanks be to the Holy Spirit, my lady, and to thee.

WOMAN: *(stares at the child, back at MARY, back at the child)* You know, God is good! That a woman who looks like thee could have a child who looks like that!

WISE MAN 3: What meanest thou by that remark?

MARY: Do not ask her this, for she speaks the truth, however naked. God is good! That a woman who looks like me could have a child that looks like this.

JOSEPH: *(to WOMAN, furious)* Dost thou think that childbed is the place to insult the appearance of a woman? Never is a woman more beautiful than after her labors have ceased and her babe is in arms to take suck.

WISE MAN 1: Get her out of this manger!

MARY: No, no, let her speak. She is as a child: unschooled in manners, merely speaking of what she sees. She is innocent; she is childlike; she is in sisterhood to my son, newly born. Who is so pure among us that he can insult me without even realizing it?

ALL: You don't think she realizes it? She just told you that you're ugly!

WISE MAN 3: She's jealous!

ALL: She's blind with jealousy!

WOMAN: No! Let me speak! It is not jealousy, exactly, but blindness does feel relevant. I mean, I was on my way to the supermarket, and when I saw the baby, I just . . . I mean, I never considered Mary before. She just seemed like a plain, okay sort of person, and I never felt competitive with her or anything. I mean, I was engaged to be married to a guy but he died, and then my brother's so weird and everything, and I'm so tense . . . so tense! I don't even know why, but there's a scream running down the center of me like hot sap from deep inside a maple tree! When I get shots or needles, or when they take my blood, I'm sure they hear that scream. I struggle so hard for everything! My mother is so mean in a way! And my own first-born son was so difficult, he was so skinny I was afraid he was going to die, he lay in the bathtub, he seemed more mortal than I am, closer to death than childhood, which terrified me, and so strange, almost autistic, and I met another man and got married, but my husband doesn't even seem to like me, he buys me necklaces and stuff, but he deserts me when I need him most, and he's tired of my silent way of screaming, and I scream out loud too, and I have a loud voice, and a loud need to use it, I need people to listen to me, I feel like eating all the time. So when I walked by this manger and just saw Mary lying there so simply, so effortlessly, and Joseph staring at her adoringly, and the baby, I never even realized she was married much less pregnant or anything, and there she is with the most beautiful child in her arms that I ever saw, and I thought I was going to throw up! I felt faint, like there was a siphon draining the light right out of my eyes, because . . . Mary even *exists*! I never had to consider that before! And her life is so simple! Her life . . . is just a prayer, and prayers are simple, they're just entreaties. They're not logistics, they're just hopes, they're simple. They're like: Grant us this, thou this and that, O thou eternal source of this and that, and blah blah . . . and for me, it's up and down the stairs and pulling meat out of the freezer, and yell, and work, and stir and struggle, and I JUST HATED EVERYTHING! And I needed to find someone to blame it on! And it was God! That's why I said God is good, that a woman who looks like you could have a child who looks like that! It was God! I blamed it on God so I could get on with my life and GO TO THE SUPERMARKET! Your miracle makes me sick! It seems so arbitrary, who gets beauty and who doesn't! So I blamed it on God, and He can take it! And now I'm going to stand perfectly tall and I'm going to the GRAND UNION! And I'm going to buy dinner rolls for my family. If you'll excuse me!

(All part and WOMAN walks through, proceeds cross-stage, and enters Grand Union.)

(Cashier line at the Grand Union. A line of customers waiting to check out. The line says: EXPRESS: 20 ITEMS OR LESS. Music is Steely Dan, but it keeps being interrupted by Grand Union music.)

VOICE-OVER: GRAND UNION RADIO! Keep your holidays bustling and your guests hustling! Shop Grand Union! In this week's flier . . . etc. and GRAND UNION IS CURRENTLY SEEKING PART-TIME EMPLOYEES! JOIN THE GRAND UNION TEAM, AND YOU'LL FIND OUR FLEXIBLE SCHEDULE AND COMPETITIVE PAY JUST RIGHT FOR YOU!

CASHIER: Next in line please?

WOMAN: Am I invisible?

CASHIER: Not at all, ma'am. Please place your order a little closer to the register.

WOMAN: No! I want to see you ring it all up!

CASHIER: I can't ring it up if I can't reach it.

WOMAN: You can reach it! Bend over!

CASHIER: Pardon me?

WOMAN: Bend forward and reach them! That way I can watch! You people ring the order up so fast no one can see what the hell they're paying for this rotten lettuce!

CASHIER: Our pricing is all automated, ma'am.

WOMAN: So what the hell do they need YOU for?

CASHIER: *(bending around, looking at the order)* Are all these things yours?

WOMAN: Yes.

CASHIER: This is a secondary express line. Twenty items maximum.

WOMAN: You're just annoyed because you're unnecessary and because I want to watch you ring up my purchases. You can't get around that! You can't! Just because you're lazy doesn't make me a fool! You know at my mother's store, the King Market, she paid for a broom every time she shopped there! She must have paid for 175 brooms before she realized, that's the way she was! They just had a broom by the cash register and every time a customer checked out they charged the person for that broom! Then when the customer came to complain, the girl would say: Oh, there was a broom by the register and I thought it was yours! They charged 400 customers a day for that broom every day for ten years! Somebody bought themselves a condo! And the ladies all thought: Oh how nice, they keep the place clean, but it was a con! It was a regular *scam*! It was a daily robbery of these poor people!

CASHIER: Look, Miss. This is a secondary express line.

WOMAN: Don't you SECONDARY EXPRESS me! You probably didn't even finish high school! I can't even tell if you're a man or a woman! And this Grand Union music! It comes on like an attack of Meunière's Syndrome! It wheedles into my ears in the most annoying manner!

(People behind her become restless; start giggling.)

WOMAN: Don't you laugh, you grexers! You're all grexers! And you shouldn't be buying those Dolly Madison ice pops, you're as fat as a house! You're going to get diabetes! *(turns back to CASHIER)* What level of education did you reach?

CASHIER: Well, I did my undergraduate work at Amherst, took my Ph.D. at U. Michigan, and I'm currently a postdoctoral candidate in linguistic complication and magisterial restraint right here in the Tri-State area.

WOMAN: That's a bunch of lies! Filthy lies!

CASHIER: Ma'am, let's just ring up your order.

WOMAN: Don't patronize me!

CASHIER: Ma'am, you are the patron here.

WOMAN: Damn right! The patron is always right! I don't mind paying for what I get, but I'm not paying for that broom!

CASHIER: *(finally losing it)* Why should you? You rode in on one!

WOMAN: I BEG YOUR PARDON?

(Other SHOPPERS back off in horror and exit; WOMAN's rage turns slowly, visibly, into despair, and she crosses downstage to CRITIC, sits at his feet, puts her head in his lap and sings:)

WOMAN: The painful thing is how often I think of graves, of bodies buried; how often I wonder if we have enough land on Earth to bury the billions of future dead. The painful thing is that I look at a crowd of people and think: all those funerals. The painful thing. The painful thing. The painful thing is: the child waiting for his mother to come, and she doesn't come. She won't ever come. J says: to me, the critic is the one who doesn't come. The painful thing is sudden music: music that drifts in off someone's hi-fi or at the French Fries stand and suddenly rips open your whiteness of mind, rips open that flat white envelope and blue sprinkles fall down in some terrible, sudden light: they look like water, and water comes down out of your eyes, and you're undone. You yearn, you're undone. The painful thing is, I can't do it, Jake, I can't help you. The painful thing is I'm lost, I'm done. The painful thing is, something's killing me. The painful thing is I want you to love me. I'm here, I'm over here. I'm temporarily immortal: I'm never ever going to die until I die.

(Sound of heartbeat is heard, soft at first but gaining volume, as song ends; CRITIC moves WOMAN aside, gets up and crosses to DOCTOR's table; he sits down on table, takes off his shirt.)

DOCTOR: How's the shoulder?

CRITIC: Feeling better.

DOCTOR: Good.

CRITIC: A lot of it's just sitting at the computer all day.

DOCTOR: Hold still, I'm going to check your pressure. *(DOCTOR takes CRITIC's blood pressure; notes it on a chart.)* Now take some deep breaths for me. *(listens)* And ... just breathe normally. *(listens)*

(Sound of heartbeat rises again. Lights crossfade from DOCTOR and CRITIC to a performance stage; CRITIC takes out pad and pencil and makes notes, shirtless, while on DOCTOR's table.)

PERFORMANCE ARTIST: In Manhattan? Yes, listing please for Herkheimer, H-E-R-K-H-E-I-M-E-R, first initial S as in Sam, on West 20th Street. *(pause)* Pardon? No? Well, anywhere, anywhere in the West Twenties. Twenty-first, twenty-second, twenty-third, any of those. Nothing? Are you sure? Look, I've gotten this number from you many times before. Well, not you personally, but one of your colleagues. I call every day and get this number, I know it's there, don't tell me it's not there, I get this number every day, sometimes several times a day. *(pause)* Well, if you must know, it's because I don't have any pencils in the house, that's why I have to call, I'm scared of pencils, they look like miniature dead trees and DON'T GET YOUR SUPERVISOR! I hate it when you people say you're going to get your supervisor! It makes me feel VERY MARGINAL! Please just check again. Thank you so much. *(pause)* Yes, S like in Sam, not F like in ... far far away! *(pause)* Well, thank you for checking! Just because something's there every day for eleven and a half years doesn't mean it's going to be there this afternoon! Maybe it's a full moon, or something, things disappear! *(pause)* Okay, FINE! Get the Supervisor! I look forward with all my heart to a discussion with the Supervisor!

Yes. Is this that Supervisor? I'm delighted! Delighted to talk to you! Look, supervisor, look. You are the last person I am going to speak to before I kill myself and I am finding this conversation rather clinical. Why don't we just ... cut loose! Why don't we swing! I'll tell you things about myself and you can tell me things about yourself, like *Silence of the Lambs*! I'll start! Everything's wonderful! My daughter said she wants to shoot me dead with a gun! She said Mommy I'm cold, get me the summer! She said that, get me the summer! And I went out and looked for it ... just like that idiot you work with, I feel sorry for you, you're working with idiots, and he couldn't find Herkheimer, I've called every day since my bas mitzvah, it's like the summer in February, Herkheimer ...

(As PERFORMANCE ARTIST talks, voice gets softer and softer; lights fade down on PERFORMANCE ARTIST and up on CRITIC, whose pad and pencil drop to the floor, and he lies down on DOCTOR's table; it becomes a psychiatrist's couch. CRITIC folds his hands on his chest and speaks.)

CRITIC: The painful thing is the dreams. In my work, I just say what I see, but the painful thing is the dreams. I keep driving a car that slides into this gray water that's just beyond a fence of some sort. There are other people in the car, in the back seat; I'm like a taxi driver, or maybe there are kids back there. I'm alone in the front, and I lose control of the car, and it slides under the fence and sinks, really gently. The gentleness is the worst part of the dream. I keep having this dream in different forms, where something really gentle is the only clear indication of something horribly violent. Again and again, in these dreams, there's a tiny sound, thud, thump or crash that signifies the end of a life, eternal loss. It's horrifying, the sound is so small and the death so huge. Small as a doorway to the infinite, that's the message I keep getting. That's what art tries to be, a lot of the time. Hell, all the time. All the time. All the time. And I open my eyes and my heart's slamming, you can't believe a heart can go like that, my blood pressure's like 200 over nothing. It's a dream that stays with me all day, no matter where I go or what I'm doing, it's there. It's like I never wake up. Like what I went through last year. Someone kept calling me last year, a wrong number; I kept telling him he had the wrong number, that he wanted the guy who lived here before me, I think the guy before me had the same first name, but he said there wasn't anyone before me, fucking bastard, he sent me flowers, sent them to me at WORK, I never told him where I worked, they had my name on them, he'd call late, tell me he loved me, he wanted me, those flowers were so terrifying, this stranger, heckling me with flowers, fucking cocksucker. They looked beautiful, wrapped in pink paper, two dozen roses the color of just-oxygenated blood, almost black, with little babies' breath around them, this prick, and he sends me a card says: DARLING, THE FIRST ROUND IN THE CAROL OF LOVE IS ROSES. And I said to the delivery guy, Take these back I don't want them, he has the wrong person, and the guy said: aren't you such and such, my address on the card, and I said Yeah! Yeah, but they're not for me, they're not mine, take them back, and he says, Just sign here and THROW THEM IN THE GARBAGE IF YOU WANT! But accepting those flowers meant accepting violence in the guise of love from some voice beyond apprehension and prison time, some voice with all the control, some voice who knew where I worked but I didn't know where it worked, that could just strike anywhere, it meant accepting that, and I said GET THESE THE FUCK OUT OF MY OFFICE or you'll EAT THEM and SHIT THEM and I must've raised my hand or something, because he ran out the door down the hall and into the elevator, and there was a phone call to my boss from the flower company, and questions about whether I was feeling alright. And I would have been alright. I told Jake It's fine, I'm just sick of some asshole calling me all night, some pervert, whatever; and it would have been alright, except after eating quickly and going to the theater, I came up the stairs after getting out my mail and there, scattered all over the floor outside my apartment were the black roses, petals all the hell over the floor, a soft ocean of petals, like the gray water in that dream, and pink paper torn, and I didn't see the babies' breath anymore, and the card, with scuff marks on it, unedited, still, still saying DARLING, THE FIRST ROUND IN THE CAROL OF LOVE IS ROSES.

(NARRATOR enters, goes over, flings on the work lights; house lights come up too, surprising CRITIC mortally on his shrink's couch. CRITIC sits up and squints into the cruel, sudden new light.)

NARRATOR: *(to audience)* How are you feeling? Is it time for an intermission? *(looks around)* Did you enjoy that monologue with Herkheimer? Didn't you think that was funny, the way she calls Information for comfort, it's like a suicide phone call to a total stranger . . .

CRITIC: Excuse me.

(NARRATOR turns around and looks at CRITIC, who says nothing. NARRATOR continues.)

NARRATOR: The link to criticism here was that she said she found the conversation with the supervisor too clinical . . .

CRITIC: I beg your pardon, get out of here and turn off those lights. I was in the middle of a very private conversation, and I'm finding this very inappropriate right now.

(Long pause.)

NARRATOR: Well, EXCUUUUUUSE ME!

CRITIC: Look. I'm sorry if I spoke harshly... I'm just feeling ... I was just involved in a very personal ... disclosure ... and these lights and talking upset me.

NARRATOR: Well, this isn't ABOUT you! Why does everything have to be about YOU? We've put up with you here throughout the entire presentation! You've been sitting here snorting nasal spray and judging us and scrawling your little chicken scratch through the whole thing!

CRITIC: I was *assigned* to this!

(ACTORS rush in from wings.)

ACTOR 1: *(very sarcastically)* You poor thing!

CRITIC: Cut it out now. If you're going to behave irrationally ...

ACTOR 2: Go ahead! Write that! Write that the show was irrational!

ACTOR 3: Immature!

ACTOR 4: You hated it!

CRITIC: I did not set out to render judgment on you people, I was in the middle of an important conversation and I was just taken by surprise when you suddenly...

ACTOR 1: I had that happen to me! A critic came to see my show about the death of my mother and began his review with I HATED...

NARRATOR: This creepy guy from some downtown rag came to see my show, and he laughed so hard he practically needed medical help, and the Stage Manager went over to evict him but then he shut up, and then he went home and wrote the most disgusting review and he said he hated himself for laughing and always would!

ACTOR1: A sick man!

ACTOR 2: Well, I performed in the Seattle Fringe Festival two years in a row, and the critic wrote: 'I was shocked; last year he brought such an excellent piece, and this year he was just in a coma!'

ACTOR 4: My women's theater company got a guy who wrote: 'Not even Shakespeare would put three women on the stage together for an hour and think it could hold our attention!'

ACTOR 1:   He said I was eerily real . . . he said it was too real . . . he would like it to be more DEAD so that he could be MORE COMFORTABLE!

CRITIC: Look! I'm trying to serve your community! I'm trying to let my readers know about you people! I was . . .

NARRATOR: Quit calling us You People! It's like Ross Pee-rot addressing a rally of black folks!

ACTOR 2:   Frank Rich called Kathy Weights OVERBATE!

ACTOR 1:   Cathy Bates Overweight!

ACTOR 3:   That was Vincent Canby!

ACTOR 2:   Whoever!

CRITIC: Look, I'm just trying to facilitate a dialogue by telling the community what I've seen on the stage. That's my whole job. And it doesn't pay very well; you probably think I make a ton of money, but I get fifty bucks for some of my shorter pieces.

ACTOR 1:   Well that's a big fifty bucks more than I've been paid for doing this work tonight.

CRITIC: I know, look . . .

NARRATOR: Have you read *Criticism: Four Faults* by Michael Kirby from the December 1974 issue of *The Drama Review*?

CRITIC: *(very annoyed)* No, I can't say I have!

NARRATOR: Well you should! And although it has serious flaws in logic, namely that what's a B flat to a C for one person, for another person is just BLEH . . .

ACTOR 1:   He doesn't give a shit about that.

CRITIC: Why don't you all just SHUT UP!

(silence)

CRITIC: This is so stupid . . .

NARRATOR: You're one of the best critics! We all want you to show up, you're smart!

ACTOR 2:   It's so hard to get you to come and write about us!

CRITIC: *(exasperated completely)* What does it matter if I show up? You're closing on Sunday!

ACTOR 4:   I have no furniture!

ACTOR 1:   Yes it matters. It gets us WORK IN THE FUTURE!

ACTOR 3:   I need work right now!

ACTOR 4:   I don't even have ONE FUCKING CHAIR in my house! Give me that chair! Give me HIS chair! I want that chair! I want HIS chair!

(ACTOR 4 goes center stage and picks up chair with RESERVED written on it. CRITIC goes over and gently attempts to take chair away.)

ACTORS: Boo! Boo! Boo! Boo! Boo!

(Lights fade down on ACTORS and CRITIC. Booing continues. NARRATOR is transfixed by the fertility of this brawl, and stands rapt; a basketball jersey that says 33 EWING on it is thrown to her; all other ACTORS exit; she puts the jersey on as BOOING crossfades from the mouths of the ACTORS to a soundtrack of a stadium crowd booing. After donning jersey, NARRATOR stands up on CRITIC's chair; CRITIC lingers on the outskirts of the stage, observing NARRATOR, much as she has often done to him.)

NARRATOR/PATRICK EWING: You know, you folks stink! You really do! You stink, man, you fucking suck! Here I am, this tall black guy! My knees ache, sweatbeads pour outta me like commuters off the rush hour A train, I give pep talks, press conferences, I take jump shots when it's hopeless! That last shot before the buzzer, it was fucking hopeless. Sure! Sure they pay me a lot of money! So you boo me because I missed it! YOU try it! See you guys sit up there! You hear sneakers squeaking, but you don't hear what's being said! You don't hear *words*! You don't hear *language*! There's talk here! So I got this big shot coming up, Van Gundy draws the play and it's my play, I feel a little nauseous, I feel it in my left shoulder, that's where I feel nauseous, man, and Coach draws the play, what's his name inbounds, Childs gets it, fakes to Starks, I get it at the numbers, I got three assholes around me, one of them's five feet four and I just want to reach down and cover my dick 'cause I'm afraid he's gonna bite me, and you creeps are up there yelling! And you're not yelling to support me, to say, HEY WE BELIEVE! AND NO MATTER WHAT HAPPENS, IT'S ALL ABOUT LOVE! No, that ain't the way you're yelling! You're yelling the way people yell at a bullfight, it's just yelling, because somebody's gonna die out there, and that's pure adrenaline, the spectacle of death, you know some asshole's gonna be dead out there, the creep with the cape or the angry black animal. So you're yelling for blood, man, and I got this creepy guy the size of a 10-year-old, and I got their big fucking center, and some other johnny asshole, and the yelling, and Van Gundy looking like he's trying to fart without making any noise, you

188

know that look he gets, he's always got to tell the press how bad we are so they don't write about how bad we are, they just quote him, and sure they pay me a lot of money, but at a moment like that it don't mean nothing. AND YOU'RE BOOING! The next thing I know you're booing me! Yo, WHY the fuck are you booing me? I'm your man! You fans in New York, you stink, man! Who do you think you are? It's money, man, that changes everything. You look at me when I miss the fucking shot and all you see is a millionaire blackie who can't play ball. And then when I win big games for you, you assholes, you go out into the street and get drunk! As if the glory was yours! You share the glory! That's what they buy when they pay me! They buy glory for each and every beer-swilling deluded would-be wanna-be racist creep who watches me! How much is glory worth? They buy a little bag of glory for YOU! And every kid who wants to be me until I miss the shot!

(CRITIC is deeply enjoying NARRATOR's monologue; he now enters stage fully and sits on DOCTOR's table near NARRATOR; she notices him, and directs her final tirade toward him.)

NARRATOR: You know what they're saying while I'm trying to take a shot? You see their mouths moving but you don't know what they're saying, you think it's just Reggie Miller saying we're choke artists and they're loosy goosy, or Spike Lee in his gentleman's hat smiling pretty, placing bets. That's what you think, but it ain't like that. Just imagine it. I'm dribbling, the shot clock's at 8, right. I'm dribbling, I'm like the mailman with three dogs biting his legs, three fucking dogs trying to use my pantlegs for dental floss, and what the fuck you think they're saying to me? Happy Birthday? They're saying Go Ahead Asshole they're saying You and Who Else, they're saying You Haven't Made the Big Shot since the Winter of Ninety-Four, they're saying Down You'll Come Baby, Cradle and All, and they're saying all that with Four Letter Words, like Fuck you Suck you Fall you Blow you Bite and all the booing, man and all that Noise! Sometimes it's just pure noise, my whole job is noise, it's just noise, sometimes I can't tell whether it's you fucking New York fans booing me or if it's Reggie or Charlie or if it's my blood pressure or if it's midnight and my wife is snoring in my ear, or if I've fallen asleep on a plane between one dink-shit town and another and it's the engine making that low loud achy sound or what the fuck it is. YOU try it!

(A silence, during which CRITIC smiles up at NARRATOR, who continues to stand on CRITIC's chair in the New York Knicks jersey, looking back at him.)

CRITIC: I wish you were allowed to say FUCK in the dailies. FUCK is a writer's friend. I yearn to say FUCK. In saying FUCK I show my humanity and vulnerability, and I lose all other need to refer to it, or to prove it. I like that the word FUCK has had the sex, the sexual connotation, drained right out of it through overuse, like a wash-in hair color after 50 shampoos, and now all that's left is a sort of pre-objective punch and a relaxing feeling, like wearing slippers instead of shoes; it lets you out, it releases you, it makes you feel at home. Half the bad reviews I've written have been made worse by how formal I have to be. A couple of FUCKs and these people, these playwrights, would have been like friends of mine.

(GRANDMA creaks in, walks right over to where CRITIC is sitting on DOCTOR's table/psychiatrist's couch and sits near him.)

GRANDMA: Visit me Visit me Visit me. I don't understand why you don't come visit me.

(While GRANDMA is talking, NARRATOR climbs down off CRITIC's chair and sits on floor between GRANDMA and CRITIC.)

GRANDMA: Why don't you come? What's the matter? Is it all these old ladies? Don't pay any attention to the old ladies. They talk, don't listen. They talk, don't listen, pay them no attention. They're crazy, they try to talk to me I pay no attention. I don't have any money, do you have any money? Thank you. I'll wait. You'll take me to Clara's? Thank you ... Do you mean it? I'll wait.

(GRANDMA freezes.)

NARRATOR: *(turning to CRITIC, explaining with animation)* My grandmother was one of the most critical people. She was critical of everyone, her neighbors, her grocer, people she passed in the street. I loved her so much. Her criticism for me was just noise, good kind of noise, soft noise, like water lapping at a shore, it was just noise, soothing and constant, a sound of life, of cosmic metabolism. She was in the old-age home, she was 91, and she referred to her roommate as The Old Lady, and she called them all The Old Ladies.

GRANDMA: *(continues)* Listen, visit me, honey. Why don't you come? You know they think you're crazy but I'm not. They think you're crazy. They said I lay there. Right over there. And I yelled HELP ME for two weeks. Now who in their right mind is going to yell HELP ME for two weeks? And they say *I'm* crazy. Who's going to yell for two weeks HELP ME? If no one comes after fifteen minutes I say forget it!

I'm so glad you came to visit me. It's hard to make friends with these old ladies. They're crazy. They yell all week, the yelling, you should hear the yelling here. I'd like to get to know somebody but what am I going to do, cut them open? You try to get to know someone it's like killing them. I mean you can't just walk up to someone and say What are you? You have to sit and wait. And they're all crazy as loons, these old ladies. One of them lay for two weeks screaming HELP ME! Can you imagine that? Two weeks I'm listening to HELP ME! It's like a Fats Domino record! HELP ME! HELP ME! They're crazy here! That's why they bring them here. You have to wait for someone to talk to. You have to wait.

How old am I, honey? You've got my skin, honey! You've got my soft skin! Your sister doesn't have my skin! But that's okay! She's got her own skin! Will you come again? Will you come again? Will you please, God bless you! Visit me soon again! See that lady? She's crazy. She's a mun-YOCK! When she laughs it sounds like someone ripping your clothes! HA HA HA HA HA HA! But I got plenty, believe me. It's not bad but I wish it would go quicker. Bit by bit by bit. They take away. Bit by bit. Why can't it go quicker? You know someone once told me MY HEART HURTS and I said you're crazy. But the other night my heart hurt, it gave a SQUEEZE like a BANANA! And I thought *this is it*! I'm ready! So I closed my eyes and then I burped, and that was it.

How old am I honey? Honey, how old am I?

I feel so sexy sometimes, really. I went up to a man once but it turned out he was a television. It was just a television. One of those tall boxes with a voice BOOM BOOM coming out of it. The nurse said: Why are you wringing your hands? How can I tell her I feel sexy? She never felt sexy in her whole life, she's crazy. So she says: You're talking to the television set, you're crazy, and I said: I AM NOT, THOSE PEOPLE ARE!

But do I feel sexy! But I'm not lonely! I go to bed with Arthur-itis! And he's there when I wake up! But I feel like holding hands! Feel my hands honey! They're soft like butter. They're soft like old velvet with buttons. I feel like someone's in love with me. Just because I'm . . . how old am I now? Listen. I was born May 23, 1898, how old am I honey? Because I feel like I'm in love with someone, but I forget. I forget. I got a big blotch on my chest, the doctor says what's that? And I say last night I was making love all night. All night. And he starts to laugh! But the one time I'm trying to say something important they think I'm crazy. They could ignore me Monday, ignore me Tuesday, ignore me Friday, but Saturday I'm trying to say something, and he's laughing. He's laughing. He's laughing.

(GRANDMA gets up and wanders away into the audience; NARRATOR rises to her knees staring after her; from stage right, NARRATOR's MOM enters, in the form of two women; one of the women speaks as MOM, the other touches NARRATOR silently, caressing her face, hair, shoulders, and says nothing. This double-selved MOM finds NARRATOR on her knees on floor next to CRITIC; NARRATOR notices MOM's arrival, rises quickly and sits on psychiatrist's couch next to CRITIC.)

MOM: Is that the new dress I bought you at Marshall's?

NARRATOR: No, Mom. This is my costume. It's my show costume.

MOM: It's nice. It fits you well. What's it made of? *(picks up hem)* The hem is coming down . . . it looks *epis* a little uneven . . . you know, it's not well made, you should return it.

NARRATOR: Mom, I think you should . . .

MOM: You got your hair cut, it looks nice.

NARRATOR: Thanks, Mom.

MOM: Did they cut much? *(looks)* They didn't cut much. How much did you pay for this haircut? They didn't hardly cut anything, you were robbed!

NARRATOR: You just said you liked it, Mom!

MOM: What's to like? They didn't take anything off.

NARRATOR: Okay, Mom, I think . . .

MOM: I can't stand to see my mother like that. Her bra's all dirty. She talks on the phone for 15 minutes, and when she comes back, I say, Ma, who was that, and she says I don't know.

NARRATOR: Okay, Mom. Mom, okay, I think it's time . . .
MOM: That wasn't very funny, before.
NARRATOR: What wasn't funny, Mom?
MOM: That business before with the man talking about sex, that whole thing.
NARRATOR: Okay, thank you.
MOM: I love you dear.
NARRATOR: Love you too, Mom.

(The MOMs exit. Silence.)

CRITIC: That your mom?
NARRATOR: Yes.
CRITIC: She seems very nice.
NARRATOR: Thank you.
CRITIC: Does she come to all your shows?
NARRATOR: Mostly.
CRITIC: Mostly?
NARRATOR: Sometimes I tell her not to come.

(Enter CRITICAL LADY into light. CRITIC and NARRATOR watch.)

CRITICAL LADY: She said I couldn't face adversity. She said I couldn't face adversity. Now I was in second grade, and she wrote on my report card that I had a hard time facing adversity.

And she had the most beautiful handwriting, exquisite cursive: the letters were perfectly formed, and they sashayed through space in the most deliberate, graceful way; the letters all looked the same; they all had the same measured beauty and movement. And in that writing, in ink the blue color of Hawaiian mountain lakes, she wrote on my report card that I was unable to face adversity. And my parents showed that to me. And I remember feeling an empire collapse.

First of all came the defeat of not knowing what adversity was, which was so painful. Often we're criticized for being deficient in things we don't understand, and that incomprehension nullifies the criticism without dulling the pain of it: adversity. And you should have seen how beautiful the word looked: adversity. It sounded like a combination of Advertisement and University. Adversity. It also made me think about how my corduroy coat which my mom ordered for me off a cereal boxtop was *reversible*.

My father explained it. He said adversity was the state where things are not going well for you; where things are going wrong; where there's doubt, uncertainty, fear. And I wanted to say: I live where there's doubt, uncertainty and fear, because I live with you. Because I depend on you and am in love with you; because you can never say you're wrong and because your wife hates me. Adversity.

I love the word Adversity. It's a white-glove word for a blue-collar problem. Adversity. It's as tall and general as a mountain. It's far away, non-specific, snow-covered, clean. No gasping for breath, no gagging, no screaming, no one visibly dead, no children standing and screaming for hunger and fear, no rejection, no poverty, no surgery, no finality. Adversity. Just an Advertisement for a University where human despair is studied in depth.

Adversity.

(CRITICAL LADY comes and stands close to CRITIC.)

NARRATOR: Do you know her?
CRITIC: Yeah, I know her.

(There is a long, long silence; the stage, finally empty of action and language, settles into itself; the CRITIC and the NARRATOR sit near each other, occasionally smiling or laughing; CRITICAL LADY stands behind them, detached. This silence stretches into the evening like an arm reaching for something; it is both deeply comfortable and richly tense.)

NARRATOR: *(to CRITIC, gesturing toward the empty stage)* So . . . what did you think?
CRITIC: *(considering the entire production, slowly, delicately, deliberately)* You . . . you write beautifully! Some of these monologues just sing . . . some very lyrical moments. Thematically, it's very complex. It's a hard subject, criticism. One thing that . . . that bothers me . . . watching this, I can't tell if I'm looking at you or at an artistic creation . . . and that makes me uncomfortable. Have you . . . have you thought of . . . putting another actress in the role?

(NARRATOR turns away from him at this; rises slowly from bench where she has been sitting with the CRITIC and comes back downstage center, as if having returned home.)

NARRATOR: Five forty-five in the morning. I took a taxi to Grand Central from my dingy, unspecific apartment on Thirty-third Street and Third Avenue. I actually lived at

Thirty-third and Third, a walk-up I sublet from a woman who didn't realize how much she hated me, just sort of got nauseous and threw up every time we were together.

That morning was colorless and bitter; it was the end of January, that time of the winter when it seems as if it's always been winter and always will be; despite the profound cold the air was filthy and unbreathable. The entire city was silent and gray. As I approached the entrance of Grand Central, I saw a man huddled in a tattered coat just outside the entrance. He was barely moving; stooped as though old. His long beard looked frozen. I decided to give him money. I reached in my pocket and found a dollar something in change; took it into my ungloved hand and started walking toward him. It felt like waltzing, because it was silent and cinematic in that light. As I approached him, I noticed he was walking toward me, suddenly, as if aware of my intention; his hand outstretched. But as we got right up to one another, I looked at him and saw that he had money in *his* hand, and was offering it to *me*.

(Lights fade slowly down on CRITIC and CRITICAL LADY; finally on NARRATOR.)

FINIS

Commentary: *Going Critical*

In optics 'critical' pertains to that 'angle of incidence beyond which, light rays, while passing through a denser medium to the surface of a rarer are no longer refracted but totally reflected' (OED). Without our awareness of the optical concept, many of us were trained as 'critics' to aspire to precisely such an angle of incidence. Whereas the artist presumably could only work within that denser medium of refraction, we, as critics, were enjoined to penetrate the depths and then return to the surface, like Plato's traveler from the belly of the cave, to illuminate the work of art . Our 'art,' if we were allowed to call it that, was the art of total reflection – distant, removed, reserved – unhampered by the subjectivities we brought with us to the reading or spectating. While such a notion of criticism has been made theoretically obsolete by post-structuralist, postmodern, feminist, race, gender, ethnic and queer visions, it nonetheless persists in critical writing. Much of which, let's face it, is tedious, dull and dispassionate. Still even those of us who fully embrace the inevitability of our own subjectivities at play in critical writing have difficulty finding a way to locate 'ourselves' in relation to the work which we have chosen, or been assigned, to 'study.' Though perhaps we know, as Herbert Blau reminds us, that the 'most naive spectator is the one who believes she/he is *merely* watching,' the complexities of desire – identifications and disidentifications; the perils of incorporation, assimilation, displacement, disfigurement – make critical writers join with artists in a marriage of heaven and hell. An odd 'mass' indeed. Even performative writing, the much-applauded solution to these difficulties, too often becomes mere solipsism. How to refer 'only to oneself' and yet commune with another? How to recognize the other(s) within, between, among, against one's 'selves' and yet not make them self-identical. Among the paradoxes of performative writing is that it is, in many ways, *more* indebted to a notion of the writer 'suffering' in isolation, signaling, perhaps, but often most feebly, through the flames.

Critical Mass brings these questions directly to the center of the performance. The critic sits in his 'reserved' seat, but it is onstage. His privacy is violated by the narrator, as hers is by him. He too speaks in monologues, while critiquing hers, and she his. He has one overwhelming lingering discomfort by the end of this play: why can't the narrator be performed by a *different* actress? She is too much 'like herself' for his comfort. Among the many issues this 'dark and caustic comedy' addresses so poignantly, the one that overwhelms me is the critic's last plaintive cry for the narrator to be *someone else*. Someone other than herself. There is nothing more unbearable, perhaps, than mutuality; nothing more impossible, perhaps, then equality. Margolin wants to know why this is so. *Critical Mass* is her public meditation on these questions. What constitutes the impulse to evaluate, measure, dissect, categorize, judge? This is no simplified, liberal world-view – 'why can't we all just accept each other's differences and get along with each other.' *Critical Mass* gives us no such panacea. There is no way out. No exit from this stage. It is where we all live, and die.

In nuclear physics, the critical mass is the minimum size of material required to sustain a chain reaction. Hence in a different discourse, we speak of the 'masses' as an amorphous but tightly collected body, a multitude or aggregate, within which individualities get lost. In aeronautics, mass refers to a state in which 'inertial coupling between the angular movement of a control surface and other degrees of freedom of the aircraft is eliminated, so avoiding flutter of the surface.' Masses seem to be, at once, inchoate aggregations, *and* stabilizing mechanisms. *Critical Mass* dwells in, and upon, this seeming contradiction.

Criticism, suggests the narrator of *Critical Mass*, is a 'substitute for touch. ... You can't eat a play, you can't kiss the eyelids of a piece of music.' She tries again: criticism is a 'replacement for religion sometimes – a theology of fashion don'ts and dark comparisons ... people who have given up on the myths of their church, and find an even more intense arrangement of pieties in a quest for "truth" that takes a critical form.' Pre-empting, or practicing, for 'The Last Judgment?' The critic laments in *Critical Mass*: 'a review almost exists before it's written, that's the painful thing.' But the narrator's daughter in *Critical Mass* teaches us that shadows will appear again when we are least expecting them. We cannot touch our arms in the reflections of them on a windowpane. The effort to do so amputates touch. Holding, waiting, adjusting the furniture. Soot on our faces, all. A terrible beauty is born in these moments. Must they be belated? Arriving too soon, too fast, too slow, too late, or never finding the theater at all? Margolin sees them streaming by us. Falling comets. Linguistic meteors. Reach out and catch them if you can. She stands with her arms spread wide, inviting us to join her in her yearning to hold the impossible moment fleetingly in this faithful space. Catch her if you can.

Appendix: First Performances

Of All the Nerve
Performance Space 122, New York, NY
30 November 1989

970-DEBB
Performance Space 122, New York, NY
13 September 1990

Gestation
Theater Club Funambules, New York, NY
6 November 1991

Of Mice, Bugs and Women
Atlantic Theater, New York, NY
November 1993

Carthieves! Joyrides!
Here Theater, New York, NY
8 November 1995

O Wholly Night and Other Jewish Solecisms
The Jewish Museum, New York, NY
22 April 1996

Critical Mass
Performance Space 122
27 February 1997

All shows, with the exception of *O Wholly Night* and *Critical Mass*, were developed at Dixon Place, New York.

Bibliography

Books and Academic Articles

Blair, Rhonda, 'The Alcestis Project: Split Britches at Hampshire College.' *Women and Performance: A Journal of Feminist Theory*, **6**(1) (1993), pp. 147–50.

Blau, Herbert, *The Eye of Prey: Subversions of the Postmodern.* Bloomington: Indiana University Press, 1987.

Case, Sue-Ellen, 'From split subject to Split Britches.' In Enoch Brater (ed.), *Feminine Focus: The New Women Playwrights.* New York: Oxford University Press, 1989, pp. 126–46.

Case, Sue-Ellen, *Split Britches: Lesbian Practice/Feminist Performance.* London and New York: Routledge, 1996.

Davy, Kate, 'Constructing the spectator: reception, context and address in lesbian performance.' *Performing Arts Journal*, **10**(2) (1986), pp. 43–52.

Davy, Kate, 'Reading past the heterosexual imperative, *Dress Suits to Hire.*' *Drama Review*, **33**(1)(1989), pp. 153–71.

Diamond, Elin, 'Mimesis, mimicry and the "true real".' In Lynda Hart and Peggy Phelan (eds), *Acting Out: Feminist Performances.* Ann Arbor: University of Michigan Press, 1993, pp. 363–82.

Diamond, Elin, *Unmaking Mimesis: Essays on Feminism and Theatre.* London and New York: Routledge, 1997.

Dolan, Jill, 'The dynamics of desire: sexuality and gender in pornography and performance,' *Theater Journal*, **39**(2) (1987), pp. 156–74.

Garner, Stanton B., *Bodied Spaces: Phenomenology and Performance in Contemporary Drama.* Ithaca, NY: Cornell University Press, 1994.

Hamilton, Sabrina, 'Split Britches and the *Alcestis* lesson: "What is this albatross on?".' In Darkin and Clement (eds), *Upstaging Big Daddy: Directing Theater As If Gender and Race Matter*. Ann Arbor: University of Michigan Press, 1993.

Hart, Lynda, *Fatal Women: Lesbian Sexuality and the Mark of Aggression*. Princeton: Princeton University Press, 1994.

Hart, Lynda, 'Margolin's "Lesbians Who Kill".' *Theater Journal*, **44**(4) (December 1992), pp. 515–17.

Hart, Lynda and Peggy Phelan, 'Queerer than thou: being and Deb Margolin.' *Theater Journal*, **47**(2) (1995), pp. 269–82.

Margolin, Deb, 'Commencement address.' *Women and Performance: A Journal of Feminist Theory*, **6**(1) (1993), pp. 169–76.

Margolin, Deb, 'A Perfect Theater for One: Teaching Performance Composition.' *Drama Review*, **41**(2) (Summer 1997), pp. 68–81.

Margolin, Deb, Lois Weaver, Peggy Shaw and Vivian Patraka, 'Little Women: the tragedy.' *Kenyon Review*, **15**(2) (March 1993), pp. 14–26.

Merrill, Lisa, 'An interview with Lois Weaver, Peggy Shaw and Deb Margolin.' *Women and Performance: A Journal of Feminist Theory*, **6**(1) (1993), pp. 151–67.

Patraka, Vivian, 'Split Britches in Split Britches: performing history, vaudeville, and the everyday.' *Women and Performance*, **4**(2) (1989), pp. 58–67. Reprinted in Lynda Hart and Peggy Phelan (eds), *Acting Out*.

Patraka, Vivian, 'Split Britches in "Little Women: The Tragedy": staging censorship, nostalgia and desire.' *Kenyon Review*, **15**(2) (March 1993), pp. 6–13.

Phelan, Peggy and Jill Lane (eds), *The Ends of Performance*. New York: New York University Press, 1998.

Reviews

Split Britches
Stasio, Marilyn, *New York Post*, 24 February 1981, p. 18.
Stone, Laurie, *The Village Voice*, 19 April 1983, p. 105.
Swan, Christopher, *The Christian Science Monitor*, 28 January 1982.

Beauty and the Beast
Hartigan, Patti, *The Boston Globe*, 16 February 1988, p. 62.
Stone, Laurie, *The Village Voice*, 19 April 1983, p. 105.

Upwardly Mobile Home
Cumbow, Paul, *Seattle Post Intelligencer*, 20 June 1985.
Pasternak, June, *The Guardian*, 24 November 1984, p. 20.
Solomon, Alisa, *The Village Voice*, 13 November 1984, p. 95.

What's with Hamlet?
Jacobson, Lynn, *New York Native*, 27 February 1989.

Little Women: The Tragedy
Barcott, Bruce, *High Performance*, **52** (Winter 1990), p. 72.
Massa, Robert, *The Village Voice*, 27 June 1989, p. 100.
Rosmiarek, Joseph T., *The Honolulu Advertiser*, 14 July 1990.
Tallmer, Jerry, *New York Post*, 7 July 1989, p. 22.

970-DEBB
Houppert, Karen, *The Village Voice*, 25 September 1990, p. 102.
Poattie, Tara, *New York Press*, 12 September 1990, p. 124.
Simonson, Robert, *TheaterWeek*, 1 October 1990, p. 43.
Skye, Jonathan, *New York Native*, 1 October 1990, p. 41.

Of All the Nerve
Cohn, Meryl, *Bay Windows*, 23 May 1991, p. 27.
Fanger, Iris, *Boston Herald*, 18 May 1991, p. 26.
Levin, Anne, *Trenton Times*, 3 December 1989, p. D2.
Solomon, Alisa, *The Village Voice*, 12 December 1989, p. 120.

Gestation
Richheimer, Judy, *TheaterWeek*, 7 October 1991, p. 23.
Stone, Laurie, *The Village Voice*, 12 November 1991, p. 113.

Lesbians Who Kill
Chansky, Dorothy, *TheaterWeek*, 15 June 1992.
Hart, Lynda, *Theater Journal*, **44**(4) (December 1992), pp. 515–18.
Russo, Francine, *The Village Voice*, 19 May 1992, p. 106.
Siegel, Fern, *Ms. Magazine*, **2**(2) (September 1991), p. 81.

The Breaks
Gussow, Mel, *New York Times*, 21 April 1993, p. 17.
Solomon, Alisa, *The Village Voice*, 27 April 1993, p. 109.
Strand, Ginger, *Downtown Performance*, 21 October 1992, p. 20.
Ungaro, Joan, *TheaterWeek*, 5 October 1992, p. 37.

Of Mice, Bugs and Women
Anon., *TheaterWeek*, 31 October 1994.
Brantley, Ben, *New York Times*, 19 October 1994, p. C14.
Jacobsen, Aileen, *New York Newsday*, 10 October 1994, p. B8.
Wells, Bonnie, *Amherst Bulletin*, 28 July 1995, p. 14.

O Wholly Night and Other Jewish Solecisms
Anon., *The New Yorker*, 23 September 1996.
Backalenick, Irene, *Backstage*, 6 September 1996, p. 52.
Bruckner, D.J.R., *New York Times*, 23 August 1996, p. C2.
Chansky, Dorothy, *TheaterWeek*, 30 September 1996.
Rinn, Miriam, *North Jersey Jewish Standard*, 23 August 1996, p. 37.

Critical Mass
Blake, Leslie, *Time Out*, 6 March 1997.
Daly, Ann, *New York Times*, 2 March 1997, p. 2:5.
Ebling, Margot, *The Village Voice*, 18 March 1997, p. 89.
Marks, Peter, *New York Times*, 8 March 1997, p. 1:16.
Stone, Laurie, *Village Voice*, 4 March 1997.

Other
Hillerman, Monica, *Gay Community News*, 1 April 1990, p. 11.
Johnson, Wayne, *Seattle Times*, 20 July 1990, p. F5.
Langworthy, Douglas, *American Theater*, **13**(5) (May/June 1996),
pp. 38–40.
Ledes, R.C., *Artforum*, **28**(3) (1989), p. 154.
Lumenello, Susan, *Bay Windows*, 22 March 1990.
Margolin, Deb, *Harper's Magazine*, April 1998, p. 47.
Reibman, Greg, *Boston Herald*, 19 March 1990, p. 41.